Dr. & Mrs Matthew Hoch
Theresa & Hannah & Sofie,

Jesus'
promise to you is
John 11:25

Nelson L. Price

THE CHRONICLES
OF NICODEMUS

Inquiries regarding purchase and discounts
for bulk purchase should be addressed to:
Dr. Nelson L. Price
1400 Beaumont Drive
Kennesaw, Georgia 30152
Phone: (770) 422-2564
Fax: (770) 427-6578
E-Mail: NLPrice@AOL.com
http://www.nelsonprice.com

THE CHRONICLES
OF NICODEMUS

Jesus' Resurrection:
A Transcending Miracle or a Tactical Theft?

by
Dr. Nelson L. Price

ISBN–10: 0-9671696-2-3
ISBN–13: 978-0-9671696-2-0
First Edition
Manufactured in the USA

Published, distributed and marketed by:
Journey Publications LLC
5000 West Esplanade Ave – PMB 214
Metairie, LA 70006
(504) 355-0532

CONTENTS

ACKNOWLEDGMENTS

My heart overflows with gratitude to the many who helped make this historical novel possible. Among those to whom I acknowledge thanks are these friends.

Nelda and Terry Moore whose optimism regarding my original draft kept the vision alive. This delightful husband and wife team's combined efforts provided untold hours helping craft the work. Dr. Nelda's exceptional creative writing skill and editorial experience helped my story line take life. As a grammarian, Terry's meticulous reading and detail corrections purged the work.

Dale and Guelda Harris, Aaron Brookshire, and Joel Young whose tenacity and technical expertise guided the work through many high tech traps.

Tony Boyadgian, my first guide in the Holy Land and dear friend on 37 subsequent study tours. His knowledge of Bible antiquities, archaeology, customs of the era, and geography enabled me to set the story in a historically reliable setting.

Further I am grateful to my wife, Trudy, the advanced reader whose patience and persistence kept me on task. She provided a home environment conducive to creative writing. To these and any I have unfortunately overlooked —THANKS.

Nelson L. Price

WHO IS RESPONSIBLE FOR THE DEATH OF JESUS?

Who killed Jesus? This historical novel depicts various persons involved in the drama of Jesus' crucifixion. It does not seek to place responsibility on any one race.

Romans actually arrested Jesus. A Roman pronounced the sentence of death. And Roman soldiers carried out the execution. That does not put the blame for Jesus' death on all persons of Roman ancestry.

Jews desired and designed the indictment of Jesus. That does not place the responsibility for Jesus' death on all racial Jews. Jesus was a Jew. His mother was Jewish. His disciples were Jews. His social circle consisted of Jews. And those who buried Him were Jews. The hostility and condemning spirit of some Jews around Jesus cannot be attributed to all Jews. Many befriended Him and became His ardent followers.

Some Jews are depicted as acting aggressively in opposition to Jesus. Others are represented as very supportive. To stereotype all Jews in either category is improper. There is no anti-Semitic inference intended in this work. Readers are encouraged to accept each character as being responsible for his or her actions and accept the characters as individuals, not representatives of an entire race for all generations.

INTRODUCTION

A historical novel may sound like an oxymoron.

Being in part a novel, it contains some material that is not historical.

Being in part historical, the history must be accurate, and none of the fictional material should be in conflict with history.

A balance is desired that will keep history from being laborious and fiction from being perfidious. It is desirable that each complement the other.

There are times when secular history is used to explain the background for certain biblical truths. An example of this is the conflict between the army of Aretas IV, King of the Nabataens, and that of Herod in which most of Herod's army was destroyed. The Bible makes no reference to this. However, this secular historical fact explains the biblical account of the composition of the guard appointment to secure the tomb of Jesus.

An example of fact and imagination blending relates to Jesus' teaching in which He says, "Behold, the lilies of the field . . . ." That is fact. The idea He gestured toward fields abloom with lilies at the moment, though highly likely, is imagination.

The reader's discernment is at times challenged by determining which is historical and which is fiction. A concerted effort has been made to avoid discrepancies in history. History, biblical and secular, takes precedent over the author's imagination. The body and spirit of Scripture should always be given preference. If any contradictions exist, the author asks the Father's forgiveness and the reader's pardon.

Efforts have been made to insure that fictional interplay and dialogue between characters do not compromise Scripture. Enjoy the story and the characters who became the embers, the blazing coals, on the hearth of a new era.

PROLOGUE
The Quandary

The forlorn outcasts stood in the noonday shade of a terebinth tree musing over the most mysterious matrix of the ages. Still in the colorful priestly robes, these prestigious sages were now rejected by their fellow jurists. The brows of their kind faces were furrowed as they questioned whether the transcending miracle of the resurrection of Jesus had happened in this garden or whether the reported phenomenon was merely a tactical theft of a corpse.

That issue prompted Nicodemus and Joseph of Arimathea to meet in Joseph's quiet, garden nearby his stone-pillared home just inside the walls of Jerusalem. They had come to re-evaluate the travesty of recent days. They did not come to this place only steps from the barren death site seeking only amnesty from grief, but also a solution for the conundrum of the ages.

These two were among the few jurists on the Sanhedrin with residual piety. Cognate reasoning and compassion had long vacated the court. Avarice, greed, and arrogance had come to characterize this prestigious body. There, corruption made a mockery of justice which the court had been meticulously designed to insure. Now fully isolated from colleagues because of their involvement with the burial of Jesus, they met in a rendezvous arranged by a sympathetic scribe.

Joseph was a master gardener having learned well in his not-distant hometown of Arimathea, renowned for its lovely gardens. The smooth garden path hewn through the rocky hillside and the elm trees lining the way offered clear evidence of skill and commitment and unrelenting labor.

Overhead the sky was dazzling cobalt with patches of cotton. The sun hit the leaves of a single rare red sumac, igniting it with color like a candle. Rosefinches and house buntings drank from a small shimmering pool.

Joseph was a gracious host, Nicodemus an admiring guest. A bouquet of floral fragrances overpowered the aroma of embalming spices coming from the nearby tomb where Jesus was buried. The sweetness of wild thyme filled the air as they walked among the roses and dahlias and beneath the bougainvillea growing on the hewn-stone trellis. Their walk in this verdure sanctuary was interrupted as they paused, even in this riveting time, to look at the delicate beauty of the desert marigolds and marvel at their oblong yellow flowerets with toothed tips. A broadleaf helleborine, a rare member of the orchid family, blossomed nearby, its beauty competing for attention. Its deep, dark blossoms held generous amounts of nectar, attracting bees. The crimson flambeau trees formed a colorful background for the silver leaves of the olive trees. Chattering sparrows flitted about.

They were last here when they risked their reputations, if not their lives, to entomb the lifeless body of Jesus in Joseph's newly hewn tomb. Now there was little small talk. Just being together in this effusive environment was communication enough. Nicodemus stopped walking as if to let his aesthetic senses ventilate.

"Being alone isn't good when bewildered. You know that from experience," said Joseph. The depth of reasoning implied in the statement was not intimated by the gardener's calloused hands and tall, muscular frame.

Nicodemus, more slight and more fair from fewer hours in the sun and much less intense physical labor, appeared to be the more deeply reflective and philosophical of the friends. He was one of three prominent men in Jerusalem: Nicodemus ben

Gurien, ben Tzitzith Hacksab, and ben Kalba Shevuah. Nicodemus knew his peers and commoners in Jerusalem said of the three that their wealth could support the entire city for ten years. But humility had not deserted him. Munching on a pomegranate, now dampening his shorter, well groomed beard, he nodded in affirmation.

Questions challenged knowledge this day.

Was that really Jesus who hung on the center cross? Critics said no.

Was that really the body of Jesus they had so carefully placed in the tomb? This too was questioned by His detractors.

Was the body laid in that tomb really lifeless? Mockers said there is no way a dead man could live again. They insisted He had merely swooned and subsequently revived in the coolness of the tomb.

If that person were truly dead, what happened at that tomb soon after they had placed the body there?

Was the absence of the body a ruse or resurrection?

These scholars met in this cloister of color to reflect and reason. Finally they sat on a bench chiseled into the rock under the shade of another flower-draped trellis, a place of respite from where they could clearly see the empty tomb.

A cooing dove sat on her nest built in a cranny over the crypt. The entrance was embossed with engravings of clusters of grapes, acanthus leaves, fruit, and flower wreaths. The stone that once held its occupant captive had been moved a great distance up the hill.

The unimaginable and the incomprehensible had happened here—or had it?

That was their reason for meeting. They were intent upon finding and assembling answers to these lingering divisive questions. Questions of what might have been danced in their minds.

Their resolve was to reflect upon the last hours of Jesus' life, to interrogate closely eyewitnesses and record the results. Joseph, a willing companion, insisted that Nicodemus, the senior scholar and ranking member of the two, be the one to chronicle the events. They agreed Nicodemus would write in the first person but would ultimately give them both credit. And Joseph, out of his enormous wealth, would fund their venture.

So began *The Chronicles of Nicodemus*.

CAIAPHAS AND
THE SANHEDRIN BETRAYAL

Joseph and I lingered in the marketplace as the merchants began to shut down their booths for the day and wearily make their way to their homes in the residential quarter of the city. We had spoken casually earlier in the afternoon on the Cardo, the more upscale market street which we often frequented that ran north and south in Jerusalem. Now we met again just off the main corridor on a side street of the common market, meandering from booth to booth and discussing the brisk trading and the rate of exchange which we felt a little too weighted in favor of the merchants and too harsh for the pedestrian villagers who had come to buy and sell. We had paused near a grain booth when a swarthy merchant, voice pitched high and eyes aslant, had charged three shekels for one half measure of barley when every commoner knew that amount was three times the fair price.

As the crowds were clearing just as the sun had spilled its evening pallets of oranges and pinks across the sky, I nodded to Joseph to follow me. We walked toward the city gates in casual conversation about our mutual appointments to the Sanhedrin when we were younger men. Now, with our beards graying and our steps having lost a bit of their youthful vigor, we were also more sober, made so in part because of the high calling of our office and also by our mutual concern for the direction the court seemed to be going in doctrinal and legal issues.

Justice seemed to be declining while political compromise with the Romans seemed to be rising. I wanted some private time with Joseph to learn what he thought of the man who had been in Jerusalem and surrounding areas performing amazing acts and claiming to be the Messiah. I had my own perceptions, and I needed to know how Joseph felt, particularly because I was aware that the Sanhedrin was about to confront—and perhaps incriminate—the man Jesus who was increasingly gaining public acceptance.

Before we could reach the stone bench beneath the cluster of trees just outside the gates, a courier I had dispatched some days earlier to report to me on the whereabouts of Jesus rushed toward us down the cobblestone street. Gasping for air, he spoke, his cropped hair and taunt muscles typical of a fit Jewish youth. "Jesus just yesterday left the home of Zacchaeus in Jericho and is headed across the mountains to come here to Jerusalem!" His voice suggested some anxiety as he spoke. Everyone on the streets of Jerusalem knew that soon a confrontation was certain to happen between this self-proclaimed messiah and the temple authorities.

The animated lad had told us that Jesus had dined with his new and unlikely convert Zacchaeus in the tax collector's opulent home in Jericho, a city so beautiful Mark Anthony once gave it to Cleopatra. The people of Jericho, and particularly Zacchaeus, had received Him well. Zacchaeus was unpopular in the city since he was perceived as a man unduly wealthy from the inflated assessments he imposed. The youth reported specifically, "I heard Zacchaeus say that he was going to give half his goods to the poor and that if he had taken anything falsely, he would restore it fourfold." I knew it was just that impact that Jesus had on people and their subsequent loyalty to Him which concerned the Sanhedrin.

The young man, having carefully made note of all he had learned of Jesus' activities, told us that Jesus would take the treacherous route from this flowering oasis of Jericho through the wadi King David called the "Valley of the Shadow of Death."

Again, I understood more than the young man knew and more than I could discuss with Joseph at the moment. The jackals that threatened Jesus' travel through this ominous valley were not to be compared to their human equivalents awaiting Him in Jerusalem.

It was an easy assignment I had given the boy. He could stand unobserved as just another curious onlooker as Jesus made His way toward Jerusalem. The young man, still winded from his excitement, told of how Jesus had gone to the home of His friends Mary, Martha, and Lazarus in Bethany, known as the "House of the Poor."

A sister named Martha, he observed, served supper to Jesus and his most intimate twelve followers, now referred to by the general populace as His disciples. Lazarus, whom Jesus—according to an astounding rumor—had brought back to life after his having been dead and buried for four days, sat at the table with Jesus. Mary, another member of the household, had anointed Jesus' feet with a pound of expensive oil of spikenard. As a show of devotion, the young man understood, she had wiped his feet with her hair, the most treasured possession of a Hebrew woman. It was apparent there was such warmth and familiarity among the friends that it wasn't surprising that Jesus chose to stay overnight. He sent His disciples to borrow a donkey for His entry into Jerusalem the next day.

Again, I found myself assessing the apparent character of this man Jesus. Surely, His choice to dine in these vastly different homes was one of His many acts which showed He was a man for all. I was certain the young courier's reports were fully accurate since I had heard of Jesus' frequent visits to this home of His close friends. I also surmised in light of the political and religious fervor in Jerusalem that this visit could well be Jesus' last opportunity for spontaneous cordiality. I gave the excited young man two shekels and thanked him for his good work.

By this time, Joseph and I had made our way through the gate to the grove area which often attracted tired merchants and villagers. We made ourselves as comfortable as possible on the bench where occasionally we had visited with other Sanhedrin members. When we finally were alone away from the ears of any sympathizers of the court, I had a chance to speak, "Joseph, I think I read you well, and I believe that you are not willing to dismiss this man Jesus as a radical, as I am not. I myself have seen too many acts which are supernatural. I perceive selflessness and compassion in all that is reported of Him. These are not qualities of ambitious man intent upon personal power. He doesn't appear to be just another one of the pretentious holy men that so frequently spring up in the desert."

Joseph appeared relieved that I had taken the risk to reveal my own assessment of Jesus. "I agree. I saw Him on His last visit to Jerusalem. I had gone to the synagogue on a Sabbath to pray. He passed by the way and stopped to interact with the people gathered outside. In response to the hostile religious people who tried to entrap Him with a question of healing on the Sabbath, Jesus revealed Who He truly is. I saw Jesus' face, could clearly see the compassion in His eyes, as He told a nearby man with a hand withered to stretch out his hand. I saw the miracle myself of the transformation of a useless, lifeless hand into a totally whole one. Jesus put love above law and explained to those who had been attempting to expose His teaching that they too should allow compassion and reason to govern their actions on every day and in every situation."

It was a great relief to me to know that I had not divulged personal persuasions to a man who would ultimately betray my thoughts. It was clear that Joseph and I were men of like minds, men appointed to government service but men drawn now into Jesus' service. Joseph and I talked of the rumors that were swirling in Jericho about what awaited Jesus and His followers in Jerusalem. What gave us the greatest cause for concern was that we had heard the Sanhedrin was contriving a way to entrap Him. Our great sadness was that one of the most astute of the Sanhedrin, Rabban Gamaliel, Nisi of "The Great Court," was a party to the plot.

"Joseph," I said, "as I see this entire maelstrom developing, I keep reflecting on the fact that this prestigious body of jurists, the Sanhedrin, was established, as its name implies, to glorify God through applying the Torah Law of Moses. What I really am disturbed about is how far from its principles the court is governing. The once-sacred institution is splitting into factions, many of the members acting secretly and maliciously. I know Jesus has become a target of their malice. Already, I know that various court members have met three times to plan their villainous deed of putting Jesus on trial for the threat they feel He poses."

Joseph, surprisingly, explained that he knew of the actions of the Sanhedrin. "One of these conspiratorial meetings was precipitated by Jesus' immense popularity at the Feast of Tabernacles in September where He attracted huge crowds and new devotees. I was at the meeting convened to deliberate the court's potential response, and I saw how provoked they were by Jesus' increasing popularity. Knowing this meeting itself was a violation of our law, I defended Jesus by showing the nature of the event was contrary to law. I asked, 'Does our law judge any man before it hears him and knows what he is doing?' My appeal was to no avail. Zeal was becoming rage."

Joseph continued, "After the group dispersed, some of the men sought an encounter with Jesus which was short in coming. After several attempts to entrap Him verbally, they incited a crowd to stone Him. As they were gathering stones, Jesus mingled with the masses and eluded them. I was there and still marvel at how He evaded them. Only the protection of heaven could have shielded Him.

"I was intrigued that the anger of my colleagues was not

assuaged as they sought Him out again. They encountered Him at the temple on Solomon's porch and once more verbally sparred with Him, accusing Him of blasphemy. Even basic civility failed them. Unable to ensnare Him in their verbal web, they again sought to stone Him. Once more He escaped as they tried to seize Him.

"After observing His patience and gentleness—and the wisdom in His tactical response to their attempts to entrap Him, I sought for the first time to meet secretly with Jesus. I learned He had retreated to the solitude of Ephraim near the wilderness, beyond the Jordan, close by where John the Baptist had baptized Him."

"Forced to await an opportunity to meet Jesus, I went about my routine and made my way to many of the unofficial meetings. I listened as His detractors counseled concerning His death. It was late February. Members of the tribunal in sullen silence had contemptuously listened on occasion to reports of His miracles and popularity. Jesus' raising the dead apparently was too much. At this session, Caiaphas, intoxicated with envy, made an impassioned plea: 'You know nothing at all, nor do you consider that it is expedient for us that one man should die for the people, and not that the whole nation should perish.' In making this assertion that Jesus should die, he made certain the jurists knew his position as high priest on the issue. It was enough to incite the court, and from that day on, many of the members have privately plotted to put Jesus to death."

It was obvious that Joseph was aware of the Sanhedrin's fear of Jesus and that he had been following the actions of the zealots longer than I. "I was aghast when for a third time some of the Sanhedrin met to devise their strategy. It was a few weeks before the approaching Paschal Feast, the Passover. The chief priests and the scribes discussed how they might kill Him because they feared the growing number of His devotees. I wasn't present when Judas, one of His disciples, reportedly met covertly with the chief priests and captains and became a co-conspirator. I heard they gladly gave him money to betray Jesus. I am comforted to hear that at least some members of the court were troubled when they learned the factions were meeting secretly, three times already, even before Jesus is brought to trial."

As Joseph had talked and I listened, shifting a bit from time on the bench which was becoming increasingly uncomfortable, I pondered how historically the intent of the court system was to give an accused person every opportunity to be proven innocent. The entire system was designed not only to punish wrongdoers, but also to save the life of the accused if at all possible. The judges were to be completely objective and hear no charge against the accused before the trial. So committed to fairness was the court that the system required that if a unanimous verdict of guilty were reached regarding the accused, acquittal was granted because the verdict indicated the court had shown no mercy. Nothing could be said against an accused until something had been said for him.

As an intent student of the Law, I understood the system thoroughly and found the neglect of its governing principles deeply troubling. Only after a case was thoroughly discussed could scribes record the votes. The rules provide that younger members of the court vote first so as not to be influenced by the senior members. Before each of the younger ones vote, the high priest always appeals to each to render a fair and unbiased vote. Each rises to vote and states his reasoning.

I knew the court's traditional allegiance to justice to be so strong that the ceremonies in the synagogue itself were not carried out with greater religious formality than that exercised by the court. Judges of the Sanhedrin had always approached their duty with the conviction that a sword threatened them from above and destruction yawned at their feet if they erred in judgment. The dictum of our body was 'Thou shalt do no unright-eousness in judgment.' Capital punishment was abhorrent to the court. I cringed to know that the austere system of justice of the Jewish nation was being compromised, had already been compromised, in the secret meetings to plan for the immediate arrest of Jesus.

When Joseph and I had finished talking, having sat until the stars had long ago appeared in the Jewish night, we retired to our respective homes, having expressed a strong sense of uneasiness about the religious and political climate in Jerusalem. Even we couldn't have projected that the very next day would begin the events we feared were about to take place. A night that had concluded so serenely under the stars soon would dawn upon a chaotic, maddening day. A flash report would hit the streets of Jerusalem about the ninth hour. Jesus would be arrested. The plan was in motion. Evil had been loosed.

Indeed, the time arrived for the court to begin its flagrant, public injustice much more quickly than Joseph and I anticipated. It was a sunny, seemingly uneventful day that dawned as Jesus made His preparation for entering Jerusalem. My faint hope for a resolution of the conflict was given new life by the ethereal atmosphere. Crowds gathered around Jerusalem from different regions to camp for feasts. The Galileans always assembled on the southern end of the ridge known as the Mount of Olives. They were rural agrarian people. They had contempt for the Romans and desired them to be driven out of the country. As people with little to lose, they vehemently opposed the Romans and admired Jesus.

For Jesus to get to Jerusalem from Jericho and then to Bethany, He had to cross the southern end of the Mount of Olives through the encampment of the Galileans. These were His people. He lived among them, taught in their synagogues, and performed many miracles in their midst. They knew Him. Not a few thought He might well be a revolutionary leader with miraculous powers who could overthrow the Romans. Others were people of great faith who hoped He might be their spiritual Messiah.

As He rode through the masses on the mountain, the people recognized Him. Gradually, and then in chorus, mystics and militants alike began to shout, "Hosanna to the Son of David: Blessed is He who comes in the name of the Lord, Hosanna." They greeted Him with branches of palm trees. Those who went before and those who came after Him shouted, "Blessed be the kingdom of our Father David. Blessed is the King of Israel that comes in the name of the Lord, Hosanna in the highest."

Across the Kidron Valley on a parallel ridge with the Mount of Olives sits the city of Jerusalem. Inside Jerusalem, there lived many wealthy merchants who had much to lose by opposing the Romans. They capitulated and accommodated the powers of government. Business was good, and there was much monetary and political profit in placating them. They were eager to gain favor by reporting of Jesus' royal reception among the people. Their unctuous actions were motivated more by the desire to curry favor with the occupiers than to suggest Jesus rivaled their power.

From crest to crest is only a short distance. The shouts from the summit of the Mount of Olives reached the ears of the people within the city. I watched as many of Jerusalem left their trades and were drawn out to see the cause of such excitement. From them a short time later would arise the cry of "Crucify Him!" I have never seen such unbridled enthusiasm as arose from the Galilean side of the hill nor sensed such hostility as awaited in Jerusalem that day. I was not hopeful for the events that would arise from these polarizing positions.

The stir in Jerusalem pleased Caiaphas, the current chief priest of the Sanhedrin, who was the primary instigator in the quest to refute Jesus, the person most bent on killing Him to stop His popularity. I knew it was Annas who was driving his son-in-law, Caiaphas, to move against Jesus. It was known among the

Sanhedrin that Annas was the major secret arbiter in the plans to stop the public acclaim for Jesus. He had been appointed high priest by the Roman legate Quininius and served for ten years. As an influential former high priest, he now served as coadjutor of the court.

It was well known too among the Sanhedrin that it was Annas and his family who commanded the racketeering that profaned the temple. Not only was Jesus, Annas perceived, bad for politics, but his major concern was that Jesus was bad for business. When Jesus drove out the moneychangers for exploiting the vulnerable pilgrims at the beginning of His ministry, He became a marked man.

Joseph and I, too, had discussed that another motivation for the Sanhedrin in stopping Jesus was political. They were uncertain about the reaction from Rome if Jesus were allowed to go on performing great acts and attracting large crowds. They were concerned how people would respond to Him as a leader of revolution. The chief priests and the teachers of the Law knew that the most certain way to control the popularity and message of Jesus was to kill Him. They hesitated only because of His popularity. To offset any overwhelming public resentment of their projected plan of crucifixion, they sought a way to entrap Jesus. To achieve this, they had devised a plan in the secret meeting based upon one inside His band of followers cooperating with them on a way to achieve their sinister ends.

It was Annas' puppet son-in-law who would be the public face in the deed. Having been high priest for nine years, Caiaphas was a most hated figure in Jerusalem. For a time the office changed so often that Tiberius said high priests "came and went like flies in a sore." The post often went to the highest bidder, the one most willing to collaborate with the Roman authorities. In the footsteps of their father, four sons of Annas, in fact, had been or were high priests.

The bright, sunny day when Jesus had entered Jerusalem

ended at dusk with a disquieting calm. Jesus had retreated to the Upper Room for the Passover meal with His disciples. I had watched the events all day and talked with Joseph as we stood among the crowd. Sleep was quick and welcomed—though brief—for me after such an emotionally charged day. A temple courier banged on my door soon after I had fallen asleep. He carried the sealed summons to the court. My very tissues twinged, bringing on unanticipated nausea and weakness as I read: "The Sanhedrin, at the mandate of Caiaphas, is convening immediately in judgment of Jesus of Galilee." I knew tonight was the beginning of the long-awaited plan to entrap Jesus and remove him from the religious and political scene of Jerusalem.

I rushed at once to the Great Hall. Most of the seventy-one Sanhedrin members were present, many more than the twenty-three required to conduct business—were present to witness this historical break with court precedent. I worked my way to Joseph, already seated in our customary place on the elaborate mosaic floor. I saw the distress in his eyes and knew he knew, as did I, that nothing good was going to happen here tonight. In fact, I felt the weight of evil as I had never before. The look of inevitability, clear by the tightness of the clinched jaws on Joseph's otherwise gentle face, showed me he understood too that something of cosmic importance was afoot. Jesus Christ, the man who we knew was more than a man, was about to be subjected to trial by His own countrymen. Joseph managed to mutter through his firmly set jaws, "This is it. Too good for the world, and they're about to get Him."

Caiaphas, at least in keeping with one court formality, was in his usual place sitting in the center of the semi-circle of jurors gathered to hear the case against Jesus. The face of Caiaphas was drawn, showing the strain of compromise of principle and the disapproval of many fellow jurists who abhorred his willingness to sell out the very foundation of the court. By no means were all members of the court committed to the course that now seemed inevitably about to be played out. The boorish-like brows which almost touched in the middle portrayed the hardness that had settled in over the priest. Virtually all knew Caiaphas was far removed from the piety required of the Jewish council, far removed from the revered rabbinical axiom: "What does God say (if one may speak of God after the manner of men) when a malefactor suffers the anguish due to his crime? He says, 'My head and my limbs are pained.' And if he so speaks of the suffering even of the guilty, what must he utter when the righteous is condemned?"

I looked at Caiaphas sitting there, soft, too soft, as one who always dispensed orders to subordinates and did little more than eat and take care of personal necessities of hygiene and robing up every day. I detested his betrayal of every tradition and law sacred to the Sanhedrin. Joseph and I were about to see in the most horrible way possible the atrocity we had spoken of only hours before. The court was about to make its leap from the side of justice and mercy to the side of evil and death.

Clearly, the general expectation regarding the anticipated messiah hardly provided an objective court. Members held themselves to be infallibly authoritative. Their haughty narrow-mindedness and personal ambitions prompted them to look for a mighty military deliverer rather than the meek, gentle savior Jesus represented. They were looking for a champion who would rid them of Rome, impose a tax that benefited them on all nations, and uphold their erroneous interpretations of the law. They envisioned a messiah who would establish a scholarly academy in Jerusalem that would draw people from all nations.

I could clearly see that the humble man from Nazareth who stood before them hardly embodied the standards the court perceived for their messiah. Instead, this Jesus had exposed their superficiality and stripped away their false piety. He had furthermore advocated the abolition of the illegal taxes they had imposed on the people. His followers, far from being noble scholars, had been chosen largely from the lesser tribes and trades. He did not embody their image of a redeemer with power and prestige that would favor them.

Knowing the disposition of many of the Sanhedrin members as I did, I was certain these smarmy men were about to prove themselves to be the best of sophists. Their foregone verdict of guilty needed a punishment. Their law only allowed strangling, burning, beheading, or stoning according to the nature of the charges. To arrange for a punishment fitting the perceived crime, they sought a violent means of execution, crucifixion. To accomplish this incredulous end, Roman approval would be necessary. Therefore, the court's actions this night could only result in an appeal to the Roman Procurator Pontius Pilate who alone could grant crucifixion through his supreme judicial authority.

As I had taken my place beside Joseph, maybe twenty feet across from Caiaphas, I saw by the way the chief justice had looked at Joseph and me that he knew of our growing allegiance to the man roughly shoved before us as if He were some renegade criminal. Here was deity surrounded by mortal, fallible men—some likely sympathetic, some merely opportunistic and eager to please temple authorities, and some just pawns of evil in the eternal events underway.

"So, you're Jesus, the man who dares assume He is God? You presumptuous, play-acting mite of men, do you have anything to say for yourself?" Caiaphas flung these words of contempt as he sat in the middle of his assembly on the floor, a place commissioned to knowledge and goodness, a place where Jesus Himself had taught about the deepest concepts of the universe and life, a place now of demented purpose. Caiaphas's velvet, gold-fringed cushion and his craned neck, now crowned with the ornate turban, elevated his diminutive frame somewhat. The bravado of words and pose added nothing convincing in his effort to compensate noise and intimidation for what he lacked in respect and character.

Standing very near Caiaphas in this rectangular room of thirty-five by fifty feet, maybe ten feet in front of the high priest, was Jesus, a compelling, desert-bronzed man gazing steadily in the direction of the high priest. The eyes of the other men surrounding Caiaphas followed the priest's piercing stare to the magnetic, majestic face of the accused man among them, their attention riveted upon this person everyone in Jerusalem had heard about.

"How is it that the 'King' would look like you? Don't you have something a little more regal-looking to wear to such an occasion?" The cynicism was clear from the pompous little man now stretching every inch of his dwarfed stature in an effort of authority, a scribe on each side keeping records.

Caiaphas effused a sense of superiority as he adjusted the gold-embroidered girdle securing the velvet robe of purple and scarlet. No doubt, Caiaphas had dismissed any plan for justice, the decision of guilt already declared in his mind. He knew his band of Sanhedrin brothers, had sat with them in this place many times. Joseph and I knew our disapproval and detachment had been evident long before tonight. We were already marked men. Others among us, if there were more sympathizers to this rebel High Priest, were less obvious. So, tonight to elevate himself with the Roman officials, it appeared Caiaphas would have his deadly fun with the King, and then they would all go home quickly. He would deal with defectors of the revered Sanhedrin another day.

"Hey, Jesus, KING Jesus, you haven't said anything yet!" Caiaphas continued his onslaught.

Jesus, with his head lowered a bit, one eyebrow slightly raised, was controlled, analytical as if waiting more than falling prey to Caiaphas's games. Far from any planned action on my part, I suddenly felt a surge of compassion for the man before me, a surge of logic too, so strong that I knew what I was must do. I was about to disclose fully my bias toward this man and no doubt alienate myself from the prestigious body—and in fact risk my life in doing so, considering the climate the Sanhedrin had generated in the city.

I stood and made a couple of steps inside the semi-circle. My time, as Jesus', in a sense had come. I had to speak for truth and justice or dissolve into something less than a man of principle. I saw the astonishment and anger in the faces around me. Then, on some few, I saw, unsurprisingly, indecision and benign interest. On one particular face, that of Gamaliel, one of the most revered personalities of the Sanhedrin for his astute knowledge of the Law, I saw what I believed was a look of identification, perhaps even of like-mindedness.

This was not the first time I had been moved to speak up for this man in danger of losing His life. However, until tonight, until this crucial moment, I had kept silent. I began with an amazing degree of control in the charged atmosphere. "I have watched this man for three years as He has quietly walked the streets of Jerusalem. Often He would smile at the children, sometimes stooping to lift a young boy to put a distressed bird back into its nest among the branches of the olive trees that shade the small, open-windowed homes on the outskirts of the city. I have watched as He stooped to talk to a crippled, ragged man and saw the man stand to his feet in adoration of Jesus, healed of a life-long disease.

"I have often watched Jesus and marveled and understood why the crowds followed Him and why He frequently had to seek the seclusion of a ship or the privacy of a garden or the home of a trusted friend. Even from a distance, I have felt His gentle spirit. In this man, there is no rival for our religious institutes, no abhorrence of the temple, no political threat to us or to Rome. I'm truly bewildered about what it is in the Sanhedrin law of compassion and mercy that this man has violated." I hoped my reasoning would possibly stop the unjust decision about to be made here.

Spontaneously, either spawned by my daring remarks to the incensed court or by their own impassioned feelings, cries of defense began to pour into the court from the darkness outside.

"This Jesus is a meek and lowly man deserving no punishment. I have seen His kindness to little children."

"He feeds the hungry and gives hope to the downcast."

"I have heard Him teach of peace, love, and justice. He does not advocate violence."

"Why do you pretend to charge Him? It is you who by your example pervert the sanctity of the court!"

As quickly as they had come, the voices stopped. The deliberate man dressed in his light-weight garment of spun flax still stood still, stolidly, reflecting neither appreciation nor chagrin at the voices. It was clear Jesus was of a different temperament than other men. The power of His presence was unmistakable, even compelling. He stood proud, though His robe once as pristine as He, now emanated pungent odors of dew-laden grass; rich, damp soil; and soured sweat of intense labor. Clearly, too, the seventy could see stains, smeared red splotches, obviously blood from some indiscernible source, from some obviously traumatic event. Joseph and I would only learn later from Jesus' followers that He had spent an agonizing night with His disciples in Gethsemane after the Passover supper and was complaisant, unresisting when the Roman solders had come to deliver Him to His destiny.

As the crowd quieted outside, Jesus, His clear voice and ethereal presence permeating and warming the cold plaster of the walls and polished mosaic floor of the hall, spoke, His tone calm and thoughtful. "You say I am King Jesus. And indeed I did come into the world to lead my people out of servitude and squalor into a full, rich life. In fact, I came to bring life, true life. I am the way, the Way to abundance and spiritual freedom. I am all the Goodness and Truth of the universe."

Caiaphas, now obviously amused with the game in play, returned, "Well, that's just too righteous of you, Jesus. You do have a rather high opinion of yourself, a man with no home, one who hangs out on the streets with your band of obscure characters. You are just a rabble-rouser who gets a thrill from how many people you can get to follow you, maybe even a sorcerer of sorts who conjures enough food to feed your groveling misfits who sit on the hillsides and listen to your rubbish. You tell me you represent truth and goodness? I guess you'll say next that you are God."

Jesus, still looking steadily and taking a deep, affirming breath, spoke unstirred: "Yes, you have correctly said I am God. As you are looking at me, you are looking at God. I and my Heavenly Father are one, one and the same. So, I will tell you I am God, God living on earth, breathing your air, and speaking your speech. I have come to teach all of you," He said, making a sweeping gesture around the room and making eye contact with every man, "to teach of my kingdom which is not of this world. Greek, Jew, Ethiopian, eunuch, child, widow, or prince, I am God and Savior of all people."

It was clearly visible that Caiaphas had stopped listening, was about to end the gaming he attempted to set in play with this rugged man who said he was God. Aghast with his mouth open and bolting from the floor as quickly as his heavy garments and inflated body would allow, he screamed, "Blasphemy! Get Him out of here! Take him right now to Pilate! The Praetorium Guard will beat Him into submission! He has no respect for the government, no respect for this assembly, no respect for my authority! We will make certain Pilate gives an order to crucify Him before He incites all the people!"

All we priests knew that as much as he would have liked to give the order for Jesus' death, Caiaphas understood that the Sanhedrin powers were limited. He knew that only at the Roman command could the death sentence sought by the Jews be achieved, no matter how incensed they were because of Jesus' miracles, His popularity, and His claim to deity. I saw Jesus as He looked at Caiaphas just as the soldiers seized Him. The message as their eyes locked was of fury only from Caiaphas. The look returned was one of compassion for a man confused and misguided.

Jesus, still steady, showed no alarm when the temple guards, joined by the Roman soldiers posted nearby to keep things in control, constrained him, wrapping their leather whips around His waist and hands and shoving Him out the door and into the street. The soldiers with their muscles bulging from under their armor and skirted uniforms took charge, pushing the crowds of pleading people and curiosity-seekers out of the way. They forced a pathway through the sweltering Jewish night and through the desparate emotions of anger, pathos, and jubilation loosed on the narrow street. Even at this unusual hour, secret followers of Jesus had whispered through the town that Jesus had been arrested. Crowds of sympathizers and revilers had gathered. Neither considered the eternal significance of what was astir.

SCROLL II

PILATE'S CONDEMNATION

The incensed troops of evil made the five-minute journey to the Praetorium, shoving Jesus through the crowds spilling onto the street. Pilate, perhaps partly out of anger for having been awakened to deal with Jewish business and partly as a matter of character, was about to reveal his complexity and conflicting ideologies. He was considered inflexible, merciless, and obstinate. He had little regard for the Jews and their religious ardor. However, it was well known he would rarely capitulate and accommodate when his authority was threatened.

Despite his reputation for callousness and severity in judgment, on this occasion he appeared strangely predisposed to be lenient on Jesus in part because he detested those who brought charges against Him. He went into the Preatorium and questioned Jesus, hoping to find reason to release Him. He made statements indicating he favored releasing Jesus. He disputed with the elders and priests saying they had presented no charge worthy of death, only accusations of healing and Sabbath profanation. Pilate could not have cared less about these.

"I have questioned this man and find no crime here, no fault. I've consulted Herod, and he too finds nothing deserving of the death you ask for. I'll just have Jesus scourged and release Him." No doubt Pilate had reasoned such a course of action would satisfy the law that he administer justice and would save the life of a man he deemed innocent. Further, such a pronouncement would get him back to other more pleasant things sooner. Pilate tried to rid himself of the despicable task of pronouncing on such a man, tried to appeal to the logic of the people crowded onto the street.

In rebuttal, the inflamed accusers of Jesus asked in a sardonic tone if anyone who spoke evil of Caesar was worthy of death.

Pilate answered, "Such a one is worthy." It seemed Pilate was putting himself into a non-retractable position in which he would ultimately have to bend to the will of the mob who knew too well how to set verbal snares.

I could see from my position the growing hostility of the crowd. So I asked the procurator if I might try to reason with the crowd. I knew any danger I might put myself in had already been conceded earlier when I dared challenge Caiaphas.

"Say what you will," said Pilate.

"Elders and priests, and all the multitude of the Jews in the synagogue, I ask, What do you seek to do with this man? This man does many miracles and strange things, which no man has done nor will do. Let Him go and do not wish any evil against Him. If the miracles which He does are of God, they will stand: but if of man, they will come to nothing. For assuredly Moses, being sent by God into Egypt, did many such miracles, which the Lord commanded him to do before Pharaoh, king of Egypt. Jannes and Jambres were servants of Pharaoh, and they did also a few tricks emulating the miracles which Moses did; and the Egyptians took them to be gods, this Jannes and Jambres. However, since the miracles which they did were not of God, both they and those who believed in them were destroyed.

"And now release this man, for He is not deserving of death. Let him go." I appealed, more to the learned in the crowd than to the destitute. "His miracles have stood. There is nothing evil in Him."

Just as I finished, my peripheral vision, involuntarily it seemed, caught sight of Gamaliel once again as he stood looking pensively, analytically at me. Soon I was distracted as my fellow jurists yelled accusations at me of becoming a convert and defender of Jesus. I could clearly discern even in the shadows of the torches on the street that the crowd was unmoved by my attempt to bring order and rationality.

I could see by Pilate's demeanor that he supported my logic that he acquiesce to my passionate plea for order and reason. Nevertheless, Jesus' accusers became all the more enraged and accusative.

They lashed out at me saying, "May you come to the same end as this Jesus." Privately, because there was no need to continue the maddening banter, I said to myself, "Amen. . . . Amen. Indeed, may I receive it as you have said."

No record exists of any defender being allowed to speak on behalf of the accused according to the regulations of the more formal court. Now in a more open forum and in the throes of intense passion, some bystanders dared to speak as outside the gathering of the Sanhedrin earlier. They were not concerned with their anonymity but just with their cause.

"I was born blind, but I heard Jesus was passing by and I cried out, 'Pity me, O son of David.' He had pity on me and put His hand on my eyes and immediately I saw."

"All my life I was stooped, and He straightened me with a word."

"I was a leper, and He cured me."

"I had an issue of blood for twelve years. I touched the hem of His garment and was healed."

The lone woman among the dissenters was quickly silenced by a jurist who asserted the court had a law that the testimony of a woman was not acceptable.

Another said, "I saw for myself that He brought back from the dead this man Lazarus who had been dead four days!"

A much more hostile voice rang above the bedlam of the night, obviously not one of the sympathizers. "And on what day was this?"

"On a Sabbath."

The hostility pierced the air again. "That is one of the very things of which we accuse Him. He cures and casts out demons on the Sabbath."

The voices were overarching each other, the present one louder and more insistent than the previous.

Pilate obviously was faced with a complexity such as he had never known. I dared hope that he did have some sense of justice. It was, after all, the Jewish consensus that the ruthless Pilate had a softer side. The perception was established when he relented in his decision to replace the Jewish symbols of nationalism in the city with standards bearing the medallion of Caesar. Pleading Jews had lain prostrate in front of Pilate's house for five days petitioning for their Jewish images to remain and saw him back down on his proclamation. Pilate also had shown his vicious side when he had massacred Jews protesting his use of Jewish treasure to build an aqueduct in the city. Today the vacillating Jewish leaders turned to their enemy to achieve what they knew the Procurator to be capable of: death of anyone who dared contradict his current purpose or mood.

The accusers from the Sanhedrin could only reply to Pilate's initial question of Jesus' blame. "This man does evil, and He doesn't speak the truth."

Pilate, perhaps pricked by a sense of right or feeling the compassionate power of Jesus, obviously was not intent upon acceding to the Jewish demand this day. The towering Procurator's displeasure at the task at hand was evident as I watched the conflicting emotions on his face.

Joseph and I stood on the front line of the pressing crowd on the porch steps of Pilate's hall of justice in the riotous, oppressive, environment. My efforts to dissuade an inflamed crowd had failed. Pilate's efforts had failed. There was no turning back. Pilate moved again to the doorway of the Praetorium. I had pressed close enough in to hear the indiscernible tones as he conferred privately with Jesus somewhere within.

Returning to the clamoring crowd, he called out, "Hey, you rabble, I have talked with Jesus several times now. I've asked Him what He has done. I don't know for certain what He said. It was something about His kingdom not being of this world. He didn't tell me He is a king. He just talked about bearing witness to the truth. So I just don't find any crime which begins to be punishable by death."

The accusers said to Pilate, "You are no friend of Caesar if you let this man go. He who makes himself king is defying Caesar."

It was a decisive moment politically for Pilate. He dare not give the impression of disloyalty to Caesar. He had only one choice: to order the death of Jesus.

Pilate seemed to be in deep thought, even trauma, apparently arriving at a decision to make one last attempt to escape the judgment he so much did not wish to make. He tried once again to reach the crowd with reason. "Nothing deserving of death has been done by him. Even if Jesus has made a false claim, you have a custom that the court pardon a criminal at Passover. It is the custom at the feast of the unleavened bread to release a prisoner. I have another man inside, Barabbas, who has been convicted of robbery and anarchy and murder. So let me release Jesus to you. He's done no real harm.

"I offer you a choice between a hideous criminal and Jesus." He thought apparently that his suggestion would result in the populace releasing Jesus, particularly since Barabbas was such a serious offender of the law. By selecting a notorious prisoner, a rebel, who was a murderer in the insurrection, Pilate thought the people would surely choose Jesus.

"Whom should I release?" shouted Pilate, "Jesus or Barabbas?"

"Let Barabbas go! We hate this man who lies. He is not king! Kill him now!" The jurists had done well their job of inciting the crowd, and in the maelstrom they shouted for the release of Barabbas, to the ultimate dismay of Pilate. Pilate clutched his robe and questioned, "What then shall I do with Jesus?" he implored.

"Crucify Him! Crucify Him!" came the thunderous denunciation.

I cringed as the mob, now at its most fevered pitch, screamed vehemently, "Crucify Him! Kill Him!"

At this point, Pilate was at the end of himself. He moved onto the pavement in Aramaic called Gabbatha and in Greek Lithostrotos, and signed the death certificate. He never convicted Jesus, yet He condemned Him. He was the epitome of ambivalence. He then arose from the curule, the seat reserved for dignitaries. It was about the sixth hour now. A new day had dawned like no other. Pilate, a man outwitted, a man to be pitied, ordered that Jesus be brought out. "Here is your king. Take Him away," Pilate said, his voice almost subdued in defeat.

Pilate, a man stunned and now standing numbly before the people walked to a bowl nearby and took water from the basin and washed his hands. He obviously wanted the public to see— wanted them to see his effort to distance himself from the atrocity, no matter how futile a gesture. "I wash my hands of the blood of this innocent man." His robust voice had now grown defiant.

The reply returned from the crowd was blood-curdling: "His blood be upon us and upon our children!"

Pilate wasn't quite yet finished with his own residual cynicism to the crowd. "So you low-life ignoble brood, I'll let you have your way. You've got your man Jesus!" The verdict was met with glee by the perfidious, pious accusers. Their thirst for blood was about to be assuaged.

With his head bowed, Pilate nodded to the four guards standing by with ready whips and to Gaius, the centurion who was chief trainer of scourging in the Roman guard and himself the most exact of the scourgers. The astute soldiers knew the procedure: strike with the most intensity and most violence thirty lashes upon the strong, firm body waiting inside the stately columns of this building dedicated to justice. Humiliate and mutilate the body of this uncommon, innocent man who said he was God, that was their commission.

In the clamor of the noise and hostility, I managed to slip inside the Praetorium and stand undetected just outside the door of the scourging room where Jesus had been confined. I could hear it all, see it all. The soldiers efficiently, as they had been trained, tied their prisoner to the lashing posts, arms and legs stretched wide to prevent any unanticipated retaliation from the lashing about to follow.

THE CRUCIFIXION ATROCITY

"Hello, King Jesus, welcome to your coronation day," sneered Gaius, the chief executioner, looking stalwart and proud in his regal Roman uniform. "Men, prepare this man for the scourging with the flagrum." Gaius' command was more snarled than spoken since he understood too well the pain and suffering the bits of bone, metal, or stone woven into the whip would inflict. In reality, it wasn't just one whip, but nine small whips of leather prepared with the chards at the end which would assure maximum pain. The Romans knew well how to torture their victims.

I knew the events of the next hour would be fully devoid of human compassion. Only the demons of hell could orchestrate such a scene as a Roman scourging. Most often as the whip ripped the skin, the soft tissue beneath oozed as the blood poured profusely over the bulging, warm flesh. When the skin wasn't lacerated, still a serious wound resulted, producing traumatic swelling and bleeding beneath the skin. While the pain of the flagellation was almost unbearable for the victim, the Roman executioners often enjoyed a riotous time of perverted glee, almost of coliseum-event proportion. The soldiers took delight in their skill and competed to see who got the best results, meaning who could make the most ghastly wound.

"Proper coronations, of course, necessitate a crown. Here's yours, O, King!" chortled Gaius, now not only the chief executioner, but also the chief frolic-maker. I had seen Gaius as he had accepted the makeshift crown from a Jewish priest after the pronouncement of Pilate's sentence. I could only fear its purpose. It was a crown of a crudely woven chaplet of thorns, which cynical priests had prepared days before and had dispatched to Gaius. Gaius' quick and muscular act of shoving the crown of humiliation into Jesus' bowed head evoked derisive laughter from the soldiers. Blood spurted and flowed down the face of Jesus as the two-inch thorns penetrated his brow, quickly soaking his disheveled brown hair. Then, as if in a drunken prank, the soldiers ripped off Jesus' one simple garment and left him only in His loin cloth, their demonic fever growing. Somehow exultation in nakedness always accompanies attempts at humiliation. The soldiers' delight confirmed that something base in human nature is excited by lewdness.

With the prisoner exposed, the whips, so cleverly devised by the Roman soldiers, began to flail the air, striking the back of Jesus. Gaius led the way, expertly sending the first slicing blow almost exactly between Jesus' shoulder blades. The chards did their work well. They ripped through the smooth, mid-Eastern skin to the pulsing life beneath. As their training promised, wet flesh instantly erupted and drained down the strong, healthy back of Jesus.

"That blood of God looks pretty much like ours, wouldn't you say, men?"

"Wonder if he feels like God now?"

"Surely God wouldn't stand there and let us do this? Well, He did say He was just the son of God, and that's evidently not a very high-up place in heaven."

"He said he could give life. Let's see how he does with his own. Come on, Jesus; let's see you give yourself life! Stop the blood. Fix your body back!"

The taunts rang out in rhythm to the crackling of the whip and the audible deep breaths of Jesus. Gaius, satisfied in having taken the first blows, stood back to observe his trainees do their work. After the required thirty-nine lashes at the full power of the guards and soldiers, the executioners assumed Jesus sufficiently subdued and physically disabled. They were well trained in what they should do next: place the T-bar of His cross on Him and set Him on the road for the very public trek of a thousand paces to the execution site, to Golgotha. This was the eschewed "place of the skull," a dreadful quarry outcropping visible to the people on the roadway carrying on their day-to-day life in Jerusalem.

"Hey, soldier!" Gaius was speaking to a young guard standing at attention with hands behind his back ready to act upon command. "You and the other men, get that biggest crossbeam. Yeah, that one over there by the wall." He was pointing to a rugged, eight-by-eight, six-foot-long hewn timber lying in the silt and grunge of the dried blood of the Praetorium scourging hall. "Yes, that's the one. That one deserves to be used by a king, and a king is what we have here!"

The four sinewy guards struggled as they moved the beam from its long-undisturbed place on the floor and hoisted it onto their shoulders. They shared the load of this cross rejected in other crucifixions because its weight was too great for most weakened criminals to carry. The obliging young men struggled toward the wall where Jesus waited in a pool of His warm blood. Still not yet fully calloused, the apprentice soldiers quickly looked away from the naked back, now a cascading waterfall of red spilling over the patchwork of bubbling flesh, torn sinew, and slivers of bone. Before they could recall their stolen glances, the tortured man turned His focus upon them, riveting their eyes to His. No malice was there in His gaze, no regret, no blame, just sadness for the men, the politics, the evil at work to execute such a deed.

"Can't you say anything, Jesus? Do you still feel like a King, huh?" The taunts went on.

From my stolen position within the Praetorium anteroom, I witnessed the repulsive, horrid scene. An atmosphere of evil permeated the place like no other I had ever felt. I could hardly bring myself to look upon this person under such senseless assault. But neither could I look away, compelled somehow by the force of all history to witness this ghastly scene. Jesus' visage was one of knowing, one of surrender, one of destiny as He lifted His drooping shoulders without comment and spread His weary arms for the heavy crossbeam.

"That should hold it!" Gaius spoke as if acknowledging a night's work well done. The soldiers laid the cross just above His shoulder blades in the sticky blood and spongy flesh, obviously assuming such placement would minimize the movement and sliding of the splintery beam. "Hey, Jesus! We'll see you later at Calvary. Enjoy your morning walk!" Gaius's cruelty had not diminished.

With that sneering command, the reveling soldiers shoved Jesus out of the torture chamber and down the steps of the Praetorium. The death march had begun. The narrow cobble-stone street was the venue for the crime, not the crime of Jesus but the crime of an entrenched government and of an entrenched religion that had forsaken compassion and justice.

I made my way outside the flagellation arena shortly after the executioners had thrust Jesus onto the street. It was easy to remain unnoticed in the pandemonium loosed. The human wall along the street had only continued to grow while Jesus was inside. Now it erupted in rage as He staggered onto the pavement in the early-morning chill to begin His prophetic journey. The screaming people fell into step with the procession of evil, some screaming in their rising anger, some screaming in victory for their won cause, some screaming silently inside for the travesty that was enacted in the golden city of Jerusalem.

Jesus was taking His final steps toward crucifixion—an act doubly unjust and cruel because He had done no crime for which such a death was a just punishment. Every citizen of Jerusalem knew crucifixion was a Roman death, not a Jewish process. It was a punishment improvised to exact the greatest suffering possible in a prolonged series of events—a complicated process which began with flagellation and ended many hours later when the centurion in charge injected his lance skillfully into the heart chamber to assure that death was complete. The mercy of a quick death was not the intent of the Romans at all. Crucifixion was reserved for persons guilty of robbery, piracy, assassination, perjury, sedition, treason, and desertion from the army. No, that isn't accurate. It wasn't imposed on people guilty of heinous crimes. People is too inclusive a term since Roman citizens themselves were protected from a death so despicable.

I was a little surprised to see the next torture tactic. The Sanhedrin had found a place to actively enter the crucifixion process. Two students of the rabbis were chosen to walk alongside the accused, urging Him to confess His guilt and preparing Him for death. Their appeals were actually taunts. "Admit it. You are guilty of blasphemy. Admit it and purge your conscience."

"You are no god. Deny your claim to free your soul as you face your destiny."

"Confess you are a bastard impostor."

Jesus, weighted beyond His ability to move and weakened from His massive loss of blood, forced Himself forward, obviously unable to continue this fiasco for long. Yet no groan or sign of protest or trauma was heard from Him.

All the emotion loosed on the street was deafening. People of various persuasions defined their passion by their posturing: some flailing arms in glee, some looking heavenward in pleas for mercy, some beating their chest in rage. Yet above all the den of the street, one cry pierced the chaos: "Oh, my son, my son!" Mary could only groan as she saw Jesus, bowed under the crude crossbeam, stumble along on the unforgiving stones of the street. I saw the woman on her knees, fighting off the crowd and reaching with both arms outstretched toward the bloody man with the heavy wood on his inflamed back. Human agony at its worst was evident in her hopeless face and words, all other words imprisoned in her grief. I fought back the surging pressure of sorrow in my own chest.

Though the proficient Roman soldiers felt their charge sufficiently subdued and disabled, awareness had not left the grotesque figure slumped under the unreasonable weight. Cloaked in the deep red blood streaming down His face and onto His beard, His shoulders, His legs, and to His bared feet, Jesus turned His tortured body, nearly unrecognizable, to look in the direction of the voice He knew to be His mother's. Their eyes met. Her screams stopped, replaced by a love too deep for utterance. The resolve, the comprehension of the divine purpose of their life together which she saw in her son's eyes, made her own pain secondary, the torture bearable, as she was apparently reminded of who her son was. Suddenly an air of resignation and some solace seemed to come over her shuddering frame. The prod of the carnifex suddenly broke the unspoken communication which the stunned mother might assume to be their last.

"Mary," I said as I reached down to help her to her feet and enfold her contorted face into the soft fabric of my robe. "I'm a friend of Jesus." She pulled away and looked to see who now consoled her.

She looked into my face to test the authenticity of my words. Feeling assured, she spoke. "How did you know my son?"

Before I tried to respond over the noise of the crowd, I guided this gentle woman back beyond the crowd where we stood near one of the many merchants' booths lining the streets that would soon open for business. I explained, "I only spoke to your son once. I sought Him at night, for my safety, where He was camped with His disciples. A Pharisee, a member of the Sanhedrin, surely could not be seen by day talking to Jesus. I confessed to Him that I had seen His many acts and heard His words. I had acknowledged within my spirit that He surely was from God because no ordinary man could do these things He did. And I felt His divinity that night as He spoke quietly and explained that the non-seeking person could not understand the deep things of the spirit. I comprehended much of what Jesus meant, but I feel there was meaning in His words far beyond the surface of what He said."

"Yes, I understand. Those are some of my most treasured times; the time Jesus and I spent working or just talking together. He always had a sense of the profound as One in this world but not really a part of it. His words always said more than what my mind alone could comprehend. But I understood much of what Jesus talked about. I have enjoyed His deep wisdom since He was about twelve years old." Her tone was reconciled now, was sweet even in its reminiscence.

Mary reached up in the cool morning to touch her face. "This head wrap I'm wearing now, Jesus brought it home to me maybe three years ago. In fact, he got it here at one of these very trading stands. He thought the royal blue was perfect for me. I knew He never traveled with money. When I questioned how He made the exchange, He explained that He offered the shopkeeper labor to repair this awning in payment for the scarf."

"Straighten up and walk like a man, walk like a king. That is what your inscription says 'King of the Jews.'" It was the carnifex, the hangman in charge of condemned prisoners, who could be heard yelling above the street noise to his exhausted prisoner. His blasting command snapped our full attention back to the ongoing events, Mary's moment of relief lost.

"Jesus, why don't you say you are an insurrectionist?"

"Come on. Admit that you are a blasphemer. It won't change anything now, but these people need to hear you." The taunts were coming first from one and then the other of the two student rabbis assigned to the accused to prod a confession in preparation for death.

The death procession looked stately, royal even, to anyone casually looking on. But to the seeker of truth, to those in pain, to those who sensed something supernatural at work, to those sensing this dark day in the history of humanity, this was no time of regality. This was a time for endurance.

As Jesus struggled toward the gates of Jerusalem, among the incited crowd was a man who was not a citizen of the city, obvious because of his giant stature and his glistening black skin, luxurious-looking beneath his white tunic. His muscles and broad shoulders strained the loose garment. It was apparently this appearance of strength which prompted Gaius to speak to him. "Hey, you, carry this cross for Jesus. He can't make it, this king that He is. And we've got to get this crucifixion going to beat sundown."

"Yes, Sir. I will take the cross." The man's look of compassion for Jesus indicated His ready compliance was likely more for Jesus than for Gaius. I would learn later when I spoke with Joseph that it was Simon from Cyrene, the father of Rufus and Alexander, who was compelled to carry the cross which Jesus could not. I knew the Cyrenes were a colony of a hundred thousand persons who lived within a day's journey of Jerusalem, a highly civil population who had dwelt there since the rule of Ptolemy Soter. The Cyrene synagogue was in Jerusalem. Simon and his sons worshiped there regularly, thus creating no curiosity as they were among the crucifixion procession.

I saw as Jesus passed His cross to the gentle man that He recognized a person much like Himself, one willing to relieve suffering where he found it. Jesus appeared fully aware of the spirit of the man and of the events around Him. Even in this feeble state, Jesus' attention moved to the street side, drawn by some distraught women along the route. His compassion obviously was not diminished by the agony. "Daughters of Jerusalem, do not weep for me; weep rather for yourselves and for your children." This remark, another to me not clear in its meaning, arrested my attention. It was not a comment spoken in hostility. So, therefore, I could only observe that this indeed was no common criminal, but a man who saw purpose and meaning far beyond the events which were happening.

Outside the city at the place of the skull where the vilest of the vile had been executed, the taunting, blood-thirsty crowd gathered. Ghoulish glee contrasted the mourning friends accompanying Jesus. Mary and I had followed the procession until it had exited the city. I stood behind the crowd at the edge of the quarry site. Mary, who had by a miracle kept her composure, moved on with the group to the execution site. The look of knowing from her son, it was clear, had changed her disposition from one of desperation to one of reserved acceptance.

I knew the crucifixion process well and understood that part of the victim's agony was the stress of forced observation of the preparations for hanging and subsequent death. Carrying the cross was only the beginning of the long, ghastly process. Executioners, themselves more worthy of death than He, cheered on the crowd by holding up first the nails and then the hammers and binding cords in a show of triumph. They taunted the condemned standing by, shaking the implements of death in their faces. Already their gold and garnet tunics were spattered with the crimson blood of their victim.

Jesus was not alone in watching the preparation of execution. He was flanked on each side by two men, two authentic criminals placed there by dutiful Roman guards. Jesus was easy to identify. He was the one beaten and bloody. He was the one scaled over by dried blood from head to foot. The scourgers had been unmerciful. The other men, maybe each thirty and strong, well conditioned, had just awakened perhaps from the last night of sleep and had been led uneventfully to their destiny. Jesus, quite by contrast, had aroused government, religion, and the long-suppressed evil sprit of men into a passion that the city—and I surmised even the world—had never seen before. I was there, an unwilling witness to the grossly misguided plan to eradicate from the earth a good man and His influence.

Jesus stood staunch, having straightened a bit, maybe having regained some strength in Simon's relief. The gashes of dried blood crisscrossing His back could only be compared to the clumps of wet clay in a newly plowed field. The cattails had even made their way to Jesus' front side. A large bruise caused by a harsh blow to the right side of His chest was already turning black.

This trauma, I knew, was only precursory to the pain to come. Three-quarter-inch-thick, seven-inch-long spikes were used to affix the prisoner to the traverse member of the cross, the patibulum. The crude cross structure was then raised and dropped into a prepared hole, a thud echoing from the rocky soil. The feet of the victim were then nailed to the upright post, the stipes.

Exposed on the cross, disfigured and nearly nude, Jesus at that moment was a man now alienated from heaven and rejected by earth. He belonged to neither. He belonged to death. But as He hung there, His feet barely above the ground, it must have been a moment when angels lamented and demons laughed. It was a moment when death mocked life and compassion was exiled.

The gruesome processes that occurred at crucifixions were well known to every citizen of Jerusalem. Anyone could stop on the street at the time and watch for as many hours as he or she wanted since the execution site was just outside the city. The Roman delight in their stern punishment echoed into the city. Experience-hardened executioners laughed as birds picked at the eyes of some as they were executed and animals gnawed at their legs. Gnats would commonly gather around the faces of dying victims as insects bored into open wounds around the eyes.

I stood back on the fringes of the crowd, barely able to watch as someone who had done no wrong was subjected to this inhumane death. Though I chose not to go too close to Jesus, I could see that Mary knelt near the cross, apparently still sustained by the power imparted by Jesus' look of acknowledgment. I could see there were various groups at the cross. Some were just traveling by on their way to something they considered more important. Many passing by wagged their heads in derision and shouted insulting language to degrade and defame Jesus. Religious leaders and a few of His devotees added to the numbers.

Just as the crowd had moved closer to the execution site, I was amazed to see the courier I had employed a few days before. I suddenly felt his appearing was by some divine arrangement. I so wanted to know fully what was happening at the cross, and this was my way to maintain my own distance but yet be nearby.

I pointed out who was who to the young man—Mary, in particular, and Gaius, and John. I sent him away as the mocking crowd grew louder and more crude. Their cries were clear: "Blasphemer!" "Bewitched!" "Son of Beelzebub!" "Profaner!" "Impostor!"

Just then the young man in my employ rushed back with a report: He was fast and mindful of his work, but, too, the scene was only a little way removed from where I stood. Even the religious contingency, he said with dismay, showed irreverence by mocking Jesus. The chief priests, scribes, and elders, he reported, taunted Him by saying, "You saved others, now save yourself. If you are the King of Israel, come down from the cross and we will believe in you. You trusted in God; now let God deliver you, if He will have you. You said you were the Son of God; surely your Father will rescue His own son."

I could identify Gaius by his colorful uniform and by his lance held at attention. He stood transfixed, intently watching everything. The young Jewish boy reported on one of his trips back to me that he saw Gaius wince when his comrades gambled for Jesus' garments. He said he believed that Gaius generally was showing signs of discomfort as he observed the derisive looks of the faces of the priests.

The lad was most excited to tell me that Gaius had shaded his eyes to better see the three on the crosses. The interplay between the three intrigued Gaius. The thief on the left used the title Christ and asked Jesus to come down from the cross and save Himself and them with Him. The young lad knew it was not uncommon for the thief to make this request. Even the most secular of the Jews expected a revolutionary to assert power, save Himself and them, and lead a successful revolt. But I knew this, their secular concept, was foreign to who Jesus was.

The young courier continued. "The thief on the right, in making his appeal, used the name Jesus. I knew the significance but didn't take time to explain. Jehovah is salvation. Of Jesus the second thief had asked pardon. What the priests, Herod, Pilate, and others did not see, he had seen: the thief had recognized this King and wanted citizenship in His eternal kingdom.

From my vantage point, I could see that Gaius was transfixed on Jesus. He observed Jesus' palpations grow weaker, His breathing more shallow, His involuntary spasms more frequent. Jesus panted more intermittently as His body weight pressed on His chest. Obviously Gaius could hear the death-rattle in every breath. I could see that he strained to hear Jesus' words. No doubt, the blood gurgling in His throat made speaking more difficult. His lips, parched from hours in the sun, surely moved with greater difficulty. I could see by Jesus' strained movements that cramps wracked His body. The courier rushed in just at that time to say Jesus' body was beginning to turn a grayish yellow. I knew from having seen many people pass from this life that this was the skin tone of one dying.

In the only act simulating compassion, the Romans traditionally made an offer of amphora. This was a death drought of frankincense and myrrh blended with vinegar. The sedative was offered and refused. Jesus, though weakened in body, had found the strength to refuse any comfort in His death. His expression was resolute.

My friend and co-sympathizer now, the young lad said he heard Jesus say, "Father, forgive them for they know not what they do." He said, "I believe that Gaius is becoming affected by this man."

Perhaps, I thought, the chief executioner is beginning to note the divine nature of the victim on the center cross. "Father, forgive them for they know not what they are doing" reverberated in my mind. I could hope that Gaius would seek the forgiveness Jesus prayed for—forgiveness even for that first, slaughtering blow. In Gaius' bewilderment, he might have wondered, "How could I be forgiven by the very one I am torturing to death?" Surely Gaius had seen many men die, but never one like this. I reflected that the liquid gargle of this prayer for forgiveness offered through lips crusted with dried blood was not like anything Gaius had ever heard.

The astute young lad told me of how he watched as Gaius' sharp eyes scanned the crowd. He saw Gaius fixated upon a woman standing near the cross as she lifted her white veil covering her head crowned with a black mantle. Quiet tears escaped and flowed down her expressionless face. She swallowed back the pain with Jesus' every agonizing movement and sighed with His every groan. My young friend said it had to be His mother. Only a mother could share such suffering.

I could observe that Jesus was silent. But the ruckus crowd was not. Their demeaning laughter only added insult to the disgrace of such an ignominious death. The death they sought eluded Jesus for a while as His posture on the cross revealed. I stood by, shifting my weight, watching six hours as Jesus must have felt raging thirst, throbbing pain from the lacerations, and burning lungs needing air.

My courier reported with surprising minutia how the weight of Jesus' body and spontaneous spasms caused the nail holes to gape open. He described how the fresh blood from His hands formed rivulets flowing down His side and how the blood from His feet trickled down the cross onto the gray furcated rocks.

I could see from my observation point that slowly and deliberately Gaius Cassias approached the cross, his spear in hand. Because I had observed the execution process on other occasions, I knew what was about to transpire. Indeed it did. After a momentary pause, Gaius thrust the lance deep into Jesus' side. My vantage point did not relieve me of hearing Jesus' anguished cry, "Father, into Thy hands I commend my spirit." I could see Gaius was at the foot of the cross where he was only slightly below eye level with Jesus. I saw him draw closer to look into Jesus' unresponsive eyes. He had seen the blood and water flow from His side. I heard his thunderous voice: "The deed is done. The life is gone. Jesus is dead."

Gaius had done his work with efficiency and exactness. I could see. Jesus had expired. My courier reported that indeed blood and water had poured out of Jesus' pierced side. I had studied enough dying men that I knew such a wound and efflux of blood and water show a buildup of fluid in the lungs. The fluid in the pericardium had been released. The flow of blood only validated that Jesus' heart had been reached. The flow slowed and soon ended drip by drip till none flowed. I knew dead people don't bleed.

Unknowingly in his official act, Gaius had offered a coup de grace which ended Jesus' agony on the cross and His earth walk. It was the sixth hour when He died, the same hour the Passover lamb was being sacrificed. Part of the execution procedure was to break the legs of victims to facilitate the death. My lad reported that some soldiers had come to the cross and discussed striking Jesus' legs, but when they saw He was already dead, they chose not to do it. I heard the soldiers say, "He is dead. There is no need to break the legs." I knew the innocent man was indeed dead if these men said so, men trained to validate emphatically that a victim was dead. Before the body could be released, proof was necessary. Their verdict . . . He was dead.

The lad beside me jumped in alarm as suddenly the earth shook. Rocks began to rattle along the quarry edge. People began to scamper for shelter. Screams rose toward the clouds which had suddenly gathered, screams now for their own salvation instead of for another's death. As the earth shook, darkness came so black that none of us could see anything. Even in the fear and blackness, my mind found significance: The curtain of death had been closed on the radiant life of Jesus.

My dear friend Joseph of Arimathea found me in the darkness, having no doubt observed the young man going to and from me and the terrible death scene. Joseph, just as I had felt compelled to speak for Jesus at His trial, explained that he had dared ask Pilate for Jesus' body for burial. Joseph had made the quick trip back into the city as he was certain Jesus was about to die. Pilate had marveled that Jesus had died so soon, and he summoned the centurion to ask if Jesus indeed were dead. Joseph had hoped to spare Jesus' body the ill treatment given most Jewish victims. Yet he was surprised that Pilate had agreed. My quick assessment was that Pilate concurred, not so much in sympathy with Joseph but in retaliation upon the Jews, denying them some of the satisfaction of complete humiliation of the man whose life he had tried to spare. Now remained the disposition of the corpse. There would be no rebuttal from the still lips of the body that would soon lie encased in a dark tomb.

Receiving Jesus' body was a bold act by Joseph. Among the

rulers many believed in Jesus, but because of the Pharisees they did not confess Him, fearing they would be put out of the synagogue. They desired acceptance from their peers more than the approval of God. Joseph broke ranks with them. I joined him in accepting the corpse and in accepting the risk of alienation from our religious community. As the mid-afternoon light slowly returned after the cosmic events, Joseph and I ran inside Jerusalem, hoping the merchants were still there after the strange happenings. Joseph bought and provided the linen, and I brought one hundred pounds of spices to be used in the burial, liquid myrrh and powder aloes to reduce the stench of death until the body decayed.

After removing Jesus from the cross, we took Him to Joseph's nearby garden in which Joseph had a new tomb hewn in the stone. Gently, we did what we must do. We wrapped the body in the linen and placed it on the stone crypt carved into the tomb wall. As we were leaving, we paused one last time to glance back at the still corpse lying there on the funeral couch. Were it not for Joseph's daring, the body of Jesus, as likely were those of the two thieves, might have been taken out of the city and cast into the city dump, the flames of Tophet, or fed to the dogs. No one was left to do what Joseph and I did. All of the apostles had fled. While others hid their faces from Jesus that day, Joseph and I acted out our faith. With the help of our companions, we hurriedly rolled a stone against the door, sealing it. The calm of a Sabbath night had fallen, the infamous day ended.

SCROLL IV

THE RESURRECTION CLAMOR

"Sir, we remember while he was still alive how that deceiver said, 'After three days I will rise.' Could you, then, post guards at the tomb until the three days are past to make certain that Jesus' followers don't steal the body? If they did steal the body, the deception would continue and be worse than the first crime." The fearful voices were coming from a contingency of priests and Pharisees who dared continue their appeals to Pilate to dispose of Jesus. Joseph and I stood on the parameters of the crowd gathered at Pilate's house and listened as the intent voices pleaded with Pilate.

"You were afraid of this man alive, and now you are still afraid of Him," Pilate mocked. "Use your own soldiers. I can't supply them for you since I just lost too many in the war with King Aretas of Petra." The incensed religious leaders quickly accepted Pilate's offer to provide their own security and rushed past us without regard for the owner of the garden which they would enter without permission. Joseph and I followed the soldiers to the tomb and watched as they sealed the stone with crude rope and the official wax seal of the Sanhedrin, confirming the tomb's content as the corpse of the man named Jesus. Then the two most commanding-looking soldiers took their place at attention in front of the tomb.

Joseph and I stood just beyond the garden wall for a while, listening to the self-congratulatory conversation of the soldiers. "We've just been given the assignment for the ages. Not only are we guarding the tomb of this rebel man, but we are the most trusted police of the entire Sanhedrin." The words spoken in the night showed the guards were fully impressed with themselves. The garden eventually grew quiet as the people went home to rest, assuming they had stamped out the voice of anarchy. Joseph and I, wearied from our night-to-day-to-night watch and caretaking, retreated to our separate homes, not knowing fully what the next few days would hold.

The activities on the streets of Jerusalem were relatively subdued for the next couple of days. But just past dawn on the morning of the Sabbath, Joseph knocked on my shutters to tell me his garden was all a bustle with shouting Romans and Jewish men. My house was just inside the city walls, the lamplight always visible between our two houses. He had virtually leapt the granite stairs to my front porch. He breathlessly explained he had quietly rushed past the quarters of my wife Leonne where she slept with our two boys, now ages four and five. Joseph didn't want to alarm anyone. He knew where my room was and had knocked quietly on the bedroom shutters. I threw my cloak on quickly and ran with Joseph back to the garden.

As we rushed to his garden, Joseph explained he had been awakened by the noise of the tomb guards, talking in frantic voices between themselves, saying that an earthquake had hit about daybreak. Glowing angels, they had said, suddenly appeared by the tomb. The stone had mysteriously been rolled uphill twenty feet from the tomb door. The guards had said that in their excitement they rushed to the tomb to find it empty and the grave clothes vacated, undisturbed. They had run away to be replaced by enraged Sanhedrin officials. Joseph said he had kept watching from a distance as the Sanhedrin priests paced through the garden to confirm the guards' reports of the empty tomb.

Joseph and I, having reached the scene of confusion, were invisible in the crowd there still puzzling among themselves. And the irony is," Joseph said, "that the guards now are themselves prisoners of their own court and are at this moment being questioned by the priests.

Just then we heard the most amazing cry of joy. "He is risen! Don't be afraid." The two weeping women who were so exhilarated obviously had been startled by the words addressed to them by an angel who they said had sat on the removed door stone. We could see the women brought with them alabaster boxes of spices and perfumes in expectation of burying their hope, saying farewell to their dreams, and embalming the past.

The winds had scarcely had time to cover Jesus' footprints in the Judean sands or the rains to wash His red blood from the gray stones of Calvary when the women rushed through the crowd exclaiming, "He is risen! He is risen just like He said He would! He is risen!" Because, perhaps, any Jewish authorities assessing the situation would have considered the tomb visitors just fanatical, emotional women, they let them go undeterred to spread their interpretation of the early morning's confusing events.

Joseph and I, still indiscernible and of little interest among the clamoring crowd, made our way to the Sanhedrin Hall where the inquisition of the guards was in progress. In the chaos of the morning, we stood just outside the portal of the temple. It was no doubt Caiaphas' voice we heard: "Okay, men. Here is what we have to do. We're going to give you each two gold pieces to give this account of what happened at the tomb. You tell anyone who asks that the disciples of Jesus came and stole the body while you slept. Tell them that sleep overtook you both just before dawn and when you awoke the stone was gone."

Joseph, ever the observer, said, "The Sanhedrin plan is greatly short-sighted since it doesn't take into account that the guards can verify nothing if they were asleep." They who had committed murder now resorted to lying about the result. The guards were given assurance that if the governor heard of this, the court would appease him and defend the guards. Obviously their previous success in manipulating Pilate gave them confidence they could do so again. At all cost, the priests did not want the public to hear what the guards had just reported. Such news would attest to a resurrection from the dead. This in turn would cause the populace to accuse them of condemning and murdering Jesus. Now the guard members had to go back to their daily routines and keep their stories consistent.

Our mood somehow had become just a little lighter, even in the face of such a day and night, but suddenly any casualness was once again exchanged for the profound as we heard Caiaphas resume speaking, "And, all of you be on the alert for Nicodemus and Joseph. I'll speak to Pilate. We must find them. They have betrayed us. We must force them to denounce this Jesus that they buried."

As quickly as the court had convened, it dismissed. Joseph and I sighed deeply and walked the short distance to our homes. Monday morning, as I was in route to Joseph's home, rumors were everywhere about what had happened. Eli, a member of the guard standing near the temple, was confronted by a friend who said, "Eli, you men have had quite an adventure being on guard at the tomb. They tell me the tomb is empty and the body missing. What happened?"

"It is simple. While we slept, His followers came and stole the corpse."

"Oh, so that's it."

"Yes, it's just that simple."

The friend went on his way obviously satisfied with the answer and pleased he could relate the story to his friends boasting that he had talked with one of the guards who was actually there.

I stood a while just watching Eli and pondering. Soon the guard Eli encountered another inquirer. Feeling confident in light of his earlier explanation, he gave the same answer.

"Eli," replied the inquisitor, "do you really expect me to believe that you regimented guards slept while Jesus' friends from Galilee slipped into the garden, broke the seal, rolled a two-ton stone from the door, entered the tomb, and made off with the corpse while none of you awoke? I thought I was a sound sleeper!"

Quickly excusing himself, Eli retreated toward the temple courtyard only to be approached by another person who asked what really happened. Haltingly, Eli explained the entire fabricated scenario. "Eli," said this more skeptical prober, "please tell me that once more, slow and easy. I want to be sure I understand this right."

Methodically, but less confidently, Eli repeated, "While we slept, his disciples came and stole the body."

"Eli, do you really expect me to believe that? You said all of you were asleep. Then how do you know what happened? You didn't see anybody or hear anything. None of you were eyewitnesses to what you profess to have happened. I have a problem with that. I have a problem with the whole account. I have a solution, and it is far more plausible than yours. I am convinced the tomb is empty because Jesus arose from the dead. He lives now somewhere. He has confronted death and won. God, Who will not allow a grain of wheat to lie buried in the earth, would not allow Jesus to remain buried in the earth. That Jesus arose is much easier to believe than your fabricated story. Eli, you lie." Eli had no defense.

I could see Eli take two coins from his belt. I watched as he rubbed them as if in thought. Putting his money into safe-keeping, the shaken Eli made his way back to the barracks and his co-conspirators. He, like the others, would bear this mental scar all his life, haunted by what he knew to be the truth. Nevertheless, the guards continued to spread their lie, hoping somehow to exonerate themselves and ease their consciences. I heard their reports among the people as I walked between Joseph's home, the garden, the quarry, and back to my own home. I had hoped the shuffling of my feet might somehow settle the turmoil of my mind.

On one of my circular journeys, I saw Joseph in front of the synagogue where he often meditated, he choosing to settle his disquiet this way. I approached and asked, "Joseph, who was that man on the center cross?"

Confidently Joseph replied, "Why, Jesus, of course, the son of Mary."

"Are you sure, absolutely sure?"

"Nicodemus, I never told anyone, but like you, I sought Him out privately and inquired of Him. I knew well His features."

"But, are you certain that is who it was?"

"Nicodemus, you know I know it was. I sat beside you, feet away from Him in that crowded room that awful night the court falsely condemned Him to death. The shame of it. We knew that treatment was unjust and our actions illegal. Acting under cover of night as we did is forbidden by our own law. Yet, the blood thirst for His death was so passionate His accusers could not be deterred—though you tried.

"You know His body was cold when we last lifted the lids of His once-piercing eyes to test them with light to see if the pupils would respond. I know those eyes. In life I studied closely His sun-toned complexion, His taut muscles, and the texture of his hair. He was such a captivating physical man. It was Jesus, for sure."

"Now, Joseph, an even more important question. When we put Him in the tomb, was He dead? Think! Do you know for sure he was dead?"

"Without a doubt He was decidedly dead. You know that. At the time we had no doubt about it. You know death. When the heart stops beating, the blood stops flowing, and no blood comes from the wounds of the body. There was no blood coming from any of His wounds, not even the gash made by the spear. Thus, we know His strong heart was not beating. He was emphatically dead. That I know for sure."

I confirmed the same details. "He was indeed dead. But reason with me, Joseph. It was Jesus, not some imposter, who died on the cross, right?"

"Without a doubt it was Jesus. Of that, I am sure."

"Consider further. Be patient with me, I know I am belaboring the point, but this is too important not to be sure of every possible detail. It was Jesus we put in the tomb, but again I ask, was He dead? Of this are you certain?"

"Certain. Yes, certain." Joseph paused reflectively, as though musing over the internment, and continued. "Nicodemus, recall the glassy stare of those eyes when we lifted the lids. As we wrapped His body, seeing them with a lifeless stare reminded me of when I visited Him privately. He looked at me then as though He were peering into my soul. When we moved the lamp from place to place while wrapping Him in the tomb, there were absolutely no life responses. None. There was no breathing, no bleeding, and no muscle reflex. Before we finished, His cold body was already stiffening. Yes, I attest on my honor that He was dead."

"Well, Joseph, all things are now different. Life henceforth must be measured by this axis event. Like His disciples, we must be bearers of this good news. We can't avoid it. There is no more routine for us, no more insignificant days. Life for us has changed." It was at this time, this point of our own destiny, that we made the decision to combat the fast-spreading rumors on the street. Jesus had beaten religion and evil and death. Now we had to combat the false information with fact.

With this, we set about to find and converse with all who were witnesses of Jesus. Our journey would be perilous, but the effort rewarding for our own confirmation of the God-man and for the validation of the resurrection to all posterity. We knew we would have to travel now in as much anonymity as possible and protect ourselves until our mission was accomplished. Perhaps we knew our findings would affect history. We prayed that heaven would go before us as we set out to find Gaius Cassias, the chief executioner.

SCROLL V

GAIUS, THE CHIEF EXECUTIONER

Joseph and I intuitively felt the best place to begin our search for irrefutable truth regarding the crucifixion was to talk with the Roman Centurion, Gaius Cassias, the man in charge of the execution. We wanted to talk personally to the man who had stood at eye-level with Jesus on the cross, the man who checked the body of Jesus for life signs, the man in whom we had seen visible change as he had commandeered the death of Jesus. Who better than he to know if Jesus were truly dead?

We found Gaius sitting alone on the low wall of the courtyard known as Gabbatha munching on labaney, white sour cheese soaked in olive oil. On the stones of this courtyard, much of the drama related to Jesus' last hours had been played out. The weathered face of Gaius was furrowed with the traces of time and the stress of the contradicting emotions of his job. His eyes looked wounded, not combative. At his side was a cup of date juice tea.

As we approached, at first he was self-protective and reluctant to speak. He might well have been still in shock, having been close to the brutality of Jesus' death—so close to the human insult to the Power of the universe. Surely the greatest weight could be that he was part of the savagery, part of the ultimate affront to God Himself.

"Gaius, may we talk with you privately? We are followers of Jesus, now more openly called the Christ, and correctly so we believe. The reports of His resurrection are spreading. More and more people who were there at the cross have visited the tomb and talked among themselves. They are confident He was dead and now alive. Gaius, what we so much need to know from you is this: Was He dead, truly dead?"

This is the one question which might have moved Gaius to talk—a question which approached defamation of his professional competence. "Dead? I know death," asserted Gaius as though defending his insidious art. "I am a craftsman of death. I kill. I am surprised that I don't like to admit it now, but I have killed hundreds of people and have done it with little regret. For me playing 'the game of the king,' the Basilicus, derived from the Saturnalia, has been fun. It is the most popular game among the guard. To play, a burlesque 'king' is plied with ludicrous honors, concluding with death at the end of the farce. In accord with the rules of the game, we stripped your Jesus and put a purple robe on Him as though He were a king.

"'Hail, King Jesus.' Those words still ring in my ears. 'We are your servants, you our king' was the sporting jest."

We could see that Gaius wanted to talk about the atrocity in which he had been a premier player, so we sat beside him, one on each side. He seemed content with our close proximity which once he would have averred. "Our game was rather intricate in its rules. We enhanced His pain in many ways. Putting on and taking off robes from His scourged body initiated the pain we sought. The crown platted of thorns was part of the game plan. The deeper the thorns meant the more blood to flow into His eyes and mouth. The scepter was a necessary prop in our burlesque. We put a reed in His right hand and bowed before Him chanting, 'Hail, King of the Jews!' Then we each spat on Him. Some took His scepter and struck Him on His head, driving the thorns deeper into His brow. Others slapped Him. Oh, it was great fun for us . . . then. I truly was most impressed with the man. He was the first prisoner who did not open His mouth."

As appalling as Gaius' account of the soldiers' game was, I knew he was quite accurate in his description of the scourging.

Little did he know that I could confirm the evil he described. For he had no idea that I had made myself an audience of one to view the soldiers' work and their frolicking.

"The indignities continued. This part was from Pilate who was not actually in our play. Pilate had Jesus brought back before the public in his horrible disfigurement, still wearing His crown and purple robe. What a pathetic scene. I don't believe Pilate's interest was so much in adding to Jesus' pain as it was in making a political bargain with the Jews. Actually, I thought Pilate was trying one last time to spare Jesus, hoping such a spectacle would solicit sympathy on His behalf. It was to no avail. The religious people, intent on Jesus' life, cried out, 'Crucify Him! Crucify Him!' Then they turned a threat onto Pilate which he could not withstand: 'If you do not crucify this man, you are no friend of Caesar.' At this point Pilate capitulated and gave the order to crucify Jesus, as you know."

In a flash Gaius returned to the subject which was gripping his mind, the certainty of Jesus' death. "Yes, Jesus died, died like any other man whose death certificate I've signed. Some say on the cross He only swooned and was revived by the cool cave. I know this for sure. No man flogged by my men could have walked away days later. Many never survive the flogging itself. They are literally beaten to death. Only a body such as Jesus' could endure it. When we completed our beating, He was so weak He could not even carry the patibulum to the Place of the Skull. Jesus was near death when we reached Calvary. I have seen many cases where those who survived the whips died before reaching the place of execution. So, I know when Jesus was alive and barely alive. And I know when He was dead.

"Why, Jesus should have died of frustration and abuse before He got to us. Emotionally, He should have been exhausted by the many mock trials he endured. First there was the trial before Annas, then three trials before Caiaphas: the regular trial, the repeat trial, and finally one in the early morning to make everything legal. Legal? Hardly! There were also trials before Pilate, then Herod the Great, and finally Pilate again. All a sham. The verdict was guilty and the sentence death even before any of the illegal legal proceedings." Gaius was speaking strangely—almost as if drunk, inebriated on his date tea—or intoxicated in deep remorse which he seemed to be about to acknowledge.

Joseph injected, "We were there and observed that what you are saying is true. The decision was made far in advance of the mock trials the court contrived."

Returning to his reflections, Gaius, plaintively, but with poise, continued. "From the cross I have heard men scream in agony, beg for mercy, and curse with their last breath. But I have never heard a man on a cross pray for his tormentors to be forgiven. Never, never, never. It is unnatural. Seeing Him die and hearing those words—it was something new to my ears. Hearing 'Father forgive them for they know not what they are doing' convinced me that surely this was more than a man. This was the Son of God we were slaying.

"Yes, it grieves me to admit it. He was dead. Dead. Dead. My reputation rested on completing the task and being certain He was dead. On my honor, I say to you with no reservation, He was dead. No man could survive such a wound. These days I have washed and washed again my body trying to rid it of His blood that spurted out. An immense volume of blood drained from His body, ending His life. No man can live with that loss of blood.

The horror, the evil . . . . I even stepped in some of His blood that had spilled onto the rocky ground. I can hardly deal with my thoughts these days. I don't know what to do."

Raising his head and looking at us more closely than before, he asked, "Have you ever taken a close look at a Roman lance?" Remembering who he was addressing, he continued, "No, I don't suppose you have. Well, the narrowness of the iron shank and the weight of the wooden shaft are of such size and weight that my pila pierced deep into His body. Little wonder. Our spears are designed to penetrate armor. Where the shank and shaft meet is a lead weight designed to add to the force of the thrust and give depth of penetration. Ours lances are crafted, not for throwing, but thrusting, and thrust I did, nearly driving the sharp tool of death through His body. With that thrust, I made certain He was dead. Like the other soldiers at the scene, I wanted to get the job finished and leave. I was so confident of His death that I did not have His legs broken as I did with the two thieves.

"One image that won't leave my mind is the soldiers dividing Jesus' clothes into four shares, one for each soldier: His head gear, sandals, belt, and outer garment. His white undergarment was seamless, woven in one piece from neck to hem. Even I was shocked to hear them say, 'Let's throw dice to decide who is to have it.'"

The hardened Gaius was having great difficulty telling his story. That was obvious. "Having impaled Jesus on the cross and finishing their gambling, my legionaries sat down and kept a close watch on Him to insure no others molested His body or tried to rescue Him. Seeing His condition, they hoped He would die soon. For them, the sooner, the better. They were to go off duty after completing this assignment. They knew the moment. They were trained and very experienced in detecting when death occurred. They watched as even the normal post-death reflexive quivers ceased and the last of His blood began to clot."

Joseph and I grew nauseous just listening to the graphic details. The face of Gaius himself was showing his growing revulsion. A tear seemed to trickle down his sun-parched face, tracing one of the distinct wrinkles. His apparent regret touched a responsive chord in us, though we reminded ourselves to whom we were talking—the man who had killed the best person we had ever known. "We Romans don't know the prophecies of you

Jews, but I recently overheard a reading from your synagogue which said one of your ancient kings, David, had prophetically written of your long-anticipated Messiah in a book of Psalms: 'They divided My garments among them, and for My clothing they cast lots.' Could it be that I unknowingly was party to the fulfillment of that prophecy? These words, like a voice from the centuries, still reverberate in my mind."

I interrupted, "Gaius, you can forgive yourself for you did not know who Jesus was. Why, we, members of our revered court, knew the prophecies related to Messiah, and we failed to recognize them when they appeared clearly and simply in Him. The eyes of the court were blinded by arrogance and prejudice, yours by ignorance of the prophecy. So we can understand that you, who knew far less that we about the coming Messiah, did not understand the meaning of what you were doing."

But I did it! That is the reality which tortures my mind. As a further indignity, we crucified Him between two zealots guilty of murder, another show of contempt for Him. Not only did passers-by and religious bigots deride Him, but even the two thieves. Like most being crucified, they cursed and blasphemed, raved with gnashing teeth, and spat on their executioners. I've seen the awful torture of crucifixion drive many to absolute insanity. These thieves were no different. At first both mockingly said, 'Save yourself and us.' In those last hours, hell was about to stake its claim on the soul of one. Something in me was relieved to hear that criminal ask Jesus to remember him when Jesus came into His Kingdom.

"Doubtless this wretched man had known of Christ before this moment. There is not a synagogue, carpenter's shop, robber's cave, fishing village, nor trade route where the works and teachings of Jesus have not been discussed. There was a time Zealots were drawn to Jesus thinking He would be a great leader of their proposed revolt. Perhaps this thief was one who listened to Him teach. When Jesus would not let them make Him a king, many walked away from Him. The thief could have been among the many who went back to their trade, carrying with them the memories and visions of what they had heard and seen. I do know that in his final hour, this rebel was drawn to Jesus in faith. Christ on the center cross was a living example of what He had taught and done. He forgave.

"Seeing Christ's calm demeanor and majestic behavior, plus hearing Him speak of forgiveness, brought the man to faith and repentance. What a moment it was as Jesus struggled to lift His head, looked at him, and managed the words, 'Today shall you be with me in Paradise.' Such concern for others when His own body had such pain further arrested the attention of my guards. I have thought much since that day. Jesus harnessed His energies to forgive all the thief had done. So, I wondered, would He forgive me? I could reach only one conclusion: If that revolutionary could be forgiven for all he had done, so could I."

In all his discourse, Gaius did not tire. His voice remained strong, his demeanor determined. "I was so overcome, so numbed by the cataclysmic events—the earthquake, the darkness, the dead people rising, I stayed longer than necessary and watched as you, Nicodemus and Joseph, removed His body from the cross. As you pulled the spikes, there was no blood left to flow. There was no beating heart to cause it to flow. Only the naive would believe He was not dead when taken from the cross. You yourselves know He was dead. Yes, my deed was horrible, but it was done most thoroughly.

"I have since learned that the former Hebrew, King David, also wrote in his book of Psalms that when their Messiah came, He would have no bones broken. It is said that one of your prophets, one Zechariah, wrote that his body would be pierced. I had no prior knowledge what these men foretold. To think I may have been an agent through which these prophecies were fulfilled is overwhelming. That is the only consolation I have found in what I have done. I was part of a God-ordained plan. I was a part of evil loosed. I've been in the abyss, the depths, of evil. I want out. I saw Jesus release others. I believe He will release me from my regret, my wrong, my personal torture.

"Jesus' words and action in His death only further confirm what my fellow soldiers joined me in saying at the cross: 'Truly this was the Son of God.' I came that close to God," he said, measuring an inch distance with his thumb and forefinger, "and He let me take His life, He who could have called as many angels as He wanted. But He let me kill Him. He let me have my will. I find great relief now in yielding to His will. I am tired of my way. I am tired of being mean, cruel. I want the gentleness of the Man, the God, I saw on the cross."

At that point it must have been the wind-driven fragrance of the beautiful red blossom of a nearby eucalyptus torquata that arrested Gaius' thoughts. Something seemed to bring to mind another awareness from the cross. "I even know the smell of death. There is nothing like it. That scent I know unquestionably. The same Jesus who stood condemned before Pilate was the same man I'd ordered nailed to the cross, the same man you removed from the cross and put into the tomb. He was dead. Now come these reports He is alive. Joy and fear wrestle in my heart when I think what it would be like if I were to see Him. I feel my knees melting every time I think of such a possibility."

Gaius had hardly moved from his position on the hard stone bench. There seemed to be absolutely no awareness of his own comfort, just the need to release his sorrow. "Perhaps someday I can rid my mind of the haunting images of Jesus' suffering, but I shall never forget those words: 'Father forgive them.' It was as though they were spoken to me personally. How I long for that prayer to be answered. It gives me hope to think He forgave even me. How could it be? Now I know about mercy. I've heard you believers mention mercy. Now, somehow I'm beginning to find thoughts of mercy replacing my thoughts of remorse and shame."

Gaius dropped his head into his hands. The words seemed to come almost involuntarily: "I pray it now for myself, 'Father forgive me!' I believe that because of what happened that awful day, I have been forgiven. I, even I, who have committed so great a sin . . . I am forgiven by the one against whom I sinned."

Gaius sat erect. Joseph and I looked long at the man who was a miracle before us—a miracle of transformation sitting before us. "Soon I shall leave this place, being transferred back to Rome to the palace of Caesar. As a child, I dreamed of being a member of the prestigious Praetorian Guard in the palace. My father aspired to have such a son and had me trained for the role. My transfer to Rome is now at hand. The memory, the haunting memory of what happened in this place, however, shall never leave me."

Joseph and I sat for a while with Gaius, sharing absolute astonishment at what we were hearing, what we were seeing— the literal transformation of human character, acceptance of even the most rancorous criminal into the Kingdom of Heaven.

A new, resolute, changed man stood now. We too were glad to stretch our own bodies. Even the deep lines of his conflicted face appeared eased. "How will I, how will news of what happened here, be received there in the Imperial Court of Caesar? Talk of forgiveness in that venue where forgiveness is so needed will be strange. Should I, can I, do it? No matter what the consequences, I cannot deny what I know to be the truth."

"Gaius," Joseph said, "it is your experience, your insight that will help affirm Jesus whom you crucified. Your charisma and testimony of personal confrontation of the Christ will lead many to faith as they helped confirm ours." Upon saying this, we raised our right arms and clasped our right hands in the symbolic gesture of believers. Gaius knew the sign. This was our goodbye. We each left better, stronger men, believers more consumed with the reality of Christ.

Very shortly after visiting with Gaius, Joseph and I would feel our plan to validate the resurrection might end prematurely. As we left Gabbatha, temple guards rushed us and seized Joseph. He was arrested and locked away to be held until morning when the counsel was set to meet. Though we were frightened, as Joseph went willingly with the guards, the look we exchanged as I ran away assured us that our plan of chronicling the resurrection had only temporarily been delayed.

We felt in our spirits that Jesus' miracles were not ended as we would discover the next morning. As the court convened and commanded that Joseph to be brought forth from the house where he had been held, he was not there. The mystery of his disappearance frightened the members of the council. They were so disquieted by the disappearance of another man heavily guarded that they adjourned, agreeing not to pursue indictments against Joseph and me. Their decision to stop their actions against us was motivated more by superstition than integrity, more by fear than admission of error.

As threats against Joseph and me diminished, we were at liberty to continue our search for witnesses to the events associated with Jesus' life and death. We felt no one knew Jesus and death better than Lazarus. His home was in nearby Bethany on the eastern side of the Mount of Olives, only a short distance away. In going to Bethany, we would be tracing in reverse Jesus' last route into Jerusalem. On the crest of the Mount of Olives, we lingered looking back at the Holy City over which Jesus wept and for which He died. We were comforted that Lazarus would know what death and resurrection were like.

LAZARUS, THE PRE-EMINENT VALIDATION OF DEITY

Having bid our families good-bye the night before, we left the city early. "Are you up for a good day, Joseph?" I greeted him before dawn at the southern gate. Bethany, on the back side of the Mount of Olives, was about an hour's journey from Jerusalem. We were taking leave from our homes for several days or weeks, whatever time it took to find and talk with vital people who had first-hand information about Jesus. We would find lodging whenever we could and bivouac along the roadway should darkness overtake us on occasion.

Lazarus and his two sisters were among the people outside the disciples to spend much time with Jesus. The resurrection of Lazarus was the last miracle Jesus performed and no doubt his most astounding, which surely was the final catalyst in the Jews' demand for his death. Everyone in the area of Jerusalem had heard Jesus had raised his friend Lazarus from the dead. The news had both excited and inflamed households of the city. So because of his intimate knowledge of Jesus—and because he might have perceived much of Jesus' thought as one closest to Him, we wanted to begin our inquiry with Lazarus.

Joseph and I walked the short distance on the narrow road of sand and rock, sparing our animals for the anticipated long trek ahead. We traveled in as much comfort as possible with each of us joined by four trusted servants who had packed saddlebags on the mules and camels with food and supplies.

"Can you even begin to imagine what Lazarus might have felt

when he found himself outside the tomb when Jesus brought him back to life after four days?"

I sort of grinned. "Lazarus wouldn't have known he had been put into a tomb. But I can imagine how he felt suddenly feeling alive and invigorated after having been sick. And certainly as he saw Mary and Martha dancing in the street and the people of Bethany standing in astonishment, he would have known that something spectacular had taken place." I too was speculating. "Or maybe he did know he had been gone for a while, gone to another place, another dimension of space and time. So surely some immense understanding gripped his mind and spirit as he stood outside the tomb and realized that this was a miracle that not even he, one of Jesus' best friends had seen Him perform.

We didn't personally know Lazarus and his sisters, but we knew by reputation that they were kind people, so we knew our visit would be well received since talking about their dear friend Jesus would no doubt bring them comfort.

Just as we came to the city of Bethany, a small town of a few merchant stands, a government hall, and several modest houses and stables, we spotted a little house sitting back under some juniper trees—mud roof, adobe walls, one window, and the door ajar. The unpretentious, inviting clay house was far different from the opulent stone palaces of Jerusalem owned by Caiaphas and other wealthy Jews. Three people sat there, humbly dressed people in home-spun cloaks. They might have been exchanging a few words too quiet to discern, but mostly they appeared to be content just to stare into the distant hills awash in the morning sun, now well over the horizon but not high enough to bring the typical desert heat.

These contented people were not disturbed to see two strange men coming their way. Long ago we had abandoned our priestly garments for the clothing of the commoners; Joseph's a sandy tan garment and mine a rusty iron color. Belted and in turbans to protect from the blistering heat to come, we looked like typical men passing through the city, perhaps having come to trade for some wool for which Bethany was particularly known. "Pardon . . . ladies, and sir, could we sit with you a bit and rest?" We had now approached the three, all still unalarmed. I am Nicodemus ben Guerin, and this is Joseph of Arimathea, both of Jerusalem."

"We welcome you, sirs."

"I'm Mary. This is Martha."

We nodded in greeting, but felt like old friends very comfortable in our common acquaintance with Jesus. I said, "We heard that Jesus had very close friends in Bethany, have heard your names referenced on the streets of our city. And we knew it was you, Lazarus," my voice soliciting confirmation that indeed it was Lazarus to whom I was speaking, "and your resurrection that really got the Jewish authorities rushing for Jesus' death. They were afraid to hear of a man who had been raised from the regions of the dead."

Clearly, it wasn't Lazarus the people would have feared, not this Lazarus now in his natural state as he was before. There was nothing to fear in this man of moderate stature with his neatly combed hair not yet in turban in the early morning and his gentle, well-groomed face. Lazarus's mild demeanor assured he was well loved in the city. His hands were tender as one who could console with a caressing touch the lambs now herded in the stone fence at the side of the house.

"Yes," Lazarus, cradling a warm cup of tea and looking out over the lonely landscape, began to speak as one calm, insightful, knowing, "Jesus was our friend, is our friend. He's more like a brother than a friend. You know, more than once as we sat out in the cool night breeze under the stars, Jesus told me he would be arrested—that He would die—for His good deeds and His talk of heaven and God. But I couldn't comprehend it."

Then Lazarus' voice became even more calm, more certain. "He told me too that he wouldn't stay dead. He said he would come back to life after three days in the tomb. Joseph, now I know. I've heard it was you who dared ask Pilate for Jesus' body for a holy burial." Lazarus reached again for Joseph's hand, perhaps seeking again the warmth of the initial handshake. Once again, he gripped Joseph's hand and forearm in confirmation that it was an eternal deed that Joseph had done. His warmth let us know that he understood we were not men just passing through on some casual mission. Jesus, he knew, was the person we needed to speak of.

It was Martha, a stately but somewhat tense-seeming, agitated, woman in her late thirties, who spoke and rushed inside to bring lotus tea for all. But, ever attentive to the comfort of her guests and recognizing we would stay a while, she returned immediately with a polished, artfully crafted wooden bench obviously reserved for guests. "This was a gift from Jesus, our friend. He would be honored that we use it now." We welcomed a place to rest and the hospitality after our early-morning journey. Soon Martha returned with our tea in the immense efficiency typical of her widely known reputation.

The preoccupation of the siblings as we had arrived perhaps had been too deep for conversation. Or maybe they had assessed the miracle of life so long that there was nothing else to say. Too, no doubt, they were emotionally distraught over the news of Jesus' death. Whatever the reason, they had been sitting quietly. Then abruptly, the sister identified as Mary asked, "Have you heard of what Jesus did here?" We nodded our heads in sad response. "We still don't understand why, and we don't know where He is. But we do not think for a minute that He is truly dead. He is alive, and we'll see Him again. We know we will." Effusively she spoke, "Jesus spent more time in our home and in our village that any other place outside Galilee. Others here knew and adored Him. He was neither class-minded nor indifferent to the different.

He was compelling, yet one of us."

Urgency was apparent in her voice.

There couldn't have been a better opening for our inquiry. "That's what we're here to talk about. "Mary," I said, nodding to the sister of about thirty-five, obviously alert and energetic, the yellow of her cloak suggesting the sunshine of her personality, "you might help us understand Jesus' resurrection by telling us of your brother's return to life after being dead four days. We knew the background and wanted to get directly to Mary's perspective on the restored life of her brother."

Pensively she began, "Jesus delayed after hearing the news of Lazarus' death. Why? I questioned. Candidly, His apparent disinterest angered me at first. Didn't He care? Was He not the loving One we perceived Him to be? These questions hammered my grieving mind, only creating more pain for me.

"Peter told me that while some of the disciples demurred, Thomas said, 'Come, let us also go, that we may die with Him.' And Peter said he had urged Jesus not to come at all, reminding Him of the attempts to stone Him. They all, except Thomas, questioned His wisdom of going back to that area. They pleaded with Him not to go. But He did come. I knew He would. I know now how foolish it was of me to doubt His love and wisdom. In retrospect, I recognize how unsafe it was for Him to have come. But, ultimately He was compelled by the very love I questioned."

Martha nudged her sister out of the conversation, herself wanting our attention. "When He arrived at our house, I chided Him for His delay. I was still angry but controlled my temper. Jesus looked directly into our faces when He came that morning, said nothing, and then calmly walked to the tomb. We heard as He told the disciples to remove the stone. They protested profusely, trying to persuade Jesus not to disturb a four-day-deceased body which surely would be putrid by that time. Nevertheless, they obediently took away the stone from the place where we had left our brother.

"Jesus then, still calm and with measured words, lifted His eyes to heaven and prayed, 'Father, I thank you that you have heard me. And I know that you always hear me, but because of the people who are standing by, I said this that they might believe that you sent me.' Then with a loud voice, He shouted, 'Lazarus, come forth!'

"For a minute everyone around the tomb stood mute. We were there. The disciples were there. All of Bethany was there. By that time, the people had heard that Jesus had come into town soon after daybreak. All of us stood at the tomb—all mute, silent, waiting. The disciples knew that nature would obey Him. We hoped Jesus' power extended to the grave. The other onlookers were just skeptical. "There was no sound, no angelic light, no drama. Lazarus simply suddenly appeared. He stood there before us on the huge stone which lay flat on the ground. He had a momentary glow, as if undergoing some transformation from a perfect world back onto a terrestrial plain. He smiled and spoke, greeting Jesus and us. The crowd clamored to touch Jesus and scrutinize Lazarus. But as if unaware of the amazement around them, Jesus and Lazarus left the tomb and walked privately, slowly, back toward our house, oblivious to everyone around them and nonplused by what had just occurred. What those two shared after such a momentous event, no one knows except Jesus and Lazarus."

"Lazarus was back from the dead—was back in our home doing all the things he did before, and many saw what happened. As a result many believed in Jesus. But some were upset, angered even. This miracle was too much for Jesus' detractors to endure. Almost immediately, rumblings began of Jesus' tricks, of His proclaimed deity.

"Jesus stayed the rest of the day with us. Twice he walked into the streets to play with children curious of what had occurred and of this man who could do such wonders. Then life for us changed again. It was two days after Jesus brought our brother back to us that we heard the Sanhedrin had seized Him."

Where Lazarus had been buried was just beyond the family's humble house. From our bench in front of the house, we could see the tomb. Even then, as if it were a public attraction, a landmark, people were gathered there. Some were just sitting and contemplating what happened there. Others were conferring, trying to reason it all out. One man who had just left the tomb speculated loudly enough that we could hear, "Lazarus had been in the tomb four days. Even if the old tale about the spirit remaining in the body a period after death before departing were true, Lazarus' spirit would have left his body."

Joseph and I knew of such speculations and had analyzed the possible reason for Jesus' delay in responding to news of His close friend's death: Obviously, He might have deliberately delayed the two more days before coming so that none could possibly say Lazarus' spirit was still in his body when resurrected. Jesus likely wanted to leave no space for anyone to deny His greatest miracle verifying His power over life and death.

Just then a young woman, who seemed to be in the group of visitors at Lazarus' tomb, stopped to look at Lazarus' home and to observe him in his restored body. Mary recognized her as a young woman known in the village and called out to her, "Rachel, come here." Contritely and with an air of reluctance, the young woman of perfect physical proportions and unusual beauty moved toward us, her eyes shifting randomly and nervously.

"Rachel, we've talked of Jesus' death and resurrection. These are the two men who buried Jesus." There was some reluctance in meeting us on the young woman's face.

"Did you know Jesus personally?" Joseph asked as he and I

stood momentarily in respect for the young lady.

With a pained expression, the woman identified as Rachael looked at Mary who gave her a nod as if to say, Go ahead and tell them. They're okay. They're safe. Mary knew Rachael had a story we needed to hear, so Mary helped her start. "Rachel was not always a believer in Jesus. In fact, her life was very contrary to His teachings. Go ahead, Rachel. They will understand."

Rachael looked at us and then cast her eyes down as if recalling something disconcerting to her. "It was the harvest feast in my sister's home here in Bethany. I had eased into the crowd with men looking at me lustfully and women withdrawing from me suspiciously. I was, simply put, a woman of the street, a prostitute. Being who I was, I was too well known for what I was. Most of the nice people pretended not to notice me in the loud festivities—that is, they didn't acknowledge me until I did something which was repulsive to them. I knelt before Jesus and began to wash His feet. I knew what I did would cause an even harsher judgment on me. The act was most unconventional, but not spontaneous. I knew what I was doing. It was what my sad heart needed to do. I had heard of Jesus forgiving the lady brought to Him who was accused of adultery. I had heard of His conversation with the Samaritan woman at the well. I had become sick of my lifestyle, and for a long time I had watched Jesus when He came to our town. I wanted the blessed life that He modeled, and I wanted the forgiveness of which He spoke."

"So, you literally approached Jesus and washed His feet without invitation?" I exclaimed.

I knelt before Him. I washed His feet with my tears and wiped the dust from His sandals with my hair. I sought the cleansing He offered."

"Why were you not stoned?" I asked.

There was grief and a bit of bitterness in her voice. "The answer is simple: I was not married. Our moral code does little to protect women, but a single woman is not stoned. Stoning for an adulterous wife is mandated by the law, not for her adultery but her infidelity. It is because of her offense to the male who is protected by the law that she is punished, not for the sin. She belongs to one man the same way sheep, goats, and land are his property and simply comes under the laws of property. Harlots, the label given women such as I, are considered the property of all men. Such women rank lower than animals in our land and subsequently have not offended the law.

"I was an outcast ignored in the daylight by my patrons, leered at by Roman soldiers, hissed at by mothers shielding their children's gaze of me, and despised by the pious. Then one day I met a different man in the street, someone whose mere presence communicated He was different. To my astonishment He treated me like a lady. He stepped into the gutter to let me pass, smiled, and shared a friendly greeting as He went on His way. I later learned that was Jesus. I thought of Him, 'He doesn't seem like a man—clean, courteous, gracious.' I thought of Him as more like a god. Later on the Mount of Olives, I heard Him speak of the love of God. The love of which He spoke I had never known, but I instantly desired it. I had the feeling that if He forgave me, God would.

"My moment came when I hesitatingly approached Jesus on the Mount of Olives. Would He scold me, condemn, or castigate me? I didn't know. But I took the risk."

"Did you tell Jesus who you were?" I asked.

"Yes."

"What was His response?"

"Seeing my obvious contrition and hearing my words of repentance, He said He forgave me. I felt as though heaven had acted on my behalf and I was forgiven. That was the reason I had to show my devotion openly. It wasn't well received by those glaring at me, but obviously it was acceptable to Jesus. He tried to mitigate the moment by telling a story of two debtors. One owned fifty pieces of silver and one five hundred. Both were forgiven by their creditors. Then Jesus explained that the one forgiven the most would be the one most grateful. That was an allusion to me I knew—and an appeasement to the crowd. I had much of which to be forgiven. Expressing my devotion was worth the scorn I felt for doing so. Now, in light of His death, I am all the more glad I expressed my love for One so unloved by so many.

"I come to this tomb often because I can relate. I can reflect here. Lazarus was physically dead, and Jesus brought him back to life. Spiritually, I was no less dead, and as great a miracle as He performed for Lazarus, He performed for me. I am alive. I hope you understand me, not as the people of this village, but as Jesus did."

Apologizing for having to rush to care for a sick woman, Rachael excused herself, leaving us uplifted, stirred once again about the power Jesus has in life as well as in death. All people of the village knew well the love Jesus had for Mary, Martha, and Lazarus. Rachel knew the love He had for her too, and that was plainly enough to change her, to restore her. Even as we had talked, her countenance had changed from dismal and reluctant to effervescent and animated. That, we knew, was the work of Jesus. Rachel left, hugging her apparent dear friend Mary goodbye.

We were grateful for the interlude of Rachael, were affirmed in our perception of Jesus as a true life-changer. But we wanted to talk with Lazarus more. "Lazarus, while you were beyond the veil of death for four days, Jesus delayed His coming at the invitation of your sisters. Joseph and I want to share with you our understanding of why He chose delay instead of immediate response as His heart must have so longed to do. He did so because you were to be involved in His signature miracle. In bringing you back from death, Jesus knew His detractors would be forced to deal with the miracle definitive of His deity. It evidenced He had power over death, that He had power over all things.

"As He anticipated, the accusers had no explanation for this miracle, but they were unwilling to accept its implications. Their fear of a man who independently had power over life and death only hardened their resolve. What Jesus said, 'I am the resurrection and the life; he that believes in me, though he die, yet he will live'—His implied proclamation of deity—really inflamed them. Your resurrection, Lazarus, proved these words of Jesus. That truth scared Annas and the Sanhedrin to death—scared them into the death of Jesus.

"There is profound eternal significance to your resurrection. Our own resurrection, though the span of time between our death and our resurrection is much longer than yours, Lazarus, is guaranteed by your return to life. Coming here has given us cause to continue our search for validation of Jesus' resurrection." Lazarus looked at us steadily, knowingly. Quickly my mind rushed to Martha's observation that Jesus and Lazarus had walked away in quiet, confidential conversation immediately after Lazarus came from the tomb. I sort of pursed my lips and closed my eyes in confirmation that Lazarus knew the significance of what happened to him. Just maybe he'd already had this conversation with someone much more perceptive than we. It was a good moment for me. I knew I would mention it to Joseph that night as we took our rest from the momentous day.

Reluctantly, Joseph and I, no longer strangers but now supernaturally new relatives of Lazarus' family, arose from where we had sat for three fast hours. So intense was our sharing that we had never become distracted by the curious onlookers or the street activity around us. This time hugs and blessings replaced the detached handshakes of our first meeting. We headed out of Bethany, stopping soon by the roadside just outside the village.

There we spent the night on the rough-spun blankets our servants kindly spread. We knew our journey had only begun.

Tomorrow we would continue our inquiry into eternal matters. We would walk the routes Jesus had walked. We would talk with people with whom Jesus had talked. We each held an unspoken hope that we might even encounter the man we had laid into the tomb days before. To expand our odyssey for truth and hope, we would next find Simon Peter whose reputation for vacillation was well known among his constituents. We wanted to assess his resolve and passion for Jesus.

There was no more likely place to find Peter than Galilee. Our journey there would take us across unforgiving terrain, past stunning gray rock formations jutting up like timeless citadels keeping watch over the centuries. We would travel through towering mountains crowned with olive trees that seemed to defy gravity, their buckled roots clinging to the hillside. We were not to be distracted from our objective, a visit with Peter.

PETER'S CONFIRMATION OF JESUS

"Finding Peter has been a chase, but there he is, Joseph," I eagerly pointed to a stocky bearded man sitting on a fishing vessel rocking gently on the blue waters, its bow wedged just a bit into the pristine sands of the sea. His nets were on the shore folded as only a skilled fisherman knew how. They were ready for Peter's next launch, but he wasn't putting them into the boat to move out to sea. In fact, he was strangely sitting on the roughly hewn planks of the boat, his dangling sandaled feet showing abuse and wear as he talked to an intent crowd. He appeared to be responding to specific questions they dared ask a man whose countenance was forbidding, a man emanating little warmth.

From a safe distance and at an angle from which Peter could not see us, we sat behind the people enraptured by what we heard. Here, too, we should be safe if any Roman or Jewish investigators had infiltrated the group hearing Peter and wishing to know more of Jesus.

"Some think it strange Jesus spent so much time here in Galilee," we heard him explain. Knowing the region, Peter understood why Jesus elected to center his ministry here. There were reasons other than the scenery and solitude.

"Jesus knew what He was doing. This remote area gave safe haven from the religious establishment in Jerusalem who sought His whereabouts in pursuit of His life. However, for Him there was a more pressing reason for His frequent presence here. The caravan routes from the East beyond the mountains of Moab; those passing along the shores of the Great Sea, the Via Maras; and others passing through the Valley of Jezreel's ancient city of

Megiddo, and those passing from the distant land of Egypt by way of Samaria, all traverse the shores of this lake. And, nearby," he said sweeping his weathered arms through the air, "are the hot wells known from Rome to Athens, from Babylon to Egypt. Persons from all these regions come here for health and recreation. People of many languages visit the baths daily. The abundance of fresh water also allows them to replenish supplies for the long journeys.

Jesus consciously chose this crossroads of the world to launch His teachings. It is little wonder that near the end of his ministry, the Greeks came asking to see him. Doubtless, members of a caravan from Greece or persons seeking healing had heard Him teach and told of Him. People from everywhere in the commercial world heard him teach sitting on the western slope overlooking the sea. They heard something more than their buying and selling, something revolutionary:

Blessed are the poor in spirit for theirs is the kingdom of heaven.
Blessed are those who mourn, for they shall be comforted.
Blessed are the meek, for they shall inherit the earth."

Peter looked and sounded emphatic in sharing the information he apparently deemed crucial. "The mercenary-bent traders, people who only saw life in terms of getting and spending, for the first time encountered truth here in Galilee, discovered something of the very essence of life. They found something beyond the temporal give-and-take world in which they lived. Jesus taught a new spirit for humanity, that meekness is love with enough muscle to control a violent temper. He taught of a human power blended with gentleness, discipline, and strength. He taught the truth the traveling traders and wealthy pleasure-seekers knew instinctively in their restless spirits: If we wish to possess the earth, we should beware lest the earth possess us.

"Jesus did nothing by accident. Everything He did, every word, was for one purpose: to advance His Kingdom in this world—to point people to truth. Galilee was a calculated choice. He knew His message would be dispersed from this place all over the world. Jesus taught that the heavenly, honorable way of life is most often just opposite what we would do, feel, or say normally. He said we shouldn't just love our neighbor, those who are good to us. He said we should love our enemies and do good to people who do wrong to us. Such a message helped to civilize societies far from these shores."

"Cephas," a fisherman having long known him called out, "why did Jesus call you Peter?"

With pride typical of the man of impetuous reputation, Peter responded, "Jesus called me the 'rock, Peter.' Those who traveled with us knew me by Peter, not Cephas. That's sort of strange now because no one was more on-again, off-again than I. There were times I was rock solid in following Him and times when. . . when I plainly rebelled or lied. Those are the times I regret," he mused, the clawing hand of guilt apparently tearing at his heart.

"Jesus always saw beyond what we can see. Jesus changed my life here at a time my fishing was flourishing. The markets in Rome were pleading for fish from these waters. To Roman palates they were considered delicacies. The demand was excellent and the price superb. I was set for life. This fleet of boats you see here were all new when Jesus called me to follow Him.

"Jesus called first my brother Andrew, who had been a disciple of John the Baptist. Andrew followed by his own compulsion, but also at John's insistence. Jesus had such a compelling spirit. I had no choice when He said, 'Follow me and I will make you fishers of men.' There was something strange, something magnetic, something supernatural in the man. I just followed.

"What did you hear? 'Follow Me, Cephas?'

"What did you do?"

"Where did you go?" The calls swelled from the crowd.

"There was no way we could envision then what course we

would follow. There was something inescapable in His call. Andrew looked at me and I at him. I nodded and he gave me an acknowledging smile. Andrew and I pride ourselves because we were among the first to follow Him. But I tell you, the man was irresistible. I think now it was His total goodness that was so compelling.

"Just down the shore a bit, we encountered James and his brother John, sons of Zebedee, and He called them to come follow Him. We could sense urgency in Jesus' life. He seemed to be selecting men to become an intimate group of learners from Him. There was something He had to do—that's how we understood Him.

"Jesus' words were magnets. His spirit was truth. Once having heard him, anyone was changed either to love and believe or to rebel and hate. There was no indifference with this man of such an intense character. But He was fun, of course, giving us all monikers such as mine 'Peter' or 'Sons of Thunder' for James and John. But He was, more than anything, a philosopher, teaching the very essence of truth to stop the onslaught of evil in the world. Too, He was an exacting man who demanded the most supreme human conduct in social and religious matters.

"Jesus didn't come to refute the Jewish religion. He came actually to complete it. He had the highest regard for the traditions of His faith, though He knew that the religious leaders had corrupted the truth. And He didn't merely acquiesce to the wrong He saw. I saw Him become incensed in the temple once when we visited it as we did on occasion. The column-lined portico of the courtyard had become a market with two hundred thousand people there. The 'moneychangers,' the commercial people and the priests in conjunction, collaborated to extract the most money possible from the people who came to pay temple taxes and to offer sacrifices for their sins. We could not believe what we saw. The corruption was repulsive."

Peter, growing weary in his sitting position, could only shift, not daring to stand on the swaying boat, and hardly paused in his discourse. "The situation was so corrupt that temple authorities had declared only half shekels could be used to pay temple tax. They had set up tables to handle the large crowds as they came to pay. The rate was totally mercenary, an entire day's wages for the poor people.

"The greed was so evident to Jesus and all us. We saw lambs, often purchased on site for sacrifice, drastically overpriced. Then we observed the priests charge the people to have their lambs sacrificed. Most horribly, we often saw priests lead lambs around the altar and back into the fold to be sold a second or third time. They paid a cheap price for pigeons raised at Ramat Rahel and then charged worshippers an exorbitant price for them. Even these were sometimes sold more than once.

"Jesus was moved to a demonstrative anger. His fun times and his philosophical times were gone at that point. He was a rebel, a rebel against wrong. He was angry. He shouted at the greedy priests. He turned over the tables, drove out the animals, gave the merchants their dove cages and told them to get out. He screamed to them, 'You have made My Father's house a house of merchandising!'

"I have since been reminded our father David spoke of the zeal of the Lord being vented. Malachi, one of our prophets, wrote that the Messiah would cleanse the temple. Another of our sages of old, Isaiah, forewarned He would deal prudently with such people. To think those moneychangers would carry out their conspiratorial thievery in the Court of the Gentiles is unimaginable. Jehovah had our ancestors to build that court as an open invitation to the Gentiles to worship Him. He has chosen our race, not as pets but as a pattern to all nations, and that pattern had become distorted. So degraded was the conduct in the outer court it had become known as the 'Bazaar of Annas.' Annas was a disgrace as a high priest.

Peter's intimate knowledge of Jesus was clear. And the people demanded more. "It was so bad that sons of Annas were known as great hoarders of money. No one could worship in a carnival atmosphere such as this. They were so perverse as to carry out such thievery right in the place where the Ark of the Covenant rested.

"Jesus embodied His own teachings: 'Be angry and sin not.' The sin of the people was in not being angry over such misconduct. A deep sense of shame, sorrow, and anger built up in Jesus for good cause. In Him determination and dynamism were amazingly combined. Gentleness controlled, but did not eliminate His capacity for righteous indignation. Neither did it lessen His zeal for a just cause. Love for righteousness and purity motivated Him to act."

Peter moved again, this time propping an elbow on a bent knee he had lifted to the bow. He was normally not a patient or instructive man. Jesus usually did the teaching like this—from a hillside, a boat. This was Peter's moment to carry on what his Master had begun. "As these self-righteous thieves fled, they shouted to Him to give them a sign that they might believe. A sign He did give them, but their cold hearts would not receive it. Of the temple, the hieron, that required Herod the Great forty-six years to build, He said, 'Destroy this temple, this naos, and I will rebuild it in three days.'

"The temple building, the hieron, in which He spoke was not the one of which He spoke. It, the temple building, is known as a sacred place used for worship, an edifice. In referring to a different part of the temple, the naos, known as 'the dwelling place of deity,' He was speaking of His body. Not even we at the moment knew of what He was speaking. Soon we would. He did indeed speak prophetically."

Joseph and I looked at each and nodded as if to say, "Now we understand." We had for the first time understood this mashal, this veiled remark. An hour must have passed. Peter was interrupted little. The people were intent upon his every word. They seemed to understand that his message was merely an extension of the teachings of the man Whom he obviously adored. Too, we observed, his words carried much of the power and spirit of Jesus, his mentor. Joseph and I still sat on the ground, still behind the crowd unobserved by Peter and undetected as strangers in the diverse people typical of Galilee.

"Peter," an eager young enquirer called out, "Judas, we have heard of him. Tell us about Him."

"I will tell you a bit about him and admit a bit of my shame. Solemnity and sadness prevailed at one point in our meal together—our last meal, though we didn't know it. But Jesus knew. Jesus broke bread and told us we should do the same, always in remembrance of Him. He said that in like manner His body would be broken for us. Then, He lifted the cup and said, 'This cup is to be drunk in remembrance of Me.' There was no way we could comprehend or envision how those symbols would be played out in the next hours.

"Soon after He dipped the bread, a most unusual thing happened. Judas left the room—more than left. He bolted. Because he was our treasurer, we thought he was going on an errand for Jesus. We were to see Judas only once more in Gethsemane.

"Reflecting on that night, I think there was one last appeal, one last opportunity for Judas to return. We sang a Psalm as we concluded. The streets of Jerusalem are narrow, and the still night air caused the sound of singing to travel far. Thinking about it now, I believe Jesus chose that hymn as an invitation to Judas. Oh, if he had only responded favorably. A traitor to the greatest cause of heaven, Judas made his way through the winding streets to the high priest.

"Judas' avarice prevailed over the largess of Jesus' love. He sold not Jesus but himself for thirty pieces of silver. Later realizing what he had done, in revulsion he threw the coins at those who posed as his confidants. They were now his taunters. They mocked him and laughed at his emotional distress. Had he not done what followed—hanged himself in remorse too deep to confront, I am convinced Christ would have forgiven him. Judas was greedy and envious of Jesus' stature. Jesus had often warned us of the traps of greed and envy so cleverly used by the Great Deceiver Satan. And I counsel you against each now."

Peter, apparently beginning to suffer more from having sat so long, pulled himself up and stood holding the mast. He dropped his head, shook it, and said, "If only, if only. . . ."

"If only what, Peter?" an old fisherman asked.

"With grief I share with you my moment of shame, even disgrace, from which only Jesus could enable me to recover. In the Upper Room that night, Jesus said one of us would betray Him. His remarks live with me yet:

All of you will be made to stumble because of Me this night, for
it is written:
I will strike the Shepherd,
And the sheep of the flock will be scattered.
But after I have been raised, I will go before you to Galilee.

I missed the most important part. I was so concerned with declaring my devotion, I didn't comprehend the significance of the rest of His statement. Instead of hearing what He said about being raised, all I heard was 'one of you will betray me.' With bravado I said, 'Even if all are made to stumble because of You, I will never be made to stumble.'"

We could see that the rugged Peter choked back tears and continued with emotion in his voice. "Jesus looked into my eyes and calmly said, 'Assuredly, I say to you that this night, before the rooster crows, you will deny me three times.' I failed. I failed so miserably to be loyal to Jesus—to fulfill my commitment. I know

now a true commitment is the capacity to carry out the intent of a decision long after the emotion that inspired it has faded. Behind every commitment has to be a firm personal resolve. Resolve I then lacked, but not now. I hope that those hereafter who make known a commitment to Him will carry it out and not deny Him as I so disgracefully did."

Again pausing to abate his emotions, Peter moved to another venue of Jesus' last hours. "From the Upper Room on Mt. Zion, we went through the Essen Gate and across the Kidron Valley. Through the Brook Kidron, blood from the sacrificial lambs in the temple had flowed on this day of sacrifice. By the light of the full moon, we could see the water flowing crimson. What a foreshadowing of what lay ahead. Thus began what will always be known as 'the night of vile.'

Joseph and I were drawn by the message of this rustic, disheveled fisherman. For the moment we had dismissed any potential danger for ourselves in this place among these people. We knew we must speak with Peter personally. Slowly, to remain undetected, we made our way through the crowd and soon stood near the boat, our sandals sinking slightly in the damp sand. Peter saw us immediately and sensed something imperative in our spirits. He ended his discourse and opened an opportunity that we might speak to him. "If there is anyone who would like a private word with me, I'll be happy to talk more of Jesus."

We had made our way to Peter's boat and had taken the signal. His picking us out of the crowd was no accident. Peter, perhaps, recognized some divine purpose in us, needed to talk with us. "We are from Jerusalem, newer believers than you, Nicodemus," pointing to myself, and nodding toward Joseph, "my friend Joseph. We have felt your faith. We are here for unbiased confirmation of what we too believe, that Jesus was God's Son, that He came to earth as savior for the fallen human race as your story of the moneychangers in the temple so well illustrated. Do you believe that was Jesus, the beaten man crucified on the center cross?"

Assertively Peter replied, "Oh, I have no doubt. The entire earth changed that day He was crucified. None of us disciples understood fully who He was until that time when day became night and the earth shook. Surely, all creation was reacting at the injustice of earth. Jesus had talked to us of this very thing, the crucifixion and His resurrection, but we didn't understand. We are still comprehending the true essence of Who He was and what He did, but this I know: That was Jesus. Why do you ask?"

"In Jerusalem detractors are using every explanation imaginable to deny the truth of the resurrection. We've come to confirm, come for reasons we aren't even sure of, to find people like you who can give first-hand testimony to Jesus' deity."

Peter bristled at the denial of Jesus. "I spent years with Him. I knew His countenance and voice. I knew Him well. It was He who died that ignominious death. Prior to the resurrection, my understanding was clouded. I knew He was Jesus of Nazareth, born in Bethlehem, but He was more. He was the ultimate act of incarnation. He was Immanuel, God, literally God, with us. It was decided before the world was formed that Jesus would come to earth and be raised from death. God sent Jesus to offer us new life, life in the resurrection. Jesus came to teach the human heart to obey and love once again."

By now we were walking along the shore. The crowd, too, seemed to sense the urgency of us strangers among them. They respected our privacy and kept their distance. Silently we walked to a place on the shore where the rocks were blackened by some previous fire there. Charred bits of wood remained just out of reach of the sea. "It was here, right here, we saw the Master for the third time after the resurrection."

We noted that Peter had said "The Master," evidencing his devotion.

"The women at the tomb said that He sent them to tell us He would see us in Galilee. I exulted, 'I'm going fishing,' meaning I want to be where Jesus said He would be. I could hardly wait to get here. To secure food when we got here, we went fishing and toiled all night. Still our nets remained empty. Then by the slightest of morning light, we saw someone on the shore standing by this fire. A familiar voice called out asking if we had caught anything. There are few things more disturbing than to fish hard and catch nothing. One more frustrating thing, however, is to fish hard, catch nothing, and be asked if you caught anything. That is the ultimate of embarrassment.

"When we answered no, He shouted, 'Cast your nets on the right side of the boat.' The words were familiar. We had fished here with Him earlier, and this same scenario had been played out. We cast our net, and the catch was so great we feared it would break our nets.

"John, always perceptive and alert, was the first to realize who had called out to us. With joy he cried out, 'It is Jesus. That is Jesus on the shore!'

"My heart raced at the thought. I put on my garments and plunged into the sea. As I swam, I thought, This is the Jesus who healed the sick on these shores. Here on the mountainside He taught. This is the Jesus who with a word calmed the storm that stirred these waters. It was these waters on which He walked. This is the Jesus. . . . This is the Jesus. . . . This is the Jesus I denied three times.

"The others soon came ashore. As I think of what happened then, it was as though each action, each element, of Jesus that day had a teaching-learning significance. He walked to the fire. Our prophets often used fire as a symbol of judgment. As He walked to the fire, so He had gone to the cross to be judged for us. Bread was warming by the fire. A commonly known concept is that bread speaks of provisions. As He provided the bread, so I am persuaded He will supply all our needs from His riches in glory. Fish have long symbolized productivity. There were fish on the coals of fire. However, He did a most unusual thing. He told us to bring some of our fish. This too had a message. To be productive for Him, a joint effort is required. Without Him we can do nothing. I have a new conviction. It is that through Him I can do all things He desires.

"Jesus and I had shared fleeting glances as we sat around the fire. My eyes had darted away each time in shame. Then our gazes met and locked as He spoke, 'Peter, do you have a selfless love for Me?' I evaded the direct question and replied that I was back in fellowship with Him. He said, 'Feed My little lambs.' I knew what He meant. He often used such language of shepherding to teach the young or immature in the faith. He posed a second question: 'Do you truly have a self-giving love for me?' Once more I affirmed I was back in fellowship with Him. This time He said, 'Shepherd My flock.' This truth also came from His prior teachings. He had told us to be fishers of men and now He said, 'Shepherd My flock.'

"Being both a shepherd and a fisherman is common here. We fish in the spring and winter when the fresh waters bring organic matter into the sea and the fish feed near the surface. We perform as shepherds in the fall and spring when the sheep have their greatest needs. By using these two professions, He was defining for us our roles.

"I could hardly bare His third question. 'Peter, do you love Me more than these?' He glanced at my fishing boats, then at my fellow disciples. For me that defined what he meant by 'these.' He was asking if I loved Him more than my possessions. He queried as to whether I loved Him more than I loved my friends, my family. Assuredly, I answered yes. My reply from the depth of my new resolve came forth, 'Lord, you know all things. You know I am truly back in fellowship with You.'

"Perhaps it was my use of the title Lord I delighted to apply to Him that convinced Him of my unwavering renewed devotion. Still He instructed me, 'Feed My sheep.' This time He spoke of teaching those mature in the faith that they might continue to mature and produce. To these roles I have devoted my life and resolved to give Him my all, even if I have to die for Him as He died for me. I now know His reason for probing me three times. It was three times I denied Him."

Peter sat on the warm sands and signaled we should do the same. Now a man matured by experience and pain, he was overflowing in sharing Jesus. "Reconciliation is rare. Making up is hard. The power of the resurrection is the power of reconciliation. In this relationally challenged world because of my reconciliation with Him, I want His resurrection power to be visible in me. I am living proof that the most severely estranged can have a restored relationship.

"Three times I had denied Him. Now by His grace He had given me three opportunities to profess Him. As always He had my interest, as He does of all, at heart. It was with joy I had professed my loyalty which I shall forever demonstrate." Peter concluded his philosophical applications. Remorse was replaced by repentance.

"Yes, I believe in His bodily resurrection. Here, right here by these charred reminders, I saw Him, dined with Him, and talked with Him. On this spot I saw the resurrected Jesus."

"Such empirical evidence is what we seek," noted Joseph. "Your first-person, on-the-scene recollection of this revered moment gives us a sense of sharing in it and offers irrefutable evidence Jesus lives." I nodded affirmation.

Peter was tenacious, holding us until his soul was purged. "One further obvious proof of His resurrection I must share. Days after the resurrection, I visited the steps of the temple. It was a hot day and many people were resting there. They were from many nations, but mostly local people. They were individuals heavily involved in the trial and crucifixion and then witnesses to the empty tomb. They had heard that Jesus had been seen by many since the resurrection. They knew the man they had crucified was not an ordinary man. They knew only a man who was who He claimed to be, God, could come to life again.

"On those temple steps, I told them they had taken Jesus lawlessly and killed Him. I told them God had raised Him. They did not shout me down because they knew what I said was truth. I reminded them of the Law which said David declared God would not allow His 'Holy One to see corruption.' I explained how David 'foreseeing this, spoke concerning the resurrection of Jesus.' I wanted those people to know God was not taken by surprise. I quoted from their well-known scrolls again: 'Therefore let all the house of Israel know assuredly that God has made this Jesus, Whom you crucified, both Lord and Christ.'

"My hearers did not protest my words. They were indicted by them, deeply convicted. They cried out to me and the other apostles with me, 'What shall we do?' That was easy. My response must have shaken the columns of the portico: 'Repent and let every one of you be baptized in the name of Jesus Christ.' I told them the baptism was a symbol of the forgiveness for their sin, not a means to obtain forgiveness. They understood, and we baptized three thousand that day. There was no revolt on the steps of the temple because these people had seen Jesus arrested, seen Him beaten, seen Him led away, seen the panic of the soldiers, and seen the angel and the empty tomb. They knew who Jesus was, and they believed in the resurrection."

We sat for a minute, stunned and deep in gratitude for men like Peter. We felt his truth. We had known of the great event of three thousand being baptized, but we didn't know Peter then. We didn't understand the significance of what had happened there. The very people closest to the death of Jesus, many of them those who demanded His death, now were believers. They no longer could deny His deity. Now they embraced the truth.

"Thank you, Peter. Thank you for your courage. Thank you for your confirmation of the truth we know and feel, the truth we too have seen. Surely, life is more than survival. Life is an eternal process. Jesus came to restore wholeness to a broken people. Thank you for your first-hand knowledge of that. Thank you for sharing your life, your words, your essence with us. What we experienced here in Galilee is a forever thing."

As we left Peter, a crowd was once again gathering around him asking questions as he lifted his nets. We were more than satisfied in our investigation. But we had to move on. There were others who knew Jesus. We had yet to interview any of the women who were involved in the reported resurrection. Though the testimony of women was not considered credible, Jesus gave women credibility. One of those closest to Him was Mary Magdalene. She was among the first at the tomb and a logical one to seek. Her experiences, no doubt, would offer insight into the person of Jesus. But there was the question in our minds of whether her traumatic experiences in the horrifying death of her friend Jesus had left her in a state of shock, making her insights unreliable. The one who could either further confirm or confuse us waited down the shore of Galilee in the village of Magdala.

SCROLL VIII

MARY MAGDALENE'S ACCOUNT OF JESUS

Joseph and I found Mary on the shore of the Galilee. After she had seen Jesus, she had retreated to the quiet of her home village. There were fewer persons to disturb her there, just a few unpretentious houses on the outskirts of town with quiet families, creating a pleasant, comforting community. We ourselves felt safe, not pursued, and free here in the tranquil, secluded place with mountains securing one side and the sea the other. The solitude enhanced Mary's reverie. And it was reverie which we saw on her face and in her posture as she rhythmically worked in the small garden of her sea-washed home. She didn't notice us approaching the arbor leading to her house because she was intent upon removing the few blades of grass which interrupted the beauty of the freesia-scented lavender cyclamen carefully placed beside her doorway. The energy and the peace visible in her carriage let us know quickly that here was an individual who had been with Jesus, one who had been touched with his peace, and one now at peace with herself after the deepest trauma of her life.

The countenance of no one we encountered surprised us more than Mary's. She was not at all what we expected as she stood to wipe the sweat from her temples with a delicate linen handkerchief. She was far removed from the disheveled, distracted woman we might have anticipated who would still be battling personal demons. She was obviously of a wealthy class just at the peak of her physical evolution, a woman of maybe thirty. Her complexion was flawless. It was that of women who used night-ly facials made of dough and ass's milk, a beauty regimen exclusive to the elite. Her expensive facial powder was white accented with a mineral-based red. Her brows and lashes were brushed black, her eyelids kohl blue, her fingers and toenails a fashionable white. Her dangling jade earrings purchased from an Oriental trader accentuated her loveliness. Among women of her city, she was a woman to be praised and emulated. This was our initial assessment of Mary.

"Mary, Mary Magdalene?" Joseph's voice was asking for confirmation from the woman with her raven-black hair made smooth by rich olive oil, piled high on her head and held in place by beeswax and a camel bone comb. Mary's loose dress of emerald shantung was secured at the waist by a heavily jeweled belt. I held back, feeling Joseph's voice might be less startling to a fellow gardener.

"Yes, I'm Mary. And may I inquire who is addressing me?" Mary asked as she came through the arbor to greet us.

"I'm Joseph, and my friend is Nicodemus." Joseph and I exchanged quick glances of agreement that we had both seen the flicker of recognition in Mary's eyes.

"I have heard of you. It was you who took Jesus to your tomb, Joseph. I thank you for that kindness, but I don't understand how it was you who took care of Jesus' body when you are both known to be members of the Sanhedrin who demanded Jesus' death."

The apparent contradiction of our position and our action was evident in her lovely face. "We understand, Mary, your confusion about our seeming conflict of interest, but we were unwilling participants in the Sanhedrin condemnation. We have been secret believers. We've both spoken to Jesus, spent time with Him to learn who He was. We recognize His deity. We acknowledge Him as the Christ. Our lives too were changed because of His intervention. And because you were an eyewitness to Jesus before His death and after His resurrection, we wanted to talk with you for more exact knowledge of the resurrection." It was Joseph who continued to establish the initial trust with Mary.

Now, I spoke. "Mary, you were close to Jesus, as was His mother. Tell us of Him."

"I would like to tell you of my relationship with Jesus." Mary began speaking as she walked toward the shade of the nearby cliffs and sat on a large stone, motioning at the same moment that we too should find our own place and make ourselves comfortable. While shade provided our eyes relief from the bright sunlight, the shadowed retreat otherwise was hardly necessary since the temperature was very comfortable on this early spring morning. "I know many have misunderstood and used the feminine issue as one of many attempts to discredit Jesus' authenticity. Jesus knew that too, but His grace covered all the misguided intentions of the detractors.

"In reality, I was deeply humbled by Jesus' spirit, and I gave Him my devotion. He had such a lordly manner and regard for women—for all humanity, in fact, no matter the age or status. All people, particularly those considered inferior in society—women, children, the infirm felt elevated in His presence. His regard for His mother was unlike that of any other son for His mother. Even on the cross. . . ," she paused and wiped the moisture from her eyes and steadied the tears in her voice, "He was concerned more for her than for Himself.

"I knew of the whispers. But as close as we were and as endeared to me as He was, there was always a respectable distance. Never was there even so much as a glance that projected anything but respect. Ours was a bond of the spirit, a bond that transcended the physical. Nothing could compare to the holy regard I had for Him. There was sanctity to it. I honored Him in all ways and gave him my utmost respect. He was my teacher, my mentor."

Mary's face and her voice were clear of emotional involvement, were just strong and decisive. "Jesus only touched me one time. That was as He was greeting others, He kissed me here," she said pointing to a spot just above her brow. "There was nothing sensual about the kiss. A man in Jewish culture never shows endearment for women in public, yet He honored us as He did His disciples. None of us who followed Him daily felt enamored of Him. We felt enabled by Him. That's why we stayed close to learn of Him, to absorb a little bit of who He was."

Joseph and I knew the custom: slaves kiss their masters on their feet, scholars kiss their teachers on the hand, and equals kiss on the cheek. We knew the significance of Jesus' kiss. Mary and all Jesus' followers were equal, were spiritually one. "There was even a rumor Jesus and I were secretly married. If we had been married, there would have been no reason for it to be secretly. In the Mitzvh there are six hundred and thirteen laws, religious commandments, related to such things as prayers, the Sabbath, alms-giving, temple visitation, and marriage. If Jesus were married, there would have been no dishonor requiring secrecy.

Mary was most articulate, almost adamant, about the public misconception—or contrived misinformation–about her relationship with Jesus. "I certainly was never married. My name indicates such. Other women named Mary were identified with their husbands or their husband's mothers. I, like other unwed ladies, have been known by my hometown. My title, Mary Magdala, indicates not only that I am from the town of Magdala but that I am a woman of means in control of my own property. That is what enabled me to travel with the Jesus cadre and help support them."

Mary's eyes suddenly took on a somewhat ominous look of regret mixed with joy. "He freed me," she said with deliberate, exact intonation. "When I first saw Him as He walked in the village of Galilee, I was a woman possessed of evil spirits despite the careful guardianship of my family. I was a mess, made so by an increasing series of bad personal choices and careless experimentation in the occult. I had neither rest nor sleep nor peace. I abused myself mentally with defeating self-talk, and, yes, I hurt myself physically in an urge to find some peace within—cut myself, didn't eat well, took no pride in my personal appearance. I was a defeated woman. Jesus and my friends counted seven spirits which Jesus demanded leave me."

It clearly wasn't easy for Mary to tell two strange men what Jesus had done for her. "Little children ran from me. Youth in the streets mocked me. Even dogs barked at me. I must have appeared to be a lunatic loose on the streets. I had lucid moments, and when I heard what things Jesus was doing, I had enough presence of mind to seek Him out. He saw that destructive demons had possessed my life and spirit. I didn't have to tell Him. He called my name, and repulsive animal-sounding growls emanated from deep within me. The demons knew who He was though scholars at the temple in Jerusalem did not. I am a miracle. I am evidence of Jesus' compassion and restoration."

Just then a crude young woman, maybe just past her teens clad in black, her face contorted and her posture stooped, shouted as she passed us. Her impish voice was joined by other distorted voices emitted from her throat. Angry vile poured out as she hissed and cursed at Mary and us.

"Who is that?" asked Joseph.

"She was once a lovely young woman living here. Now, you see her stooped, haggard, sinister, dark—a woman whose lost herself. I envied her beauty and cringed from her mockery of me. Then she began to spend time with the witches of Endor who came to Galilee to fish. Intrigued at first, she soon became a devotee of their craft. Now she, as I once was, is possessed of evil spirits. Oh, I praise God for my freedom from such anguish, such self-loathing. It's little wonder that I esteemed Jesus so highly.

Even now I choke back emotions thinking of that joyous moment. He gave me life. So, in service I gave Him my life and was delighted to be a member of His traveling circle. I found a wonderful place of value as I could do the chores of cooking and caring for the needs of Jesus and the disciples."

Mary began her defense of Jesus again, but this time expanded her gratitude to encompass others. "He unlocked the dark chamber of serfdom and drudgery in which all women were captive and allowed us into the arena of life. We were but the property of men. In public, women were forbidden to speak to any man, and no man could speak to any woman. Men did not even acknowledge their wives in public. They were kept at home and hidden from the public. No honor was afforded a woman even in her own home until she bore a male child. And sadly, one week each month because of the menses of fertility and reproduction, the woman was considered unclean and so was everything she touched. She was viewed as cursed instead of blessed. Other than a visit to relatives or attendance of religious festivals, travel was forbidden for women. To travel for other reasons was considered immoral and implied sexual misconduct. That's the characterization I accepted when I chose to follow and learn from Jesus.

"Those of us who traveled with Jesus and the apostles were indeed looked upon as deviates or worse by the pious. But fully reputable family women in the company of Jesus helped somewhat to dilute the harsh social judgment of women who dared follow Jesus. Mary, His mother; Susanna; Joanna, the wife of Zebedee and Herod's finance minister; Mary, the mother of James and Joses; and Salome, the mother of the sons of Zebedee were but a few of the women in His entourage. Having the mothers of some of the apostles with us perhaps made us a bit more respectful.

"Like Joanna, a number of the women were wealthy and helped finance the ministry of Jesus and the apostles. Many barriers had to be broken in order to upgrade womanhood. In doing so, Jesus removed restrictions and social stigma for many others. He shook the religious establishment which was bent on external cleansing without regard for internal purity by saying, 'All evil things come from within and defile a person.' This riled His detractors."

At that point Mary opened the recesses of her mind, moving on to new issues about which she spoke emphatically. "For several reasons He left this lovely region and crossed out of Israel into the area of Tyre and Sidon. This was a tumultuous area known for frequent battles. He was less known in this area and chose to stay in private homes in pursuit of rest which always seemed to allude Him. Despite His efforts at seclusion, many still sought Him out, including a Greek woman, a Syro-Phoenician by birth. She had a daughter possessed of demons and appealed to Jesus to heal the child.

By just talking to this woman, Jesus was in conflict with many social standards and broke the oral law. Nevertheless, He dealt with her in what initially seemed to be a most cruel manner. We soon learned He was testing her faith when He said, 'Let the children be filled first, for it is not good to take the children's bread and throw it to the little dogs.' In the mentality of the Jews, they came first. Jesus was likening the Jews to the children and the Gentile woman to a dog. In saying, "The children should be fed first," Jesus was acknowledging His regard for His own Jewish race. However, others were also important to Him.

"The Greek woman held fast to her faith in Jesus, apparently trusting who she deemed Him to be more than evaluating Him in the moment. Or perhaps she understood His calling her a little puppy was a significant, but common criticism. At any rate, the woman's hope-filled face was not dimmed by Jesus' words. Creatively and joyfully, she responded, 'Yes, Lord, yet even the little dogs under the table eat the children's crumbs.' We were caught by surprise by her clever response. Jesus chuckled appreciatively, perhaps grateful for her gentle persistence after His having dealt with so many closed-minded critics whose hard-hearted spirits stirred perpetual conflict. It was a relief to Jesus, no doubt, to find such a strong faith and clever mind. Her wit and her trust were rewarded. Jesus sent her home where she found her daughter free of demons."

Mary shook her head and pursed her mouth, affirming to herself and to us her understanding of the justice in Jesus. "Jesus, in almost every act He performed and every word He said, carried His message across territorial, racial, ethnic, cultural, sexual, and social boundaries in that one visit with the Greek woman and in the healing of her daughter. He was turning the world right side up. And His teachings and His acts made the world seem right—for a moment, at least, free from the oppression of prejudice and social bias."

Mary stood, arched her back, and began to walk without specific awareness in the direction of the shore. Her enthusiasm for Jesus was unbridled, and she was totally un-intimidated in her effusive accolades. "Jesus was a master storyteller. He knew people think in stories, and He used them to the fullest. Even when He told a story we already knew, we could hardly wait until the end to see what new revelation and application He would make. He often was purposefully enigmatic and paradoxical. This added to the intrigue. But, more importantly, it enhanced the power He possessed to relate to every facet of an individual's life."

Mary continued her reflection, her eyes sweetly reminiscent. "Traveling in company with those you love is home in motion. Being with Him excited the imagination and enabled us to see life, not as it is but as it should be."

I smiled a knowing smile and pressed for more knowledge of Jesus. "You have related, you know Him to have been divine. Your sharing of His human side reveals He had moments of joy and enjoyment. His respect for wit and His practical perspective of life made Him approachable by persons of all ranks. He enjoyed natural beauty and people with an open mind. His playful patience with children was rare for a male in our culture."

Mary beamed and responded, "He was relational. The common people, that is those without title or rank, loved Him to the end. It was the favorable response of the populace that the titled feared most. True, there were wealthy and governmental persons who believed in Him, but it was the people not blinded by bigotry, prejudice, of self-seeking who were most responsive."

Mary reminisced further as she suddenly kicked off her sandals and delighted in the wet sand. Joseph and I held course on the dry sand a few feet away from her but within clear hearing distance. "Back in Jerusalem Jesus crossed another line. A woman crippled for eighteen years came to Him on the Sabbath in a synagogue. She was badly stooped and could not straighten up. Jesus had compassion on her and called her out. Addressing a woman in public was a taboo in itself, but what followed upset the self-righteous even more. He touched her and healed her. Immediately she straightened up and began walking and praising God."

It was clear to Joseph and me that Mary had clear, first-hand knowledge of Jesus' everyday life. "Venom spewed from the rulers of the synagogue who told Him He had six days to heal and that He had deliberately defined religious laws and profaned the Sabbath. A modest giggle went through our group when Jesus responded saying, 'You hypocrites! You untie your donkeys on the Sabbath and lead them to water. Should not this Daughter of Abraham be set free from her bonds?' His show of respect for her by calling her a Daughter of Abraham was stunning. Sons of Abraham? Yes. Daughters, never—until now. This elevated womanhood. How clever, how subtle, how powerful Jesus was in righting wrong attitudes and reprimanding destructive behavior!

Mary herself was quite amused by Jesus' undaunted and purposeful style. "Jesus dared take this risk among men who prayed daily: 'God, I thank you I was not born a woman or a dog.' Some even considered that a criticism of dogs. Yes, Jesus bestowed honor and gave dignity to womanhood. Once after a brief respite on the Mount of Olives among the friendly Galileans, Jesus returned to the temple area early in the morning. A mass of people greeted Him. His conflict the day before with the religious leaders had not diminished His popularity with the mass of people. He began to teach spontaneously. Jesus was forever teaching and, most often, spontaneously to meet the needs of the moment.

"On this day, His teaching was interrupted by the religious leaders once more in an effort to impale Him on the horns of a dilemma. In an effort to diminish Him, they called Him 'Teacher,' not Rabbi. Their sole purpose was to discredit and test Jesus. They brought to Him a married woman caught in the act of adultery. Their primary interest was not in the woman or justice, but in trapping Jesus. If He said 'Stone her,' He would have been in conflict with Roman law which did not allow such punishment for adultery. If He had said, 'Don't stone her,' He would have been in conflict with Jewish law which required stoning for adultery. They thought they had Him.

"Adultery has always been wrong before God. In Jewish custom, males are often strangled in dung piles if guilty. But Jesus never condoned brutal, inhumane retaliation for wrong. Jesus' position was that if the accusers were so concerned about justice, they also should bring the man to be stoned as the law required. Perhaps one of them seduced her in order to use her as their foil. It was interesting to observe Jesus in every situation because He always could mentally disrobe the accusers. He removed the cloak of what they were supposed to be to reveal who they were. Jesus simply showed that those who accused the woman of sin were themselves sinners.

"Jesus' acts were most often clear and profound rather than complex and convoluted. In response to the adultery accusation, Jesus stooped down for the first of two times in this experience and wrote in the dust. This was a common behavior for persons who were thinking. Some say it was also an occasion for Jesus to avoid having to look at the lustful, leering, curious crowd. It is true that Jesus protected His mind from the seedy, sensual side of life. But this time likely He was seized with an intolerable sense of shame. Jesus stooped for the second time and began to write in the dust. He wrote the various sins of which numerous ones were guilty.

"Jesus would have been aware that many rabbis were living in adultery, and in His simple act of writing in the sand, their self-righteous armor had been pierced. As wicked and hardened as the accusers were, they were convicted by their consciences. They had not brought the woman simply to have her judged, but to judge Christ by His judgment. Instead, He became their judge.

"Jesus sealed the moment, heavy with significance for all who looked on, saying, 'Let the one of you who is free of sin cast the first stone.' One by one the accusers began to slink away. As they did, we heard the thud of discarded stones. Their plot had fallen apart by its own sordid weight. By leaving at this moment, they walked away from any word of cleansing or hope. The inner crowd of accusers departed, but the larger crowd of the curious observers were still standing around. Two members of the original cast remained–the disgraced woman and Jesus.

"'Does no man accuse you?' He questioned with compassion.

"'No one, Lord.' was her answer of obvious relief." Mary was particularly moved at this point as she reflected upon the story because she understood that a weight of guilt had been shifted from an injured woman and that at least for a brief time those who appeared socially unscarred had to acknowledge their private shame. Jesus deferred sentence. What He said meant 'I am not going to judge you just now. Go prove yourself better.' This deferring of condemnation was no indication of the withholding of ultimate moral judgment. He warned her, 'Go, sin no more.' He commanded immediate repentance which was to be evidenced by lifelong fidelity. His response verifies Jesus is not soft on adultery. And surely, in His response to the accusers, Jesus illustrated that adultery is much more subtle than a private physical act and that a person is guilty of the egregious sin merely through a lustful attitude."

Mary's tone became more intense. "There is no way we who followed Him could have heard His discerning words and not have become changed people. And now we must be the vanguard of a grand and growing company of committed followers. He taught that with God there is neither Jew nor Greek, slave nor free, male nor female. His dealing with us women was a challenge, but so was giving leadership to the apostles. A marvel little known is that He was so patient with His disciples. Even as an unlettered woman, I could see they were slow learners at times. He repeated some lessons over and over, never losing patience. Yet, He put His trust in them.

"Jesus' supernatural power had a dramatic impact upon us all. I saw it often. Once He invested the disciples with such power and sent them out on a practical activity. Endowed with the power He had bestowed, they went out to heal the sick, cleanse the lepers, raise the dead, and cast out demons. These assignments were means to an end. Their primary role was to preach that the kingdom of heaven was at hand. They returned encouraged and excited. It remains to be seen what will become of the disciples now, but they are walking treasures of heavenly wisdom. How will they run their course? He invested Himself in them. If they survive, they should do well.'

Mary retreated up the shoreline a bit and led the way to a

lichen-encrusted log which had washed ashore. Joseph and I welcomed the opportunity to sit and let our minds rest to the rhythm of the waves. "Me, I choose to return here to my home. In truth the real me is here for the first time. The demons no longer live in and control me. The townspeople know my past as well as my journeys with Jesus' band, and they have given me a haven. Little children are drawn to me. Perhaps I developed a bit of the gentle spirit of Jesus, and they sense it in me. They loved Him when He was here. He related so warmly to them, giving them a sense of importance as He did many. I love to tell them stories of Jesus."

Dipping her hand in the inlet of water lapping against the log and letting it flow through her fingers, with a distant look Mary mused, "Just think, He actually walked on these waters. How could they– why would they– kill such an innocent man?"

Her face brightened, and for the first time a wry smile lit her face as she continued. "One day Jesus and the disciples came ashore. Peter was soaking wet, and the others were smiling. I have never seen Jesus in such a light-hearted mood. I inquired what had happened. Nathaniel explained that the disciples had been alone in the boat when suddenly the most unusual thing happened. Jesus came to them walking on the water.

"Since Peter was always the let-me more than the show-me type, he implored Jesus to allow him to walk on the water. Jesus stretched out His hand and bid him come. Nathaniel told of how gingerly Peter stepped out of the boat and, with his eyes fixed on Jesus, started walking toward Him. It was miraculous! So many things were. Peter, likely feeling a little pompous as he was prone to do, wavered and looked down at his feet as if to confirm for himself he really was walking on the water. However, the moment he took his eyes off Jesus Who was walking nearby, he began to flail and sink. Nathaniel's recounting of the story was a jocular moment for us all."

Returning to the intent of the visit, I asked, "Mary, you were there at the cross. You were an eyewitness—one of those who heard all things. A simple question Mary. Was that Jesus on the cross, and did He indeed die?"

Mary was near the point of being incensed and stood abruptly, but soon her noble breeding took over—and her changed spirit. Then with a half smile she signaled that we should follow her. "Why, yes. Why should such questions be asked? Of course, it was He, and yes He died. Those hours of torture on the cross He was held captive in the kingdom of pain. Even His blood ceased to flow from that horrible gash in his side. His limp body no longer strained to lift itself in search of breath. He exhaled one last time, emptying his lungs of air. He was dead. At last His spirit soared free from His tortured body." Mary led us down the shore toward a small merchant's stand where she asked for three tonic waters.

"Mary," I injected, "you know His detractors are circulating every fabrication they can in efforts to discredit the truth about Jesus' resurrection. Some say that at the time Simon took His cross, a switch was made and it was Simon they crucified."

Distributing our refreshment and leading the way up the sand toward her house, Mary shot back, "Ludicrous!" Those from the Cyrenian community are easily identifiable by their dark skin. It was not Simon. Besides, I knew Jesus well and would not have mistaken anyone for Him." "Very well, Mary. Please indulge me, but I must ask yet another like question. John, the cousin of Jesus, has on occasion been mistaken for Him. Could that have been John on the cross?'

"Impossible. I knew them both and never had difficulty distinguishing them. It was none but Jesus on the cross. Of that I am certain. You need not ask this any more. The fact is established. I have no doubt at all it was Jesus.

"Why do they persist to try to deny so great a miracle? Why can they not see it was to their advantage that He arose? Despite the hate and disbelief of His executioners, Jesus' prayer for forgiveness offered from the cross included them."

"Yet another question," said Joseph. "You were at the tomb also, one of the first. What did you see and hear? Be no less than emphatic."

"I was there with Mary, His mother; Mary, the mother of James and Joses; Salome; Joanna; and other women. We came early to anoint His body for final internment. Our hope lay buried behind a three-ton grave stone. Our faith was nil, but our love and devotion strong. As we had trudged sorrowfully out Jerusalem's gate toward the garden, we questioned how we would get the stone moved. It was not likely we could move it and unlikely the guards would help us move it. We were unrealistic but ambitious to attend His body. There was no reason to hope for what we found."

"Just what was it?" pressed Joseph.

"It was the first day of the week, and we came early just before the formal hour of dawning. There was light enough we could see clearly. We were astonished to see that the stone had been moved away uphill a great distance.

"Upon first seeing the tomb open, we thought Jesus' enemies had been busy overnight. We thought not only did they kill Him, now they have stolen His body. We believed they had riffled the tomb. We had no reason to think otherwise."

Mary's face was taunt, analytical. "It took a supernatural effort to move that stone in that manner. Then we saw the supernatural reason. We saw an angel, two angels as a matter of fact. We were amazed, but not frightened. We were accustomed to the supernatural since Jesus dealt in miracles every day. John later noted there were two angels, but others referred only to the one who spoke. We know it was angels, messengers from God, for never a man glowed as they. Captivated by their radiance that further illuminated the area, we were enthralled by what the angel said."

"What, Mary? What?"

"He said, 'Do not be afraid.' We needed to hear that. What he said exactly was, 'For I know that you seek Jesus who was crucified. He is not here; for He is risen, as He said. Come, see the place where the Lord lay. And go quickly and tell His disciples that He is risen from the dead, and indeed He is going before you into Galilee.'"

"Did you?"

"Did we? With haste we did. We ran with joy and fear fighting for control of our hearts. As though we had wings on our feet, we ran swiftly not like ever before. Being women, we knew our testimony was not acceptable by most men. We wanted the disciples to come as quickly as possible to verify all to which we attested before anything changed. As we were running, the most glorious thing happened. I know this sounds unreal, but, believe me, it is real. On our way, we met Jesus himself."

"Mary, now calm down, Mary. Are you sure it was Jesus?"

"Oh, yes. It was now full light, and there is absolutely no doubt it was Jesus."

"Mary, I remind you His cousin John looks a lot like Him. Could it have been John?"

"Absolutely not. I know them both well as do all the women, and we had no thought of it being anyone but Jesus though He was the last person we expected to see. Yes, it was Jesus."

"Did He speak?"

"He at first spontaneously spoke the most wonderful word, one single word. And with that one word of all words, our hearts were calmed. He said, 'Rejoice.' We worshiped Him. Our adoration was interrupted by His next statement. Bidding us not to hold on to Him, He said, 'Do not be afraid. Go tell My brethren to go to Galilee; and there they will see me.'

"Amazingly at this point right after the resurrection which

must have been an astounding event for Him, Jesus had a plan. He always had a plan. I am confident, though I don't know it, that even now He has a plan."

"Just a moment," interrupted Joseph. "This is basic. Are you sure you were at the right tomb?"

"Right tomb?" Why, of course. The day of His death Mary and I sat there watching it until it got dark. Yes, it was the right tomb, the only one in Joseph's lovely garden. The hewn calyx in the shape of a flower bud decorated the top with a frieze, marking it distinctly. The garden was well known because of its great beauty. We watched as He was placed in the tomb. We observed certain traits of the scene. Upon our return on the morning of the resurrection, we saw the same scenes. The flaming oleanders, the sweet smell of jasmine, the nesting dove in the cranny, the shape of the stone, and the contour of the entrance to the tomb. . . . We knew. We knew. Certainly it was the same tomb.

Mary was so intense that she lost track for a minute and forgot who it was she was addressing–the master gardener himself. We had reached her yard by now and sat on a carefully crafted olive-wood bench. "Some artists work with ink or oils, but Joseph is known among gardeners as an artist who works with arbors, trellises, flowers, and shrubs. His hands know how to make stones embrace stones." Just then she recognized her oversight. "Yes, you, Joseph, are an artist."

"And you have planted some of the most aromatic plants in the garden, Joseph. Odors affect us by association. The aromatic plants and the pungency of the embalming spices were the same that morning as the time of entombment. My memory is clear. Yes, it was unmistakably your garden, Joseph, and definitely it was your tomb in which Jesus was laid to rest."

"Indulge us for wanting to confirm every minute detail, Mary," I said respectfully, "but if we seem at any point to be skeptical, it is to get confirmation for those who are critical. The more unlikely a story is, the more conclusive evidence is needed to prove it true. Tell us more."

"At the cross we gazed on the grimmest of tragedies. The image of that stark cross against the dark eastern sky with Jesus dying on it is etched in my mind. But finding that tomb empty interpreted it all for me. He came to bring abundant life, and for Him that meant death. I had heard Him teach it: 'I am come that you might have life, and that you might have it more abundantly.' Now I saw the truth with my own eyes.

"The reality of the resurrection and what Jesus did for us that day can't be explained or explained away. It was God's way of saying we are loved. It is God's 'Yes' to the world's 'No.' The world says you can't live forever, and the resurrection says yes you can. The world says you can't live optimistically and victoriously with hope. The resurrection says yes you can live with enthusiasm for the future.

"The empty tomb does not confirm the resurrection, but the resurrection confirms the tomb was empty. I saw the tomb empty and encountered Him immediately thereafter. When He departed from me, I wanted to cup my hands to my mouth and shout, 'Congratulations, Jesus, You did it. You escaped from the death-trap.' He arose. Yes, as an eyewitness to His life, His death, and His living presence thereafter, I believe in the resurrection."

As vivacious as Mary was and as comfortable as we felt with her sitting in her beautifully groomed garden, Joseph and I knew we had to move on. There was much work to be done, and we didn't know at what moment the heavy hand of a Roman soldier or a Sanhedrin agent might stop us without warning. We had now experienced our own vicarious walk with Jesus through Mary. We had felt Jesus' transformation power in Mary's words, her voice, her face, her total demeanor. Mary, once living in the hell of demonic darkness, now lived in the heaven of living light.

We knew there was much more to be discovered, perhaps

revelations that could only come from the ones who had gathered in Caesarea Philippi to meet with us. Peter had sent the message ahead that we wanted to meet with as many of Jesus' intimate circle as possible to record their revelations of Jesus' resurrection. We must travel to this mysterious place steeped in mythology to uncover the truth that could provide an answer to yet another unsolved issue. But first we would stop by an inn in Dan north of the Sea of Galilee for a night's rest. Now a week out of Jerusalem in our quest for documentable evidence, we were weary and needed to compose our excited spirits before we continued our journey. Located in the Hula Valley with its refreshing En Leshem springs and likened to the Garden of Eden, Dan sounded like the perfect place to retreat.

We said good-bye to Mary. She couldn't have known how she had truly enthralled us with the residual spirit of Jesus she emanated. We left her presence filled ourselves with the wonder of Who He was—and is.

Nearing Dan, we found the countryside to be all we had anticipated. As a diversion, we discussed the wildlife at the road's edge. The lovely alagernus, a tree found only in damp areas, was prolific here. Riverbank vegetation consisted of holy bramble, loosestrife, galingale, cynanchum, and willow herb. The amphibious fire salamander with its elongated black body of yellow and orange splotches intrigued us, and a nesting white wagtail was annoyed by our presence.

Choosing to rest beneath a large Syrian ash in the waning light, we began to reminisce about our old friend from the Sanhedrin, Gamaliel. Knowing he had followed our example by asking to bury Stephen on his estate on the costal plain gave us hope regarding his faith. Evidence of Gamaliel's belief first occurred to Joseph and me as our colleague had boldly defended the apostles before the court after the resurrection. That day, just two days after the resurrection, we recalled, Jerusalem was abuzz with word of the disappearance of Jesus. Conflicting opinions confused many. However, at that early stage, the apostles were attracting large, responsive crowds. As their popularity grew, resentment of them intensified in the Sanhedrin.

The court moved quickly, so quickly Joseph and I had not yet left Jerusalem on our quest of chronicling the resurrection. We were called to sit in on the first major confrontation between the Sanhedrin and the apostles, were reluctantly among the court as Caiaphas tried to indict the eleven closest to Jesus. He knew if he could silence them, then much of the battle against the perceived heresy of Jesus would be won. The disciples were summoned before the council to give an account of events related to the reported resurrection. Joseph and I sat side by side and elected to say nothing, but Gamaliel, who was not yet a target of Caiaphas as we, dared speak in defense of the disciples.

Joseph recalled that Caiaphas directed charges against the disciples rather than inquired of them. This biased the council as he had planned, and immediately the eleven stood accused by his initiative. This, like the trial of Jesus Himself, was contrary to legal precedent. We marveled over how the complaisant disciples were brought by guards before the council. Peter, boldly acting as the spokesman for the apostles, replied to Caiaphas' accusation of their spreading a heresy against the Jewish faith: "It is better to obey God than men." This was the flash point of indignation among many council members.

Joseph and I each knew too well that two opposing schools of thought regarding conflict resolution were now to be played out between the Jewish factions, the Sadducees and Pharisees. The Sadducees were known to be boorish in their conduct even with their allies and rude toward those who offered dissent. They were adamantly committed to stamping out all who professed belief in Jesus as Messiah. It was they who were responsible for Paul's appointment as the interrogator, responsible for his credentials to ferret out, force denial, or kill those who believed.

The Pharisees, we knew, though more rigid, were a more affectionate group among themselves and often sought to cultivate harmony among others. I had nudged Joseph to notice Caiaphas that night as we sat on the temple floor watching the events play out. It was obvious that his devious father-in-law, Annas, the former high priest, had instructed Caiaphas to follow the lead of the Sadducees.

Joseph recalled nearly the exact inflamed words Caiaphas spoke that night: "These men cannot be allowed to continue to advocate Jesus as Messiah. The idea of a Messiah who would suffer and die is alien to our belief. The Promised One should be our advocate and champion, not one who stands mute and offers no rebuttal to the Romans."

Gamaliel was a brave man, we both agreed, and a renowned man of the Law. As a Pharisee, he was perhaps somewhat more emboldened as he rose slowly to address the assembly. Because he was revered as a man of wisdom, the hushed assembly focused on his striking presence and listened as he spoke.

It was I who recalled, at least in paraphrase, what Gamaliel had said. "Blind. We have been blind to the words of our own prophet Isaiah who said of Messiah, 'He was despised and rejected of men.' How it grieves me to think we might be those very men of whom Isaiah spoke. How could we forget the prophet's words, 'a man of sorrow, and acquainted with grief: and we hid as it were our faces from him; he was despised, and we esteemed him not. . . .'

"We showed contempt for the very one who might well have been the One of Whom it was said, 'Surely he has born our grief, and carried our sorrows: yet we did esteem him stricken, smitten of God, and afflicted.' Our concept of Him must be weighed against this word of prophecy."

I also, not surprisingly, recalled the response of Caiaphas:

"These words cannot be applied to the imposter Jesus. Our people wait and travail for God's champion to throw off the yoke of bondage imposed by the Romans. Messiah is to be the representative of the Lord, strong and mighty."

The breeze was blowing slightly as we took a few more minutes in recollection before going on into Dan. We remembered how calmly Gamaliel had expressed sorrow that the court could not see the parallel between what had happened there and the further words of Isaiah. He quoted Isaiah frequently in his defense of the apostles: "He was wounded for our transgressions, he was bruised for our iniquities: the chastisement of our peace was upon him; and with his stripes we are healed." There is too much similarity between the prophecy and what has played out here to discount completely what we know to have happened."

Joseph recounted how we had watched as the forehead of Caiaphas tightened, his teeth clinched, his neck quivered. We had been there just a few days earlier when Jesus stood without a defender. Caiaphas retorted how this was 'coincidence, mere coincidence' by which the court must not be confused. He said the expectation of the populace was such they could never be convinced the Sanhedrin was mistaken and had hanged the long-awaited Jewish Messiah on that gibbet. Caiaphas railed that the disciples blasphemed God by declaring Jesus to be the Promised One.

We recalled how impressed we had been with Gamaliel and his intellect and ability to apply logic. He didn't give up easily. He had one last appeal on behalf of the apostles. He told the court to leave the apostles alone. He reasoned that if what they said was a lie, it would not prosper and would fade from the annals of time. But if it were of God, he had said, it would flourish. If it flourished and the court had punished Jesus' followers, the revered Sanhedrin would appear as fighting against God, and that must never be.

Gamaliel dared extend his plea a little further, as we recalled. He reminded the group that he had taught the works of the Greek poets for decades. He explained there is a principle of Greek tragedy that says the long-term course of future events tests the quality of truth of an antecedent event. Time, he said, would be the test of truth in this matter. 'Time and truth walk hand in hand' was a more common adage he cited. The truth about Jesus, he concluded, would become clear in the future. In turn, the future would judge the Jewish religions harshly if they gave the appearance of fighting against what time proved to be of God.

Joseph remembered, almost verbatim, the absolute final appeal of Gamaliel: "If the reports of the resurrection are true, our having these men killed will not suppress its influence. If it is not of God, letting them live will not perpetuate it. If a myth born of delusion, it will disappear as the morning mist." Gamaliel had returned to his seat among the court knowing he had spoken the truth and that truth would ultimately triumph.

"The court could not argue with such logic or power of persuasion," I said, knowing we must soon retire our thoughts and bodies in the comfort and safety of Dan.

Joseph managed a tired smile and echoed the outcome of that night was in the control of heaven. "The lives of Jesus' closest friends were spared. The counsel could only acquiesce and consent to a mediating position. They settled for a warning to the apostles not to continue preaching the resurrection. The disciples didn't get away unscathed though. The court took some warped satisfaction in immediately taking them out for thirty-nine lashes, perhaps purposefully emulating Jesus' beating. Their goal was intimidation," Joseph remarked, "but the consequence was renewed boldness." We remembered the parting scene of the trial. Publicly humiliated, their bodies bruised, their robes bloody, the apostles submitted to their discipline but left rejoicing they were worthy to suffer for their Lord.

That night after the trial, Joseph and I had delayed to embrace our ally, Gamaliel. We were but three of the several members of the prestigious council whose eyes were opening to the reality of the resurrection. A possible emerging fourth, Saul of Tarsus, was still only critically inquisitive—nevertheless, inquisitive as more men of the temple were now becoming. We recalled clearly how Gamaliel had bid us farewell saying, "Time, robed in longevity, today began its endless march through the corridors of the centuries to judge the decision of the court and vindicate the apostles."

The recollection of Gamaliel was an appropriate ending to an astounding day with Mary—and Jesus. The atmosphere of our hearts was thick with rich, profound evidence of the Person of Jesus. His spirit and presence infused our own. This day we had verified through two people evidence of what an encounter with Jesus can produce: vibrancy, joy, freedom, and purpose in Mary; and strength, courage, intellect, and charisma in Gamaliel.

Just as a sliver of the moon came over the treetops, we pulled ourselves off the ground for the five-minute walk into Dan. We found the inn comfortable, though not elaborately appointed. The hospitality and food warmed our bodies. But most importantly, the words of Gamaliel exonerating the apostles and validating Jesus reassured our spirits. Sleep—deep blessed, restorative sleep—came easily.

DISCIPLES' EYEWITNESS ACCOUNTS

Caesarea Philippi afforded a lovely placid purlieu for Joseph and me to meet with a remnant of apostles. I had studied the history fully and knew much about the environment we would find. When Herod the Great died, his son Philip took over the region of Gaulanitis, the territory east of the Jordon River and north of the Sea of Galilee, including the Golan range. Here Philip the Tetrarch built a city named Caesarea Philippi to honor Caesar Augustus and to distinguish it from Caesarea Maritima.

Located at the foot of Mount Herman in northern Galilee, the Spring of Paneas was the easternmost of the four sparkling springs feeding the rivers Jor and Dan which join to form the Jordan River. The cool waters of some of the springs emerged beneath the rocky face of the mountain. The ancient name of the city was Paneas, named for the Greek god Pan in whose name a cult was formed. When Alexander the Great conquered the area, his followers brought the cult to the region.

The image of Pan, the god of the shepherds with his flute, was still prolific in the area. The tradition was that Pan's music was beautiful when he was happy but was radically dissonant when he was unhappy. The street people of Caesarea still referred to a person who hit the dissonant mood, an unsettled mood, as having a "Panic attack."

It was in this setting that we were to meet as many of the disciples as we could gather on short notice. Already a network of believers had developed in the city. This enabled word to get to those chosen by Peter to meet us here where Jesus had often retreated. The population was Jewish, so Jesus could teach unencumbered. People in the area commonly referred to Him as "the Christ, the Son of the Living God." Peter had explained to Joseph and me that it was in the backdrop of the massive rock bluffs of Caesarea that Jesus first called him 'the Rock.'

As our entourage of mules, camels, and companions entered town to meet with the disciples, the mid morning was beautiful. Abundant water from the spring cooled the atmosphere of the early spring day. A Cetti warbler chirped happily as if celebrating the profuse vegetation growing along the water's edge. The fragrance of the blooming lotus permeated the air. Nearby shepherds with sheep and goats crossed the silent sands beneath the azure sky, having just shared the waters of the springs. The scene was idyllic. Apparently the apostles reuniting here thought so too as they bathed in the pool below the cascading waterfall. This, no doubt, was their most enjoyable diversion since the events of Calvary. Such revelry in play indicated that the disciples were undaunted at the prospect of meeting with Joseph and me and that they, as we, for a while felt some shelter here away from the searching eyes of our pursuers. Maybe it was our common white mantles, now dusty from our days of travel that made us less imposing figures. Maybe more so it was that the disciples remained unimpressed with social position and material resources. That was a good thought as we stopped our caravan on the banks of the pool.

"Let's cook and eat before we get into the matter of our visit." It was Joseph, his robust stature demanding nurture, who made the suggestion. Our servants dismounted their faithful camels and unpacked food they had bought in nearby Dan. Boiled fish would be our main course, fish from Galilee dropped into a boiling savory preparation of onions, garlic, cumin, coriander, mint dill, and dried mustard. The fire of acacia wood quickly cooked the fish. Goat cheese, asparagus, boiled eggs, fresh dates, figs, and pomegranates completed our nourishment.

The disciples appeared eager to meet personally with Joseph and me. Our renown resulted from our public demonstration of devotion to Jesus. They knew we were Sanhedrin priests who risked our lives to take custody of the body of a man despised in Jerusalem. The disciples dried the dripping water from their taut bodies with their outer cloaks, choosing to lay aside the garments to dry in the sun and gathered to dine in their loincloths. The sun brightened their spirits, and the prospect of getting to know new brothers encouraged them. It had been some time since this hardy band had eaten such a meal. Even the odor of food cooking ignited their appetites. There were few restraints on the quantity they consumed. More fish were added to the pot as several uninhibitedly asked for seconds.

Matthew, James the Lesser, James, John, Thaddeus, Peter, they each introduced themselves: Matthew—Levi, a hated tax collector, James—known as the Lesser because of his obscurity outside the disciples, James and John—the "Sons of Thunder, Thaddeus—also known as Judas but not Iscariot, and Peter—first known as Simon and also "the Rock." The group was diverse, men once working for Rome, Zealots fighting against Rome, philosophers, fishermen, all led by . . . a carpenter.

Joseph, a man whose work ethic allowed for no waste of time, spoke. "Our friends, we thank you for meeting us here today. You've had a great mission. And you and we still have a great task ahead. Our present cause is to eradicate the rumors and planted disinformation about the resurrection of Jesus. Evil men in Jerusalem killed Jesus to destroy His influence, and now they still try to destroy His message. We feel compelled to validate the truth that it was Jesus who died on the middle cross to confirm that he indeed is risen as He said He would. So thank you for joining us here today." Joseph then asked the group to bow as James the Lesser prayed aloud in the fashion of Jesus: "Our Father in heaven. We pray for these men, for all us here. Our mission has only begun. We also pray for those who hate our cause. We pray they will come to know the full truth in time. Thank you for our food, and please guide us all on our way. Amen."

Looking around, I saw that Jesus had called a cosmopolitan band to serve with Him. Levi was a tax collector. Soon after joining Jesus' band, Levi became known as Matthew, meaning "gift of God." He was a brother of James the Lesser. They were cousins of James and John as well as Jesus. Levi had besmirched his name by the office he held, a despised tax collector, a person everyone loved to hate. James the Lesser, son of Alphaeus, was little known outside the circle of apostles. I knew the great difference between men, between the feeble and the powerful, the great and the insignificant. Then there was James, content to be an unknown achiever, an insignificant in a significant role.

One of the highly unlikely disciples was Simon, a member of a fanatical fringe group of rebels known as Zealots, not just a Zealot but of the most savage sect, the Sicarri. They were a coalition of lower priests, Jerusalem insurgents, and refugee bandit groups from the countryside dedicated to the overthrow of the Roman rule in Israel. These fanatical idealists led guerilla warfare against the Romans. Ironically, their covert headquarters was in the temple. Theirs was an egalitarian government. When Jesus first cleansed the temple, Simon might well have been there lurking in the shadows and cheering Him on. Only Jesus could have coalesced such a group which would include a tax collector working for Rome and a Zealot warring against Rome in the same band.

A disciple known by three names was present. He was Labbeus, Thaddeus and Judas, not Iscariot, son of James. Labbeus means courageous. Thaddeus means lively, vivacious. He could not be intimidated by fear because he had grown to have but one fear, the fear of failing his Master. Bearing the name Judas, the same as the betrayer, grieved him, and he preferred Thaddeus. It fit his personality. Reaching for a ceramic plate made from the sands of Judah and now unpacked from the saddlebags by our servants, Matthew spoke as he chose from the meal spread before them in the shade of the Caesarean cliffs. "I am glad we have returned to this place. Golden moments in the stream of life rush too often past us. Memories of Jesus linger with me, yet it seems we have only come to know Him after He is gone."

Matthew continued eager to share his enthusiasm. "Jesus was clearly different from the other religious leaders in Caesarea and Jerusalem: the Jewish sects of Pharisees who believe in life after death and the Sadducees, the more socially elite, who do not. Then there are the Herodeians led by Boethus whose daughter Mariamne was one of Herod's wives, Herod who himself was thought to be the Messiah. The Sicarri and other Zealots add to the agitation. Jesus walked in a virtual hornets' nest wherever he went. His message of simple goodness and love countered everything the religions taught of form, ritual, and legalism.

"It was the common people who supported the message of Jesus, who understood that this man was different. He was not an aristocratic Messiah, not a political one, not a military one. He was a man so different, so loving. He taught us to pray, to love our enemies.

"Joseph, Nicodemus, you two are men of ritualistic prayers. Perhaps you have heard the one Jesus taught us." Sadly, we had not had occasion to learn this about Jesus, how He prayed, except from His prayer from the cross which we had heard from the shadows of the crowd. When we shook our heads that we didn't know of Jesus' prayers, Matthew said, "This is the model prayer Jesus taught us to pray for all we need and for others:

Our father in heaven,
Hallowed be Your name.
Your kingdom come
Your will be done

On earth as it is in heaven.
Give us this day our daily bread.
And forgive us our debts,
As we forgive our debtors.
And do not lead us into temptation,
But deliver us from the evil one.
For yours is the kingdom
And the power and the glory. Amen.

"Every day," Matthew explained, "we pray this prayer. All the hopes and expectations of Jesus' ardent heart are cast in this prayer. Like all prayers of Jewish people, it contains seven requests and is divided into three sections: the Shavah, praise to God, 'hallowed be thy name'; the Tephillah, requests to God, 'give us daily bread and forgive us and keep us from evil;' the Hodayah, thanksgiving to God, 'yours is the kingdom, power, and glory forever.'

Moved by an explanation of Jesus' words, I said, "Thank you, Matthew, for sharing this regarding Jesus' prayer life. I can relate to the prayer from a traditional Jewish teaching that says, 'The Holy One, may His name be exalted, will let the dead rise into His world, so that His great name will be satisfied.' Jesus, no doubt learned in the Law Himself, knew this ancient saying. That's why he prayed, 'Hallowed be Your name, Your kingdom come.' His ideals are immortalized in the prayer. It indeed is a Messianic prayer.

"Joseph and I have heard a similar prayer many times in the temple. What a mockery and shame in the empty requests: 'Lead us not into sin, nor into transgression or evil . . . .' Jesus knew the vanity and cruelty of the men who prayed the empty prayers and who perpetrated evil. Yet he was praying for them in cadence as his gentle heart beat its last, 'Father, forgive them.'" For a moment, silence hung over this diverse group of magistrates, disciples, and servants, each savoring his own memory of Jesus' forgiveness.

The sturdy man still eating ravenously, James the Lesser, most often a more reluctant speaker, then related his own insights into the uniqueness of Jesus. "Jesus always conquered the moment, handled any situation. We often couldn't resist a chuckle when he made some arrogant critic look ignorant. Jesus' quick thinking and candor disarmed those who tried to discredit him. Once when temple authorities asked Jesus by what authority he performed, He turned the question upon them as He often did. 'The baptism of John, was it from heaven or from men?' He knew if the religious elite said 'of heaven,' then He would ask why they did not believe in John and be baptized. If they responded 'of men,' then the people who loved John might stone them. Walking away, Jesus answered, 'Neither will I tell you by what authority I act.'"

James, for a man of few words, continued as he slowly picked the remaining morsels from a fish bone. "Too, Jesus wouldn't be trapped by a tax question coming from members of the temple who had infiltrated our group." Matthew winced at the mention of taxes. It evoked bad memories. In jest Simon slyly punched him in the ribs. "Jesus' detractors had asked if it were proper to pay taxes to Caesar or not. His simple answer was 'Render unto Caesar what is Caesar's and unto God what is God's.' The religious devotees failed to see the real significance of what Jesus was teaching even as He held the coin in posing the answer. He hoped they could understand that as the coin that bears Caesar's image should emote allegiance to the ruler, so should the lives of people made in God's image reflect God's likeness.

"They were confounded that they could not catch Jesus in this word snare. We chuckled. Jesus only smiled. Playing word games with Jesus was far beyond this league of men wise in their own perception.

"The Sadducees," James continued, "those who believe in no

afterlife—no angels, no resurrection—posed a question they felt Jesus certainly couldn't turn on them: 'If a woman is married seven times, whose wife will she be in the resurrection?' Jesus explained calmly that we, like angels, will not relate to each other on the basis of physical marriage in heaven. Rather, we will be new creations, not angels, but sharing common traits with them. 'Mutual love and admiration will be heightened in that age, but not in a sexual connotation of marriage.' In referring to 'that age' Jesus was speaking of the afterlife.

"Drawing on the authority of Moses, whom the Sadducees revere, Jesus recounted that Abraham, Isaac, and Jacob will all rise. Their existence does not only lie in the past, but also in the future. Using contemporary terms, Jesus referred to God as being the God of these three highly regarded patriarchs. Some listeners marveled at His teaching and openly complimented Him. There were no more questions. The session was over. Wry grins covered our faces as we thought, "Well done, Jesus. You showed them.' One-upmanship was not in keeping with His unpretentious spirit."

I noticed the bright-eyed James the Lesser engrossed in what James was sharing and asked that he explain his title the Lesser.

"They call me the Lesser because I don't talk very much and prefer to be in the background. Simply stated, I've learned to be fulfilled being a small part of a great cause." In keeping with his reputation, most often he had little to say. "I am privileged to function in a supportive role. I enjoy giving care to little details and quietly sharing with small groups. I am given to enjoying doing those things that support others, especially Jesus." With that, he smiled and nodded toward Matthew.

I allowed a small smile to escape my lips because I didn't see the Lesser relating to the discourse James had just finished. But I didn't comment and understood he was just exhilarated in his praise for Jesus.

Matthew was reminded of one of his own recollections of

who Jesus was. "Jesus made heavy moments and impossible issues a time to teach and often found in them times for comic relief. His incredulous detractors would not quit. Let me share other encounters. When Jesus met me, I was a virtual outcast. As a tax collector, nobody liked me. The Romans considered me a mere minion of Rome. The Jews considered me a collaborator with the Romans out to get rich at any cost. Both were right. Jesus changed my life. I am proof the leopard can change his spots. My call to follow Him gave me such joy I wanted to celebrate with a party. The only people who would come to a party at my house were other tax collectors—and Jesus.

"The Pharisees saw the guests as they entered and asked some of the apostles why our teacher ate with tax collectors, sinners. Jesus overheard it and answered, 'Those who are well do not need a physician, but those who are sick do. . . . I do not come to call the righteous, but sinners to repent.'

Marvelous, absolutely marvelous. I was absolved and they frustrated—again. "Some of John's disciples asked us why Jesus did not fast like they and the Pharisees did. Jesus used two simple examples in His response. One could be better understood by women and the other by men. His purpose was to show a new order had come. He said you do not patch an old garment which has shrunk with a new piece of cloth which has not. That obviously would not work. They would pull apart. A wineskin illustrated another vital point. You don't put new wine in old wineskins. The old skin is dry and brittle, no longer flexible and malleable. As new wine ferments, it produces gases that would expand and burst the wineskin. Putting new wine in old wineskins results in the loss of the wine and the skin. Who Jesus was and the teachings He shared are like the new wine. The old formal religion was comparable to the inflexible old wineskin. He was fresh and revolutionary. He was not the norm and would not fit the ritualistic religion of the day. Radical, that is the word, radical.

"Jesus was forever a teacher—and a good one who taught clearly and often in stories to be clearly understood. Jesus encountered a paralytic who expressed faith in Him. Responding to the faith Jesus said, 'Be of good cheer, your sins are forgiven.' 'What audacity!' the self-righteous critics voiced. I love what happened next. They accused Jesus of blasphemy. How could He forgive sins? He knew what they were thinking, so He asked them a question. 'Which is easier, to say, your sins are forgiven you,' or to say, 'Arise and walk?'

"Any person could speak of sins being forgiven without any evidence it was accomplished. Causing a cripple to walk again would result in clear response. You would either see it happen or you would not. No one could heal such a cripple. They agreed it was easier to say 'Your sins are forgiven.' Choosing the more difficult to prove His ability to forgive sin, Jesus said to the man, 'Arise and walk.' Imagine their chagrin when he did. If Jesus could accomplish such a visible physical act, He had authority to forgive sin."

"Judas, or if you prefer, Thaddeus," I said, "you have been quiet. Would you please share?"

"I do prefer Thaddeus. The name Judas has fallen into such disrepute I prefer not to use it. I was just thinking of Iscariot, what he did and what he is missing. He heard Jesus teach and saw His miracles. He was an eyewitness to immortality; He was trained as we were trained. We went on teaching, preaching, and healing missions together. His experience is proof that how we think and often what we do are dependent upon what we listen to.

"Jesus' choice of Judas was not that he might betray Him. I am not faulting Jesus. The choice by Jesus was not the cause of, but the occasion for, the betrayal. Our group provided a favorable atmosphere in which Judas could have become a true devotee. It was his choice. Jesus' motive in choosing him was pure, but Judas' motive in accepting the call was not. It is my belief he thought he was joining a popular movement that would result in his prominence. We all gave support to him by accepting his role."

It was obvious Thaddeus had thoroughly evaluated the other Judas. "Judas became outraged at the excess he felt Mary showed when she anointed Jesus with precious oil. When he protested it as being an act of squander, we should have been alerted by his avarice. His response was born of greed, that same greed that played a part in his betrayal of Jesus. Judas voluntarily initiated contact with the priest. He went to them to ask what they would give him if he delivered Jesus to them. They settled on the price of a slave under Mosaic Law, thirty pieces of silver.

"Between the time he arranged the betrayal and the dark hour of Gethsemane, Judas sat with us in the Upper Room. How could he? Truly, the wolf was in the sheepfold. Jesus did all He could to call Judas to reason. At the table in the Upper Room, He showed him preferential hospitality by offering him the sop first. As Jesus spoke of His betrayal, He offered a warning, telling us of the woe awaiting the one who would betray Him. He even said it would be better for that person if he had never been born. Judas, Judas, what could he have been thinking?"

By this time, all of us had sumptuously feasted. The fire was getting low, so we grew nearer its flames and allowed the servants to clean up as Thaddeus continued. "Never has there been a more lubricous act than that kiss in Gethsemane. Finally Judas' conscience seized him when he realized the unfolding events of the arrest were leading to the cross. He went back to the priests and tried to give back the money. Refusing the returned money, they called it blood money. The hypocrites rejected the money but had no remorse about letting the blood of an innocent man. As despicable an act as Judas perpetrated, he was a better man than any of the priests. He had a sense of guilt. They did not.

"So, so sad. Judas hanged himself. He could have shared in the love of God, but refused the privilege. Having the option of sharing eternity with Jesus, He betrayed Him instead. Upon his turning from Jesus, Satan entered him. By listening to the wrong people, He chose his companion for all eternity.

"Now, do I believe in the resurrection? Does a camel have a hump? Yes! Reflect with me. Those artisans of death assigned to kill Him did their work like ghouls. They delighted in extracting life in the most tedious way. They knew how to kill, and they knew death. They killed and they knew death held another captive."

Crouched in the sand in our makeshift bucket chairs, Thaddeus abruptly shifted the conversation. "Nicodemus, you and Joseph entombed Him. Tell us about it."

"Oh, we would like to share that. We knew there were risks, but we too had long felt in our hearts the truth of Jesus and knew the risks worth taking. The procedure involved wrapping the body from head to foot in fine linen. This was held in place by an adhesive. Removal of the wrapping would have resulted in the resin-based adhesive peeling the flesh with it. Had He not been dead, and we both know He was, He would have suffocated in those grave clothes.

"The women came to the tomb early in the morning. Faith and hope had left them. They came for one last farewell. Their purpose was to give the body one final treatment which time did not allow us to complete before the Sabbath. They brought burial spices with them. They had only one logistical concern: Who would move the stone from the tomb? Love drew the grieving women to the tomb. Their faith was fettered, but when faith fails, love prevails.

"They found the tomb empty. Upon examination, those early visitors there found the grave clothes crumpled by the weight of the spices, yet intact. The body had vacated its grave clothes without an exit portal. Like a vacated cocoon, the wrap we had carefully created bore evidence of a former occupant. God the

Father had loosed the cords of death that had bound God the Son. Jesus arose from His death couch to give life to all who follow Him. Had Satan himself visited the empty tomb, he could have said: 'Were it not for what happened here, I could have conquered the world.'

Simon, a man of action, could wait no longer. He lifted himself to his knees in the soft sand, leaning into the group in his enthusiasm. Having exercised unusual patience, he was eager to share. "They call me the Zealot because I belonged to an order of radical revolutionaries. Had I not met Jesus and had met you, Matthew, I would have most gladly slit your throat."

"I am glad you met Jesus, "responded Matthew. "Had I not met Him, I would have overtaxed you!"

Both chortled, and Simon continued, "I took the oath of the Zealots: 'We must destroy the Roman Empire, and we will destroy Jews who cooperate with the Roman Empire. We will kill all collaborators. No King but God.' I knew Barabbas. We were members of the Sicarri rebels. I was as guilty as he. He got caught. I did not, or it might have been I in whose place Jesus died instead of Barabbas. I know in a different, more meaningful way that it was for me He died.

"When I first came to this place with Jesus, my mind was still in transition from the old way of thinking to the new. Sitting here with Him, I thought of the Ptolemes of Egypt who lost a battle to the Syrians in this setting. Here the Seleucids ruled resulting in the suppression of the Jews. Here the Persians and Romans battled with the result of Roman rule in the region. Then Jesus interrupted my thoughts. He was speaking not of hate and war, but of peace and love. At first I had great difficulty with Jesus' message of love. Love to me was for weaklings. I questioned often why He called me, unworthy as I am. I believe it was because He wanted my passion for life to be a stimulus among His followers. He saw the fire in my life and did not want it vented against the

Romans. I have never lost my zeal. It burns within me now. Only now it is zeal for Jesus' cause."

Simon stood now, pacing a little in his spot in our circle around the fire. "Seeing Him relate in love to little children, orphans, widows, and the elderly moved me. Seeing the same love expressed toward those who reviled and persecuted Him had a greater influence on me. Never has a man loved like He. Never has one had the right to speak of love as He. He modeled it. I am proof that a life can be so changed by love. It is virtually impossible to recognize it as the same life. He was convivial and spoke graciously. My contumely language and manner needed His power to change it."

A look of gentleness increased in Simon's eyes as he related Jesus' essence of love. "The power of the resurrection is the power of reconciliation. Only that dynamism could have changed my despicable life. Only by His compelling love could I have been changed. That change has enabled me to live in community with such as Peter; a tax collector, like Matthew; two Sons of Thunder, like James and John; a crafty deceiver like Iscariot; and you, James; and Judas, to say nothing about the others with their idiosyncrasies."

Simon sat down once again, invigorated by his pacing. "I can tell you that Jesus had power over nature anytime he wanted. I saw it myself. On the storm-tossed Sea of Galilee in a time of great danger, even the wind and water obeyed Him. That same force calmed my tempestuous heart. Jesus changed all He touched. As a butterfly morphs into life, so my life radically changed. Only a radical force can make such a change. That force is love. His love. He was full of vibrancy, joy, and love. Little children, Roman centurions, the sick and crippled, blind beggars, rich political leaders, the simple-minded, thieves and treasurers, and those of the Sanhedrin like you, Nicodemus and Joseph, all saw in Him a quality of life that we were created to live."

Simon made a sweeping gesture, encompassing all of us there in the closing day. "We all had one thing in common, an empty hope chest left barren by pretenders and profiteers. He taught us that 'No man has a greater love than this that he lay down his life for a friend.' Then He went out and laid down His life for His enemies that He might make peace with God for them. He did not resist the nails. There was no angry glare from His eyes, only tears for others. No curse was issued from curled lips. Love lingered in the air as His words rang out, 'Father forgive them. . . .'

"Of course, cynics and skeptics are arising who question His teachings and resurrection, trying to defend themselves. Those who knew death knew He was dead. Also, we who know life know He is alive. We also know that three days after you buried Him, He began making post-resurrection appearances to various persons and groups. Personally, I know emphatically He was alive, back from the grave. I am encouraged, yes emboldened, by the fact One who loved me so much had supernatural power enough to achieve the resurrection. He lives to aid us in taunting guilt and future pain."

Simon seemed to be slipping from the sublime to the surreal. "Fear, it was fear that motivated His execution. Religious charlatans crucified Him for fear He would expose their hypocrisy. Out of fear they posted a guard at His tomb. Even in death, they were tormented by His life. Out of fear, the Temple Guard trembled at the angel's message of 'He is risen.' Faithful women left His empty tomb with mixed emotions, both fear and joy. He allayed their fear with His words, 'Do not be afraid. . . .'

"Fear stalks each of us like a cunning assassin. At the end of life awaits our greatest fear, death. One day regent Death will point his caustic finger at each of us and say, 'Your turn.' Death offers no one an appeal. Our peace is found in the fact He defeated death and demonstrated by His resurrection there is life beyond the grave. Regarding death, the greatest fear, He said . . .

'Fear not.'"

Simon, it seemed, was a man with a philosophical bent, his passion extending far beyond the rudimentary thought. From his discourse on love and fear, now he seemed to be shifting subjects once more. "Jesus has come back to be with us, and though we don't know where He is right now, He is with us. This addresses another of our needs. We who are so lonely need a constant companion. Loneliness and alienation affect the popular and unpopular whether in solitude or in a crowd. Loneliness is a caution flag alerting us of our need for intimacy with the Father.

"Anger hounds us." Simon's comprehensive discourse continued. "When tempted by it, I think of what it did to Him and how He responded to it. In anger those sybarite priests cried out for blood. Anger and its twin bitterness hold many hostage. Guilt leaves its footprints on our souls. Yet, it can be a friend if it motivates us to repent and respond in love to the Lover of our souls. Not dealing with anger drove Judas to regret, not repentance. Sin is the root cause. Where sin goes, guilt follows. Jesus does not want our encounter with Him to result in our going away remorseful over guilt, but joyful over grace." Joseph and I looked at each other. Simon had a message burning within him. We mutually acknowledged his wisdom.

"I believe in the resurrection because it is the reconciling force enabling me to deal with these issues. The power resulting guides my life daily. The consequence confirms the cause, the resurrection. What we do with Jesus is an issue with eternal consequence. We have no choice but to choose. That is a choice. I choose to believe in the resurrection based on what I have heard and seen. He is alive!

"I said He gave me courage. Before coming here, I had my courage tested. I had returned to Jerusalem to contact friends. I was waiting for them inside the bustling city gates in the spacious inner court of the temple. There, pedestrians, litter bearers, and pack animals vied for space. Soldiers were posted on the thirty-six foot towers and atop the twenty-four foot crenellated wall. Also in the court was Ariel, a ranking Zealot, a member of the savage Sicarii, with a passion for inflicting pain. Ariel thought of himself in light of the meaning of his name, 'Lion of God.'

"The lion was about to pounce. He was a hard-core Sicarii Zealot from the breeding nest of rebels, Gamla north of Galilee. The right of leadership had become his because of his radical hatred for the Romans and their Jewish collaborators. His stealth had ended the lives on many choice members of the Legion. His hatred for the Romans had translated into bitterness toward me, one of his former conspirators. Because I had followed Jesus and left the Zealots, Ariel thought of me as a shameful defector. He felt I had abandoned my blood oath to rid our homeland of Rome's maltreatment. The two of us had successfully engaged in subterfuge and cunning against the best of the Roman soldiers. Now Ariel swore vengeance against me, his former ally.

"Ariel had such antipathy toward me that while I was in Jerusalem, He and two colleagues seized a moment they had hoped for. Spotting me in the crowd, they moved in on me as quickly as a hunting jackal. Knives concealed beneath their robes pressed into my side and back as they ordered me to follow them without resistance. Compliantly, I responded and was led out the gate and into a nearby karst cave created by years of quarrying and erosion carving away the soft limestone beneath the north wall of Jerusalem. By torchlight, I could see a deep precipitous pit containing bodies and skeletal remains of other defectors and Romans, making the place even more foreboding. Amid the cache of weapons stored in anticipation of an insurrection, Tobiah and Urial, two companion Zealots, held me tightly.

"Ariel began his threats. The chamber rang with the acerbic rage of an incensed Ariel. The torch was held uncomfortably close to my face as Arial excoriated me. 'The blade of my sickle sword is thirsty for the blood of one who would abandon his sacred oath to free our people in our war of liberation against the oppressive Romans. The veins of you, you disgraceful traitor, shall quench its thirst. There is no reason for life for one who would abandon our quest for liberation from oppression.'

"Ariel, pausing, gave me opportunity to speak. 'I found one who can free our people from all oppression. There will always be oppressive forces that bring pressure to bear on our people, tyrants and despots who subvert and suppress. There are universal life forces that the free spirit of men cry out against. These external forces come and go but never cease. Even if the Romans go away, on us pressure will remain in a different form. It merely changes its garments, not its nature. In Jesus I have found one who can provide true deliverance from oppression by internal means, a counterforce. Jesus promised, 'My peace I give unto you, not as the world gives. . . .'

"I continued to try to spare my life and Ariel's—though for different reasons and from different enemies. The Romans have given us the Pax Romana, the Roman peace. It is imposed peace based on fear and resulting in suppression. This is the world's false peace.

"Ariel, do you think I left the Zealot movement to avoid oppression? No, I have, however, been enabled to counter it from within by relying on the Prince of Peace, Jesus.'

"'Yours in philosophy only,'" Ariel retorted gruffly pressing his point. "'It is only theory. Our cause demands action. Roman blood must flow until every Roman boot is off our soil. No man in this land will have peace until Rome is defeated.'"

"'Not so,'" I hurriedly replied, trying not to arouse Ariel further. "I have not escaped the wrath of Rome. They have intensified their pressure on me by confiscating my possessions and dispossessing my relatives. The oppressors can cage the bird, but Jesus gives it wings and a new song to sing even in captivity. Jesus lived as He taught. Even as they crucified Him, He prayed, 'Father, forgive them.'"

"'Forgiveness!'" snorted Ariel. 'I live by the ancient Code of Hummurabai, 'An eye for and eye and a tooth for a tooth,' and the Romans owe me a lot of eyes and teeth. Simon, let me see if you can forgive me for this,' said Ariel as with his sharp sword he cut open my robe inflicting deep wounds in my chest.

"Grimacing in pain with my blood staining my robes, I fought back my old retaliatory human nature and choked out, 'The pain is external; the peace is internal. I know why you did this. There was a day I would have done the same to you if our roles were reversed. The reason I don't try to now is the reversal of life which I've found in Jesus. It is He in me that enables me to endure the pain and forgive you for inflicting it even as He forgave me.'

"Drawing up so close the spittle splattered my face, Ariel spoke piercing into my eyes with an augur-like gaze, 'Forgiveness is the way of a coward when the spirit of man cries for revenge.' Demanding that Tobiah release my right arm, Ariel placed his sword in my strong hand. Further insulting and threatening me, Ariel bared his throat and continued, 'Now you have the option to forgive or to avenge yourself. Which?'

"Returning the sword to Ariel, I spoke in a conciliatory tone, 'I choose to forgive because I have been forgiven.'

"'Simon,' exploded Ariel, 'always avenge, you fool! Though I think you are now a mad man, I am going to release you because of this so-called new life. Perhaps you can even teach some Romans how to forgive. If you don't, I will eventually teach them lessons they will never forget.'

"Ariel gave me one last over-the-shoulder look as he walked away muttering, 'Forgive? Never!' He didn't know that perhaps for the first time in his life he had just forgiven someone. With hope, I thought this one act of mercy might start Ariel, the Lion of God, on his own path following the Lamb of God."

All had spoken, each confirming it was Jesus who died and was buried. Their kindred spirits and uncommon common experiences confirmed for them He arose. Now I spoke even more confidently than when Joseph and I had arrived. "My colleagues in the temple sought to palliate the matter of the resurrection, but God intervened right in His house to confirm for me the resurrection. On the Temple Mount great confusion prevailed. A gentle breeze blew. The curtain between the Holy Place and the Holy of Holies stirred in the wind. Days before at the moment of Christ's death, the huge veil mysteriously had torn from the top to the bottom, another evidence of Jesus' power. No one could dispute this most tangible of miracles.

"This curtain of Babylonian craft measured eighty-two feet in height and twenty feet in width. Its thickness and strength were proportionate to its great size. It was beautifully embroidered in blue, scarlet, and purple. The mysteries of the heavens were depicted by formations of stars and cherubim. The earth was represented by plants. My knowledge of the history of the temple led me to see in this more than a coincidence.

"It was Moses who gave details of the construction and purpose of the curtain. As the nomadic people of Israel had traveled to Canaan, they set up their Tabernacle in various places to worship and sacrifice. It was constructed according to certain divine instructions. It was to relate the story of God's people and separate a place called the Holy of Holies from the inner court. At the center was the Ark which symbolized the presence of God. Once a year, on the Day of Atonement, the High Priest entered this sacred place. Even he could not enter until he went through extensive ceremonial cleansing. He entered carrying ceremonial blood to seek God's forgiveness for the people. This act of entering behind the curtain was considered so awesome that the priests might even be struck dead for approaching God improperly. Therefore, bells were sewn on his robe so the people outside could hear his every move and know if he had died and if they needed to retrieve his body. The curtain served as a symbol of the separation between God and men caused by sin.

"I continue to realize the significance of the veil. Those who had stayed behind not going to the crucifixion told how about noon, the midday turned to midnight. Amid the frightful hush that had fallen across the Temple Mount, an eerie, grating sound could be heard. The veil was tearing from the top to the bottom. It was at that same time Jesus cried out with aloud voice, 'Father, into Your hands I commend My spirit.'

"As the wind blew the separated curtain, it brought with it a fresh breath of spiritual vitality. No longer would access to God be limited to the high priest on the Day of Atonement. Now all who proclaim the efficacy of the sacrificial death of Jesus have a Mediator who gives direct, continual access to the Father. It is not enough to know about the grace of God. We must grow and relax in it. Jesus died on Calvary for us spiritual paupers to make us spiritually wealthy. He has opened to us access to the Father through our daily prayers to confess, to seek counsel, and to fellowship. This access is ours if we only use it.

"As priests had to go through ceremonial cleansing before entering God's presence, so we must go through inner cleansing. To enjoy fellowship with God, to be open for His divine guidance, we must have pure hearts and clean consciences. We can boldly approach His throne in prayer. Boldness does not imply a hint of casual rudeness or flippant impertinence. It means to become confident with God. He wants intimacy with us.

"Think back to the Temple Mount. Once again the warm Judean breeze blows and the torn curtain flutters in its current— a factual, touchable reminder that the way has been opened to the Father. No more lambs need to be slain. The Lamb of God, selected before the foundation of the world, has been sacrificed.

All sacrifices made on the Temple Mount were a reminder of the seriousness of sin. They foreshadowed the coming of God's ultimate sacrifice, His own Son, Jesus. I was there and saw the most significant symbol, the torn curtain in the temple. It was the Father's signature approval of the resurrection. He believed in the resurrection."

Joseph and I glanced at each other and then toward the setting sun. We were about to say a prayer of benediction when the solitude enjoyed by the group was suddenly interrupted. Grunts and bellows sounded as a small contingency of desert-weary Roman soldiers arrived. Their gold and garnet uniforms were dirty, their beards dusty from long days spent in the desert. Their weaponry was well worn from recent battles. They had come to refresh themselves, fill their canteens, and water their thirsty horses and camels.

Profanity and insults to their subordinates rose from the area of the spring. As we were rising and stretching from our lengthy sharing session around the fire, we even heard the crack of whips and clash of swords, perhaps at the least in intimidation. The boisterous manner of the soldiers was a contrast to our calm spirit as we reflected on our experiences with Jesus. Our bright, joyous spirits so opposite the soldiers' was noticeable to the new arrivals. "Why are you so joyous? I'm Malcus, the commander of this regimen." The apparent leader was speaking. The soldiers came near, and some mingled among the believers.

"Because of what happened to Jesus in Jerusalem," said Joseph, speaking for the group.

"Jesus," interrupted Malcus, "that rabble-rousing rabbi crucified in Jerusalem? Some of us were members of the execution squad. Is your joy a result of our skillful execution of Him?"

"By no means, no," responded James.

"Then why are you so euphoric?"

"Have you not heard?" I asked.

"Heard? Heard what? We left the morning after the execution and have been pursuing Zealots in the Arabian desert since that day. Surely, you are not going to tell us He escaped or something. That would be an insult to our killing skill. We know how to snuff out life, and we know without a doubt He was dead." Malcus drew threateningly near to me as I continued our interchange.

"No, by no means. You did your work well. He was dead."

"We were glad to get rid of Him, but you . . . you rejoice over His death?"

"It is not His death we celebrate, but His resurrection."

"Resurrection! You mean He came back to life? Preposterous!" A haughty smirk of anger flooded his face as Malcus continued. "We snuffed all life from His tormented body. Do you expect us to believe that spent body had life left in it? That is an affront to us as executioners." Malcus pulled his sword and placed its sharp point beneath my chin. Renounce that myth or I will cut out your lying tongue and with the cleats of my boots grind your hide into a gopher hole."

"No, he isn't lying!" Joseph exclaimed, virtually shouting.

I immediately heard the unmistakable sound of a sword being unsheathed behind Joseph. Its cold steel was instantly beneath his chin.

"Now you too lie and question our work," said the soldier.

In chorus the others replied to the soldiers, "They are not lying. They speak the truth. You did kill Him, but on the third day, He arose from His death couch."

"Are you alone suffering this delusion?" demanded Malcus.

Matthew hastened to respond. "Many believe it and many more will. Thousands already know He arose. You heard Gaius say at the cross 'Surely, this was the Son of God.'"

"We have no god but Caesar," said one of the soldiers. "What makes you think Jesus was a god?"

By now the soldiers had dropped their swords from our throats.

Malcus probed, "God, there are so many gods. Do you declare Jesus is your God?"

With fervor Joseph exclaimed, "False gods, yes, but He is proved to be our God in the flesh. Only the best of paintings are copied. Only money of the greatest value is counterfeited. Both are done to deceive. It is only natural that carnal men should make bogus gods in their own image to deceive others for devious reasons. Creating a god in our image is an ancient craft. But, in the faith of Jesus, it is we who are created in the image of our God. Jesus' resurrection is history's ultimate event. I confirm Jesus' claim to be the true God with us."

The mood slowly grew less threatening, the soldiers more curious. The soldiers settled in among the believers and became inquisitive. Wonder filled their hearts as increasingly they began to understand Who it was they had crucified.

Malcus said, "I have been a party to many executions with impunity, without guilt. It is a curiosity that for the first time, I feel guilt and even shame in killing such a man. Doubtless Gaius was right. He was the Son of God. Of all that happened that day, it is Jesus' prayer I remember best: 'Father forgive them.' Do you think such forgiveness applies to those of us who tormented and killed Him?"

"The answer is assuredly yes," I said with deep persuasion. "He forgave those of us who condemned Him."

"And those of us, His own followers, who denied and forsook Him," said Thaddeus.

"No mortal man could be so forgiving," Malcus said plaintively. Others of his band agreed. "This coupled with the eyewitness testimony of men like Gaius and you is convincing."

The interchange continued for some time. The soldiers' hunger for the truth was fed by convincing facts. At long last the two groups that were initially antagonistic parted as brothers, believers.

We two were once again about to say farewell to these men with whom we had shared so comprehensively the truth of the universe. But once more our intended departure was delayed. Shaken by what we had just resolved, we were about to regain our composure only to face a greater threat. Other members of the group and I had noticed an isolated wanderer, we assumed, periodically break the horizon of the hill as we talked with the Romans. The observer had obviously been cautious not to be seen by the Romans. We could see that slowly he had disappeared. Suddenly, with the swiftness of an eagle descending on its prey, armed men surrounded us.

The sun gleamed on the blades of their Damascus steel swords as the predators closed on the gathering. With the precision of a well planned and often performed drill, they surrounded us. The scowls on their stern, bearded faces were intimidating. In thundering tones the apparent marauder's commander ordered, "On your knees!"

Not fully over our traumatic encounter with the Romans, we fell to our knees. Knowing robber bands often preyed on small groups in this area caused us fear. Reports of their ruthless conduct were common. The leader burst into a mocking laugh. "I am Avitus. You!" he said looking down on his subjects, "I know you! And you I know also. I have seen the two of you parading arrogantly around the temple in your lavish priestly robes. You are the eminent Nicodemus and you Joseph of Aramathea. I have longed to have such as you at my mercy to humble you. Now I have the opportunity, and there is no fear of reprisal. "Why are you here?"

Before either of us could respond, a voice familiar to the Zealots answered, "We have met to talk of our Messiah."

Avitus wheeled and stood face to face with the one member

of the band who had not kneeled. It was Simon, one they knew well. "Simon," he exclaimed in angry tones, "you disgraceful cowardly traitor! At last I have found you! You broke your vow as a Zealot, and I swore vengeance on you. You gave up on our efforts to rid our homeland of the Romans. Now I shall have revenge on you. Strip him and blindfold him!" he commanded two of his most burly men.

Before more could be spoken, Simon was thrown to the ground, his arms and legs spread-eagled and bound with wet leather straps to four stakes quickly driven in the soft soil. The Zealots' skill and speed indicated this was not the first time they had performed this act. The sun would dry the leather, further stretching his limbs. It was the Zealots' intent to leave Simon as food for jackals after sundown. As the flurry of activity subsided, Avitus bent over Simon and said, "Not only did you break your vow, you set out following that rabbi from Nazareth who was disgraced and embarrassed by the court and the Romans. We saw Him crucified. How could you follow such a weakling?"

"Jesus whom we followed was not disgraced and embarrassed by anyone," declared Joseph. "Not only did He conquer His accusers, but the grave also. By conquering the grave, He disgraced and embarrassed His detractors."

"You speak riddles," said Avitus. "We saw Him die crying for Elijah to save Him."

"Do you not know what happened three days later?" I asked.

"Three days later?" laughed Avitus. "We left Jerusalem early the morning after His death pursued by that band of Roman soldiers who just left here. They had been involved in His execution. Our knowledge of life in the desert enabled us to elude those devils. We toyed with them, making a mockery of them in our desert haunts. We have been in the baron region near the Decapulous ever since. Our purpose in coming here to is secure provisions and bounty from fools like you. What is this you speak of happening three days later?"

"Though Jesus died, He returned to life and arose from the grave," replied Simon gasping for breath.

"Silence, Simon, I will not believe anything told me by one who would break his vow to rid our land of the despicable Romans. Continue Nicodemus. You are a bit more creditable man." Returning his sword to its sheath for the first time and ordering his men to do the same, Avitus demanded of me, "What proof is there of this alleged miracle of a dead man coming to life?"

Seizing the opportunity as though pleading my case against a death penalty, I began. "Jesus has been seen by many witnesses in different settings over forty days. Once He was seen by five hundred. That is in addition to the appearances to individuals and smaller groups. Peter. . . ."

"Yes, Peter," interrupted Avitus. "He was the big man, the fisherman from Galilee. I liked him and thought what a wonderful Zealot he would make. He had the fire for it. You obviously don't know we observed Jesus and His vagabond band. We had spies join His larger group and observe Him closely. Simon, when you joined Him, I thought you must know Jesus was going to become a revolutionary to lead our battle against the Romans. What a disappointment it was when I learned you had betrayed us and become a follower of just another desert prophet.

"What happened to our former friend Judas Iscariot? We understood he was the one who had enough cunning to profit by betraying Jesus to the authorities. Did this supposedly resurrected Jesus come back to settle the score with him? If so, I would loved to have been there to see it." His fellow robbers laughed boisterously with him.

Joseph replied, "No. Such reprisal would have been out of character for Jesus. Our sorrow is that Judas was so consumed by guilt for his egregious wrong that he hanged himself and did not live to receive Jesus' forgiveness."

"Forgiveness!" scoffed Avitus. "I heard Jesus speak of forgiveness from the cross." Pausing a moment Avitus reasoned, "I suppose if He forgave those who actually nailed Him to the cross, He would forgive the one whose betrayal led to Him being there." Hesitating a moment Avitus continued. "This story you tell is a marvelous one. Not that I believe Him to be Messiah, but if He is really still alive, He might yet lead our revolt."

Avitus appeared to be making an instantaneous decision. Turning to Simon, he ordered his men to cut him free. "As unlikely as what you have said is true, I am going to take a chance on it in hopes He might yet deliver us. If He does come back in that role, put in a good word with Him for us."

"He offers deliverance greater than that from Rome. It is deliverance from sin for all who believe and trust in Him," said Simon. "I was slow to come to belief in His spiritual role, but the resurrection confirmed Him as our true deliverer."

Avitus walked up close to Simon, so close his breath was warm and dank on Simon's dusty face. Looking deep into Simon's hazel eyes he said, "Simon, you broke your vow and abandoned us. In spite of that, I always had admiration for your zeal. To find it now transferred to this Jesus makes even me tempted to believe in Him. Perhaps someday, but not yet."

Mounting his charge and commanding his men to do so, he turned once more to the believing band and said, "I am letting you go so that you may perpetuate your faith. I will not judge you, nor your story. I will leave it to the ages to make that judgment. If it proves to be true, perhaps I will join you. I heard Him from the cross speak of forgiveness. If anyone needs forgiveness, I do. Simon, your contentment commends the mystical power of forgiveness. Me—forgiven? I could hope."

As quickly as they had come, the Zealots left, skilled desert rats as well as temple vermin vanishing like a vapor on a hot summer's day. Disappointed by the lack of immediate response by the Zealots to the good news of the resurrection, those of us who had known and loved Jesus were hopeful. The seed of faith had been planted. It might yet flower even in their hard hearts.

It took a bit of time for all of us to gather our wits and prepare for our next adventure. We finally hugged our fellow believers and planted a holy kiss on the cheek of each. Awaiting us was a visit we hoped would help settle us emotionally as well as give us further insight into the resurrection. Joseph and I set out to find Jesus' closest friend, John. His sensitive spirit and personal intimacy with Jesus could answer for us a lingering question that could change everything. Caesarea Philippi had been an exciting venue in our commission of faith. We left the city sensing the essence of a happy note of a flute settling over the landscape.

SCROLL X

VIEWPOINT OF JESUS' CLOSEST FRIEND

As Joseph and I made our way along the shores of the Galilee to the village of Capernaum, we had many hours to talk about our visit with the men who shared Jesus' life for three years. We wished we had long ago become a part of their group and could have learned directly from Jesus for ourselves. But we, too, were wise enough to know that God has a purpose for all the events of our lives and that He uses all things for the ultimate fulfillment of His kingdom. So our regrets were short-lived.

John had not been present at Paneas. He was a good day's journey by mule from Peter's location in Galilee. Efforts to get a message to him about the gathering had failed. Peter told the disciples and us who met with us that John had withdrawn from the post-resurrection threat to his home base of Capernaum. His plan was to stay for a while in the secluded village. He was among friends in a setting he knew well and in a setting where Jesus had worked wonders.

We knew we would readily recognize John at first sight. He would be tall, thin, deeply tanned from exposure to the harsh sunny climate. His brown, scraggly hair and beard and his perfectly proportioned nose and decisive chin would remind us of Jesus' visage. His confident carriage and assured demeanor would mirror the man we had watched so often from a distance. We would recognize his reflective spirit and his wise words. After all, he had shared most intimately as a rare confidant of Jesus. As an old adage suggests, we do sometimes begin to look and act like those who are closest to us. Yes, we would know John.

John had first encountered Jesus in Capernaum. His return here no doubt would be a comfort to his wounded spirit as he would visit familiar places and memories. The sweet, pure water of the Sea of Galilee, the pebbly and sandy beaches, the fertile soil and the climate made this a veritable garden. Walnut and olive trees thrived along the lakeshore. And the date, fig, and pomegranate trees produced ten months a year. The flocks of sheep grazing noiselessly on the hillsides confirmed the serene pastoral life of the people.

In this inviting environment, John sought time to reflect, to sort through the deep things he had experienced. We saw him sitting shaded by the mountain range around him on a grassy knoll overlooking the sea. He was writing on small sheets of papyrus. John would tell us later it was his memoirs of Jesus' deeds and words, the essence of the deep conversations they shared of the nature of friendship, the scope of love, and the reality of life everlasting that he was writing of while the impressions were still strong in his mind. He eagerly shared that he'd not only recorded the major events and the major concepts he learned from Jesus, but that he often grinned to himself as he'd remember the lighter times they had shared: James dousing him with a cup of water when he wasn't watching or his hiding all Peter's fish one morning after an all-night fishing trip.

John amazed us in his recollection of who we were. No introductions occurred. We shouldn't have been surprised because Jesus' best friend surely shared some of the qualities of Jesus' interests in people and events. He spoke first with a huge smile and open arms, both embracing our searching spirits. "Hello, my friends. I know you, Nicodemus and Joseph." To talk of Jesus was obviously John's delight. He offered no reserve. I sought to bring his focus to his life with Jesus. He responded with delight. "Oh, I feel I know you loved Jesus and I love Him. That makes us friends already."

His kind face brightened and he began. "Jesus visited the Galilee often. He walked these western shores of the Galilee from Naphtail in the north to Zebulun in the south. From this cradle came all but one of his disciples, Judas Iscariot.

"My brother Peter and I were fishermen. One day He found us mending our nets and honored us by calling us to follow Him. His promise was to make us fishers of men. The role sounded exciting and His bearing won our confidence. At once we left our father Zebedee in the boat with the hired servants and followed Jesus. We knew our father would take good care of our mother, Salome. We felt comfortable from the first with Jesus. His mother, Mary, and our mother, Salome, were sisters. There was a bond between those of us from Galilee. One of our first experiences with Jesus occurred when we went with Him to the home of Peter and Andrew. Peter's mother-in-law was ill, and Jesus healed her.

"Jesus was a master of human nature. I know now it was because of His divine nature. He called James and me 'Boanerges,' that meant 'Sons of Thunder.' He had immediately observed that we had a low flash point. Combined with Simon the Zealot and impulsive Peter, I guess we added dynamism to the group and presented Jesus with a bit of a challenge controlling the group. At times the twelve were strong-willed and difficult to control. Putting a former Zealot, a tax collector, petulant Peter, and two Sons of Thunder together with all the other variables presented a challenge. We each had deep feelings, vigorous emotional drives, and passionate impulses for action. He needed strong men with strong personalities to do what He had in mind. We qualified."

We had made ourselves comfortable just below John on the grassy hillside. My mind made a flash comparison to Jesus teaching from such a place. "My zeal and exclusivity showed one day as I joined an excited crowd to see what was happening. I heard a voice saying, 'In the name of Jesus of Nazareth come out of him.' Moving closer, I saw a man casting demons out of the youth. I sternly ordered him to stop. I rushed back to report my good work to Jesus. What He said wasn't the compliment I thought my zeal deserved. He said, 'Don't forbid him; for he who is not against us is for us.'

"Jesus obviously didn't want to exclude anyone from good works. Such works did not have to be approved by us. Peter and I were the closest of the group. We were jailed together and shared a special missionary journey to Samaria. Experiences like those draw you together."

"John," I injected, "you were as close to Jesus as anyone, perhaps closer. Even the evening of the betrayal, you sat next to Him at the Passover supper and leaned on Him. You were with Him in such private moments as Gethsemene. How do you perceive Him? Who was He? We know His vita: born in Bethlehem of Mary, taken into Egypt to flee Herod's wrath, and reared in Nazareth. But, who was He in reality?"

"A word I use for Him reveals who I know Him to be. I employ a seldom-used term for Him in my notes: *Logos*, meaning the Word. A temple priest acquainted me with it. He learned of it and its meaning from the writings of Philo Judaeus. He was at the height of his teaching when Jesus was a young adult. His family was of the sacerdotal line in Alexandria. They were among the most powerful members of the Jewish colony. Philo used the word *Logos* to mean 'all that is known or knowable about God.' To me that is Jesus. I have come face to face with the wonderful reality that He is divine.

"Here in my notes I have written, 'The Word became flesh and came and dwelt among us, and we beheld His glory, the glory as of the only begotten of God.' Employing that meaning, we can reason who Jesus was. He became a human being. He was not just the basis of a theoretical religion established upon a concept. Jesus was and is a force, a prime cause, a person. He had and has within Him the universal breath of life. Our God Jehovah is eternal. We know that of Him. He is the Ancient of Days. So too, I am persuaded, was Jesus. His birth of the virgin Mary means He had no earthly Father. He was supernaturally conceived. Thus, as no other, He had a dual nature. He was both God and man. He was—and is— Immanuel, God with us. Look here in my notes I have written, 'Before time began to begin, He was. He is now. He forever will be.'"

John spoke quietly, calmly, and retrospectively now. "I wish John the Baptist were here to tell you Who Jesus was. John taught emphatically all around the area of Jerusalem. He confirmed Who Jesus was. He knew Jesus was the creator of all our reality and He knew Jesus was the problem-solver to remake every one of us into the gentle, productive people He designed us to be. He knew Jesus would ultimately stop evil in individual lives and in the processes of the world. That's what John meant when he said, 'He who comes after me is preferred before me, for He was before me.'

"Jesus Himself said, 'Before Abraham was I am.' We missed it. The meaning of that slipped right past us. We had no experience with which to compare an eternal being among us, so we missed it. Our God is the Creator of all. His empowering resurrection is a confirmation, a validation, that He is the Maker and Sustainer of all life from the smallest invisible particle to the most gigantic mountain to the most intricate human body. Jesus is life."

At this point John appeared pensive, almost melancholy. His eyes grew very warm. His voice took on a deep sentimentality as he read to us his record of how he and Jesus had often looked for patterns in the stars as they shared a night by the campfire.

"Jesus and I spent much time alone. Many days we spent in intense activities of teaching and healing or working physically.

We shared in pain and sorrow—and joy—on a daily basis. At night, we, as all the disciples, were emotionally spent. Most of them regained their energies and perspective by sleeping. Jesus and I most often had a time of reflecting on the day or just reflecting on life. Why, we even reflected on the universe and weighty, abstract ideas which only Jesus could share and I would attempt to understand.

I remember that one October night soon after I had joined Jesus, all the other disciples were sleeping around us on their blankets on the still-warm sands of the Galilee shore, most of them snoring! The moon and stars were out, the campfire still crackled and smelled good. Jesus and I had put our bedrolls just beyond the fire up the hill on the grass and had reclined, hands under our heads, and were just gazing into the sky with no particular focus, just letting the immensity and grandeur of creation soothe away the tiredness of the day.

"'John,' He said, "the stars you see—I know they are My Father's other worlds aglow with His light. They are the mirror of His vastly creative mind. The Psalmist wrote the Creator counts the stars and calls them all by their names. We can be confident that a star-counting and a world-creating God is big enough to handle the complexities of My life and yours.'

"'Notice that brightest star, John, just above the horizon of the sea, right in the dip of where those two mountain ridges meet. It seems to be moving, pulsating as if sending messages of My Father's awareness of us here in this small place in His universe. An ancient servant of God, Job, once said the Creator stretched out the skies and that they declare His glory, His magnificence, His power. If people would take time to see the message of God all around us, they would love God and each other instead of resisting Him. They would live contentedly and completely.'

"'You know, John, that universe we see up there is just a

small, small part of what God has made. Those mountains there, there are more. There are other worlds. John, I'm going to tell you something you can't understand. There is no end to the heaven you see above you. It is infinite. And all those literal objects you see are rushing through space. They never run out of a place to go. That's how supernatural My Father is. He can create all that. He does keep creating there and here. He has the capacity to keep all that in order—to keep those stars from falling or moving out of place. And yet, He cares about whether there is enough wine at a wedding feast. He cares if a little girl is dying and her family is in mourning.'

"Jesus said one more thing that night which I still try to comprehend. He said He would tell me something else astounding: This earthly life is not all that there is. Right now, He said we can only see part of His grandeur. One day, He will let us choose where we want to visit, let us travel anywhere we want among those worlds that exist out there. God will let us keep being who we are and becoming more of what we can be—all under His goodness."

Joseph and I stood, our heads in wonder of the closeness John and Jesus shared. John continued briefly, his mind not able to deal with all the reality of Jesus' conversation. "Jesus spoke of the creation as though He were a party to it, as though it were His. He was not an idle dreamer as some said. He was a visionary. He was God who knows all things. He just shared with me a little of the reality He knew.

"Jesus has altered my world as well as my manner of thinking of the world. The ideas He shared stagger my thoughts. The most profound idea is that Jesus was the Creator Himself. Yet, He humbled Himself and came in the form of a man, one of His creation. That is no easy saying. It is a complex thought. The idea I walked with God, the Logos, and did not comprehend it until too late brings me belated reverence, brings me awe. It was the resurrection that convinced me of this. In no other way can the event be explained except that it is another of the miracles—a part of God's ongoing, alive creative processes. From the heavens to the earth, God—Jesus Himself—is in charge of the birth and death of all things. And His resurrection extends to us that eternal nature that enables Him to do all things. What a marvel that I can be like Him—literally become a part of Who He is."

"Some explain the resurrection away, John," I injected, "saying Jesus had a twin brother, who showed up after the crucifixion."

"A twin!" exclaimed John. "Absolutely not! We were cousins, our mothers being sisters. We each knew the families of the other. Thomas, one of us, had a twin but not Jesus. None of us ever heard a hint of Jesus having a twin. Of all who would have known for certain whether He had a twin, Mary would have been foremost. She knew there was no such person. Had there been, when the persecution broke out, she would have insisted the twin reveal himself, disproving the claimed death of Jesus and sparing the misery and death of the other brother.

"No! Emphatically no! There was not a twin brother of Jesus. It is amazing the extent His detractors are going to try to dispel the truth of His victory over them . . . . even over the death. They are haunted by the fact that He is alive. They fear what He might do to them. After what He has done for them, as well as us, it is apparent He would do them no harm.

"Even among His persecutors, there were those who acknowledged His supernatural power when they asked Pilate for a guard to secure the tomb. Their words show they knew: 'Sir, we remember while He was still alive, how that deceiver said, After three days I will arise.' Note they said 'while he was alive.' They knew Him to be dead. What they feared did occur. They saw the very heavens react to His death. So they knew He could—and would—come to life again as He said. It is ironic that those who feared Jesus understood more of the truth of His living again than those who loved Him.

"How insensitive we were to what Jesus had taught us. We should have known that if Jesus desires to touch with His divine power a buried acorn and make it produce new life, He surely would not remain lifeless in a grave. His victory over death as the Lord in charge of all life disproves the false philosophers who declare every living thing is born without reason, prolongs itself out of weakness, and dies by chance. I am strengthened by my friend Jesus' own words: 'I am He who lives, and was dead, and behold, I am alive forevermore.'

"I shall draw from this and other thoughts from His noble mind all of my days. Our dull minds and the minds of the bigoted religious leaders should have seen the resurrection in the Passover feast. In the Passover season individuals have for years brought the offering of first fruits. The offering was a graphic depiction of what has happened. Jesus set the precedent of believers experiencing real, tangible life after death."

Joseph and I knew well what John was about to depict. "To symbolize the new life, priests from the Temple were sent to a designated field across the Kidron Valley with instructions to reap the first ripe sheaves of the new barley harvest. They carefully chose the best. As required, the priests thrust the sickle and gathered the symbolical sheaf. On the following day, bundles were taken to the Temple, and in a service of dedication they were waved before the Lord. These sheaves, as thanksgiving for the harvest, assured there was more to come. Jesus was the first fruit from the dead signifying there are more coming in a great day of resurrection. His resurrection was just that: a praise to the Lord and assurance there is more to come."

Joseph and I had participated in the religious symbolism as John had described, and yet we had missed the meaning. John continued, "If Christ is not risen, our faith is futile, worthless, and we are still in our sins. If in this life we have no hope, we are pathetic, lost beings. Jesus changed that. He gave our lives meaning and a future hope.

"I was the first of His apostles at the tomb. I gave careful attention to every detail. Even then, I knew there would be questions as to what happened. The grave clothes were there. They were not rumpled like a covering when someone gets out of bed. They were lying on that cold slab like a shriveled body. They were mute, eloquent evidence that a living being had vacated them. His dead body was gone. Surely, Roman executions are the most efficient and brutal on earth. Rome does not remove people from crosses without ensuring they are dead. The body laid in that tomb was lifeless without question. . . . dead. You want empirical evidence of His resurrection? Many people have seen Him bodily—have physically seen Him."

John became animated, his voice elevated as he continued. "What more proof is needed? A return from the dead was so unexpected that even His mother Mary did not anticipate Him, and when she first encountered Him, she thought it was the gardener. She had been living in grief since the horror of Calvary. When He first appeared, her grieved mind could not grasp the reality of Him being Jesus. She had come to honor a dead man and encountered the Lord of life. They didn't rush to embrace as they surely did when Jesus was a child. Instead, He called her friend. She called Him master. A new era of life existed for them both. The resurrection assures us that when our friends take us to the grave, Jesus will not leave us there."

John's smile persisted. The peace he felt was infectious. What calmness guarded us on that hillside overlooking the white-capped waters of the sea. "Our faith is not in a good man who died a martyr's death on a cross; it is in the risen Son of God who is alive. He was seen, I tell you. He was seen alive.

"Peter saw Him. Of all who might not have wanted to see Him, Peter was one. Just a few days earlier, he had refused even to acknowledge he knew Jesus. Here, I have a note written by Peter that expressed his response. To insure the accuracy of our experiences, we both made brief notes. Peter wrote, 'Blessed be the God and Father of our Lord Jesus Christ.' 'Lord,' he called Him. Peter, too, believed Him to be divine, driven to that conclusion by the resurrection. Let me continue his writing: '. . . who according to His abundant mercy has begotten us again to a living hope through the resurrection of Jesus from the dead.'

"I need to make notes right now of Peter's reaction to Jesus after He arose. It is significant Peter wrote of hope. He of all of us had more reason to be hopeless. Having denied the Lord, he had no reason to anticipate he might ever make his life right again. Peter felt only in heaven could the power of God bring us to an 'inheritance incorruptible and undefiled.' It is true that in heaven we'll all be perfected. But the resurrection gave us a new life, a new wholeness on earth.

"I have spoken much, and you scholars have proven a worthy audience. Now it is your turn to speak. Joseph, tell me, as a man with a legal mind, one who has spent years searching the Scriptures, what do you think of Jesus?"

"Gamaliel, the preeminent scholar of the Sanhedren, and we two have reasoned about these disturbing days. I cannot speak for this man of letters but for myself. I know of no fact in the history of humankind which is proven by better and fuller evidence of every sort. The mind of an honest inquirer is drawn to the conclusion that His resurrection is a great sign given us by our Great God. He was and is Messiah. His mission was not to save Israel from the Romans, but to save all people, Romans and Jews included, from the evil that would surely devour them."

Redirecting the issue John asked, "You, Nicodemus, what opinion have you?"

"I have come to the conclusion that it is absolutely impossible for any man with a legal mind to sit down and thoroughly investigate the evidence for the resurrection of Jesus Christ and come to any conclusion other than that He arose from the dead. Philosophy is intended to explain the events of life, not explain them away. The arguments against the resurrection are only theoretical. Every argument for the resurrection is empirical. I know pretty well what reliable evidence is, and I tell you, such evidence as that for the resurrection has never broken down.

"I went to Him by night, John. The trenchant way He received me, His civility, put me at ease. As an inquirer, I went seeking answers to my questions. Without hearing my questions, He began right away to answer them. He said, 'God so loved the world He gave His only begotten Son.' The expression only begotten I knew meant the only-one-of-a-kind. I have come to realize this was a reference to Himself. He had existed with God the Father through eternity before time—or more conclusively before time began to begin. We mortals speak of beginnings and endings. We think in straight lines. With God, there was no beginning, and there will be no end. Jesus always had been, but there was a day and a place He came to earth as one of us.

"God gave His Son in Bethlehem. There He gave us a portrait of Himself. He was conceived of a virgin and had no old sin nature like all of us. He lived a life without sin, unlike any of us. The giving of Jesus made God knowable to us. If we want to know what God our Father is like, we can see for ourselves in the person of Jesus Christ. He was God in flesh and blood. Miraculously, He was God in a human form. He was God up close and personal so we can know Him. That I believe with all my heart. I have seen and heard too much to deny it."

My response to John was growing long, but we all knew it vital that we articulate truth to ourselves so we could articulate it clearly to posterity. "Confused at first, I know now what He meant by *Son*. It does not mean God our Father produced Him. It does not speak of generation by association. John, you said He called you and James the Sons of Thunder, not meaning there was a clap of thunder that produced you but that your personalities associated you with thunder. He is not a *Son* of God; He is *the Son* of God. There are none associated with God our Father as He. He is the apotheosis of God the Father.

"*Son* signifies a unique position of likeness and equality. Some of my colleagues accosted Him one day. He answered them, 'You say I blaspheme because I call myself the Son of God?' They agreed and responded, 'By calling yourself that, you are making yourself God, and we refuse to believe that you are God; so we consider your claim blasphemy.' Clearly they understood the title Son of God to mean more than a general relationship as is available to all. To them it meant He was God. The title singularly identifies Him as Deity, God. He was not just like God. In reality He was God. In Him dwelled all the fullness of the Godhead bodily. *Son* indicates separateness of two who have the same nature or essence. Our Father God and the Son have the same essential unity of essence.

"Jesus also referred to Himself as *begotten*. At first I thought He was saying He was generated by God. After reflection, it dawned on me. Our word begotten is derived from the Greek tongue: *mono*, meaning 'one,' and *genes*, type or species. Jesus was the only one of a kind. He was fully God and fully man.

"Then Jesus defined His purpose for me. He said that if anybody, anybody, believed in Him, the individual would have everlasting life. *Everlasting life* refers to a new quality of life beginning at the moment of belief. Everlasting does not just speak of duration, but quality of life. I observed He said 'have.' *Have* denotes the present. Life is ours the instant we believe the facts and trust the person Jesus Christ. The moment we yield our lives to Him, He then begins a supernatural work in our lives that enables us to live our daily lives with Him to guide, guard, and govern us. He becomes our ever-present companion to comfort, counsel, and console us.

"When a person believes on the Lord Jesus Christ, life takes on a new quality as contrasted with a life of futility. What He did on Calvary was not meaningless. He had a purpose. It was that we who have an abiding trust and confidence in Him might have everlasting life. Anyone who believes has this gift. Inherent in the gift is assurance we shall not perish. I now know it does not mean we shall not lose our lives or be annihilated. It means we shall not suffer divine condemnation, complete and everlasting, that we are banished from the very presence of God. Perishing is the opposite of everlasting life. The latter becomes our good fortune the instant we 'believe' in Him."

A flock of gulls, in an unusual venture from the shore, swooped near us, maybe drawn to the life and joy we acknowledged. I smiled in unspoken awareness and pressed my point about who Jesus was. "The question might be asked: 'What does it mean to believe?' It means to trust, to commit yourself and all of life to Him. It means more than accepting facts. It means trusting the person. The night He shared this with me, it was all so new, so strange, that I did not grasp it. Now that I know who He is, I know what He meant. His resurrection confirmed it for me."

"Nicodemus, I, John, believe. With your empirical application of Jesus' writings, you have fed my belief. My faith now is deeper because of facts you have expounded. I thank you. If I am ever privileged to write of these things, your testimony regarding your night visit will be included. One further thing. At the cross, Mary, the mother of Jesus, was with other friends and me. Jesus always knew well the human heart. Even as His heart beat for the last times, He was concerned about the anguish of His mother's heart. With typical kindness, He took care of His mother's present, immediate needs. Gasping for breath, He lifted Himself on the cross, inhaled, and said to Mary, Woman, a term of endearment, 'behold your son!' The reference was to me. He was consigning to me her care. He continued, 'Behold your mother,' meaning I was to treat her as my own. His first words spoken from the cross were of forgiveness. His second, spoken to the repentant thief, was of friendship. Now, His third statement was of love. He put her in my charge because He knew I would take care of her most completely since even at this time His siblings had not believed."

Then to break the intensity, Joseph stood to relax himself and spoke to me, "Nicodemus, we now call Him Lord. I pray that all generations will accept Him as Lord. He is my master, sovereign, ruler. I will obey His Word, the essence of His spirit. The title *Lord* shall stand side by side in my heart with the title *God* as the most personal and intimate name for Deity. Jesus Christ is Lord of His Kingdom, which is not of this material world. Paradoxically, Jesus created and controls the physical universe, and time and place are important to Him. Yet, His Kingdom is of the inner world of the spirit and mind. He is Lord of both the physical and the spiritual worlds. I think we both believe the title *Lord* to identify Him as one worthy of honor, one who possesses authority over our lives."

"Yes, Joseph, He who was falsely accused by the priests has now become our Great High Priest. A priest represents man to God. He was indeed a priest, yet more than a priest. He was a prophet for He represented God to us. As our Great High Priest, He was touched by our physical and spiritual weaknesses. He was weak and tempted as we. But He didn't sin. He lives to talk to God the Father for us before the throne of heaven. He is alive and still aware of our needs and pain. For years our earthly priests have offered sacrificial animals for the sins of the people. As our Great High Priest, He offered Himself."

This thought resonated with Joseph, causing him to reflect on his long-held office. "He became the sacrifice for our sins as typified by the scapegoat. On the Day of Atonement after the priest had made the sacrifice for his sins, He offered the sacrifice of the scapegoat for the sins of the people. The goat stood facing the east, confronting the people. Symbolically the sins of the people would soon be laid on it. Our colleagues would place their hands on the head of the goat and confess the sins of the people. The priest would then announce in a loud voice, 'You shall be cleansed!' The priest then led the sin-burdened goat out through Solomon's Porch, through the eastern gate, across the Kidron to the Mount of Olives. There a stranger, a non-Israelite especially engaged for the purpose, led the goat 'unto a land not inhabited,' the Wilderness of Judah where the symbolic animals would be lost, not to be recalled.

"On Mount Muntal, the goat was led backwards to the edge of a cliff and cast from its high ledge. The goat was thought to be taken by the fallen angel Azazel. Tradition said the goat always burst into four parts symbolizing the four points of the compass. Thereby, the sacrifice was for the sins of all people. Now we know the Lamb of God has been sacrificed once for all. No longer is the blood of goats, bullocks, and lambs needed. The blood of Jesus cleanses us from all unrighteousness. The resurrection of Jesus stands as the irrefutable confirmation of His mission on earth. It is the staging ground for the gathering of a new society free from the control of Satan.

"Only those who have grappled with an enemy can know the true meaning of victory. He warred with sin, death, and Satan and won over each. The decisive battle was over the grave. He forever declares to searching people, 'I am He Who was dead and am alive. Because I live, you shall live also.' And He will invite us individually when He chooses us to defeat death as he demonstrated. We will die, but we'll live again. Jesus did that."

After further reflection on Jesus and the freedom and joy of life in Him, it was time for the three of us to part. We had compared our insights and mutually confirmed our beliefs. Plaintively

John said, Till death I shall carry in my mind the presence of Jesus and the magnificence of His life and death and resurrection. I will lean on His Word daily to refresh my soul."

As we were about to leave, our attention was arrested by the arrival of visitors. While we had been talking, several indistinct bands of pilgrims had passed by. But this colorful entourage approaching was distinct. Three sun-crowned men in regal robes riding Arabian stallions and accompanied by a small group of servants came to a nearby hillside. Their courtly manner identified them as prestigious men of wealth. Regal robes such as theirs identified them as men of prominence from Babylon. In an imperial manner, they approached, identifying themselves as Melchoir of Arabia, Caspar of Tarsus, and Balthasar of Ethiopia. They didn't hesitate to begin telling their story.

Caspar spoke in a portly manner, "Our ancestors are from Babylon, and we bear the names of our forefathers. We have been drawn to your land as were our fathers. Many years ago a ruler of our land, King Nebuchadnezzar, took a young man from here as a slave into our homeland. The name of the youth was Daniel. He was faithful to his God and loyal to our king. Such devotion enabled him to rise to a position of prominence in our land. He, like our fathers and like us, was a Magi. In our land this is an imminent office. As a prophet to your people, Daniel wrote of the coming Messiah and a star that would guide pilgrims to the place of His birth. Nearly four hundred years later that star appeared. Our fathers were guided to the place of His birth, Bethlehem. Many times they told us of this adventure and the honor of seeing the infant Jesus. We grew up longing to visit this land in hopes of meeting Him."

"Did you meet Him?" inquired Joseph.

"Unfortunately, no. We arrived in Jerusalem at the time of the feast. The city was buzzing with stories about Him and the danger with which He was faced. We sent servants into the city to inquire where we might find Him. They returned late at night telling us He had dined with His followers and afterwards retreated to the Garden of Gethsamene. At sunup we were at the garden hoping to see Him. We learned He had been arrested during the night. Fearing the upheaval that might erupt, we left through the desert and have been in Arabia every since. We are returning through this region to obtain salted fish from the Galilee to take home with us."

"Then you haven't heard?" I exclaimed.

"Heard what?" asked Balthasar. "In the remote area we have traveled, there has been no news from Jerusalem."

With my head bowed, I shared, "Jesus was condemned that day to be crucified. We were at the cross and saw the horror of His death."

"Then we missed seeing Him. Our lifelong ambition is frustrated," said Balthasar.

"Yes, in not seeing Him, but not in what you expected of Him. We buried Jesus. We sealed His lifeless corpse in the tomb. On the third day He arose from the dead. Many people have seen Him and talked with Him—and He with them."

"More witnesses than three?" inquired Balthazar.

"More than three?" exclaimed Joseph. "By hundreds!" Also, He was seen by five hundred on one occasion in addition to making numerous other appearances.

"In our land three creditable witnesses are enough to establish a fact," said Melchoir. "We are men of legal minds. Such compelling evidence in our courts requires acceptance of the testimony as fact. There is much we don't know and want to know. Not having seen Him, nevertheless we believe Him to be the Savior our fathers traveled so great a distance to visit. They came home with faith established by what they had seen. We will go home with our faith established by what we have heard. Tell us more that we may share this good news among our people."

Having heard of the resurrection, they professed faith and obediently engaged in baptism." The thirst for knowledge by the inquiring legal minds of these noblemen was quenched by the flow of details which we shared. The regal men left their horses and joined us on the hillside. Hours passed as we shared minute details of the life and teachings of Jesus. For the Magi, a scribe took copious notes to insure accurate recall of all that was shared.

Balthazar concluded, "Our fathers brought the newborn king gifts: gold, frankincense, and myrrh. You have given us gifts from the King of faith, hope and love. Our lives have been enriched in ways that the gifts of our fathers could never have enriched Him. We are all the more wealthy, but now from within."

Finally, Caspar spoke for the three men. "Learning these truths has rewarded the purpose of our journey. Fearing our trip to have been futile, we find it to be fulfilling. We came seeking the man Jesus. And in a miraculous way, in not finding Him, we found Him. Upon our return to our homeland, we will search the writing of the prophet Daniel to further correlate these happenings. Thereby people of our birth may come to believe in the King spoken of by Daniel, investigated by our fathers, and confirmed by us."

Facts known by their fathers led to the truths validated by the sons: Balthazar, Melchoir, and Caspar. Feeling their mission fulfilled, they departed alive with expectation. As their faint images faded over the horizon, a new era was about to dawn in the homelands of the three.

We were reluctant, even sorrowful, to interrupt our time of sharing with John. But the lengthening shadows of the mountains behind us indicated we had to go, John back to his abode and Joseph and I back to our group. We would be secure bedding down just outside the village where we would drift off to sleep with the sound of gentle waves caressing our exhilarated spirits and tired bodies. Our servants, camped safely in front of us, would be our buffer against any danger.

Awaiting us the next days was the challenge of finding Mary, the mother of Jesus. If we found her, we feared she might be reluctant to speak of the death of her child Jesus. We prayed, as we were increasingly discovering how to pray as John taught, that time with her might provide knowledge as no other source could. John, still a close confidant of Jesus' family and now bonded with us as fellow disciples of Jesus, said he would like to take us to Mary at sunrise.

SCROLL XI

THEN THERE WAS THE MOTHER OF JESUS

Our greatest fear when we had asked John to help us find Mary was that she might be cloistered somewhere captive to her grief, even as her name, meaning bitterness, perhaps foreshadowed. John, as he had promised, found us shortly after sunrise just outside Capernaum to take us to the quiet cove where Mary was staying on the shores of Galilee. The small cottage where she now lived was a gracious gift from Joseph's family who had often enjoyed the hidden retreat, so restful in contrast to the commercial center of Autocratis, their home. She was in seclusion, not so much because she feared for her life, but because she didn't want the notoriety she still encountered in Jerusalem or any place she went. People remembered her dishonored pre-marital pregnancy in many neighborhoods. In others, she was eschewed simply because she was the mother of a hated, reviled man.

The spot where we found Mary was especially connected to the life of her son. It was a sheltered bay near Seven Springs which lay at the base of a mountain where Jesus taught. The springs that flowed here had made the area around the rocky protrusion fertile for a grove of shady willows. Not only did the warm springs irrigate the land, but where they emptied into the lake, they attracted shoals of fish. Jesus and the disciples had spent many hours here in work and leisure. Mary was walking along the seashore when we spotted her as we rounded the bend in John's small boat. Her hideaway was accessible only by boat, and for the time being that is what she desired, seclusion.

Joseph and I gave acknowledging glances to each other, surprised not only by Mary's apparent joyful mood, detectable from a distance, but by her colorful attire. Her blue cloak stirred as she exulted in the sensation of the sand massaging her bare feet and the breeze gently conversing with her spirit. She made a lovely picture with her graying hair well groomed and fastened in place off her shoulders by an ivory comb. The sparkling agate beads, mined in the Negev, observably enhanced her face as we could see even at our distance from the shore. Later we would note that the shimmering, iridescent stones matched the joy in her deep brown eyes. One fact was undeniable: This composed, exultant woman, perhaps not yet fifty, gave no signs of a woman in mourning.

Suddenly Mary was aware of our boat. Recognizing it was John, her son's beloved friend who had visited her before, she waved with abandon. She did not suppress her joy in the presence of apparent visitors with him, knowing that anyone who had gained John's confidence certainly merited her favor as well.

"John!" Mary called when we were yet a distance from the shore. "You're just in time—you and your friends too. It is time for my noon meal, and I never like to eat alone. I know you all will join me. Come on up." With that she rushed uphill to the small cottage tucked under mountain shade not yet having fallen prey to the noon sun dancing on the waves and inviting full participation in the day.

In contrast to the welcome given by Mary, a gull was deeply offended by our intrusion into its territory. As we neared, it lifted off and circled overhead, squawking its resentment until certain we would not long occupy its domain. Seeing the beauty of the area, I could understand its possessive defense as we pulled the small craft onto the shore and went, drawn by Mary's effusive joy, toward the cottage.

John spoke as we reached the weathered doorway where

Mary greeted us. "Mary, you'll be excited when I tell you who my guests—and your guests—are. You know the names of the two men who asked Pilate for Jesus' body and gave him an honorable burial."

Before John could finish, Mary, unable to contain her amazement and joy, gushed, "One of you is Joseph and the other Nicodemus! I have met you, Nicodemus. You comforted me that terrible day when I could only stand by and watch my bleeding son stagger down the street to such an unjust death.

As she acknowledged her familiarity with our story, she identified us correctly by her intuitive study of our faces and dress. "Joseph, you are the gardener. I can tell by your hands, hands devoted to long, hard labor to carve out a garden in the hostile Judean hillside near that awful place of Calvary. And, though I've been to your garden to see where my son was buried, I actually recall few details. But I know yours is the most beautiful spot in all Jerusalem. I hope to visit it again someday." Her tone softened a bit as she spoke of Calvary, her voice pained just momentarily.

"And yes, you're Nicodemus," Mary said looking intently into my face and then my eyes. "I remember you, but I must apologize, only vaguely," she said looking again only at me. "I'd know you almost by the wisdom and perception I see in your face. Too, to be honest, I can see that you're a thinker, an indoor type, who has absorbed all the histories and laws of the temple. Both of you are wonderful people. I know you loved my son, maybe very much as I did. What you did was courageous. I'm doubly grateful to see you here today. You could be sealed behind a stone in your own tomb for what you did. Eternal life is what you gained in your decision to follow Jesus no matter the cost." She had turned Christian teacher instead of mother at this point.

Mary insisted that they talk while eating. The humble cottage was not bereft of hospitality. She had obviously busied herself, creating as much sense of family as she dared in her aloneness in the cove for the meal was a virtual banquet of roast lamb with hot mint sauce. Mary, though unknowing she would have company for the midday meal, had made a chard salad with lentils and beans, mustard greens, and baked artichoke. Dessert was pear compote made of dried pears boiled in wine, water, and honey.

We sat on mats on the floor around the food in the center. With an air of satisfaction in her culinary skills, Mary passed around pliable wide flat bread which we used as both a spoon and plate as we scooped out food from the common large dishes. The herbal jujube tea was refreshing to our bodies exhausted from travel. The menu would have been a delight even to the palate of the most discerning epicure.

When we had eaten casually and talked mostly of the solacing surroundings, Mary led the way outdoors where the white caps were gently encroaching upon the sand. She gently lifted a royal blue cashmere head wrap from a peg on the wall. I was certain it was the one she had spoken about the day of the crucifixion as we had drawn away to talk in front of the merchant's booth. As we took the blossom-lined pathway from the door, dozens of yellow vented bulbul were feasting on insects in the willows near the house. We chose to leave them undisturbed and moved beyond the small yard to make ourselves comfortable in the lush grass in the shade of a large laurestine. Stones, long having made their home on the shore, made workable backrests for our cushions of sand.

"Mary, our joy in finding you is second only to having met your son himself. What a special woman you are that God chose you to nurture His Son! But you must know that we are here on much more than a social visit. We are concerned with the honor of your firstborn—just as you are. We are intent upon establishing a record—a record authenticated by the people closest to Jesus—to refute those in Jerusalem who are saying that the resurrection was a hoax. We know in our hearts who Jesus was—and is. We know He arose, but we could help secure his supernatural work in this hostile world if we could objectively verify his resurrection. You can help us. All that you can let us see of Jesus will help our chronicling of his life and resurrection."

Mary's animation was back in full sway, her spirit lifted no doubt because of her personal vindication offered by the resurrection of her virgin-born son. "Our hometown at the time of my conception was Nazareth in Galilee. It was a tiny village on the southern slopes of the Lebanon mountain range at the point where the terrain blends into the fertile Plain of Esdraelon. Nazareth was so small the census records of the area included more than two hundred and fifty towns and villages, but did not include Nazareth. This tiny, unsophisticated village was inhabited mostly by cave dwellers who found their homes comfortable and commodious.

"It was this humble geographical area profuse with caves to which God sent His Son to be born. Now that I think of it, caves appear prominently in the life of Jesus. He was born in a grotto in Bethlehem, a cave. He was reared in a cave, and at last it was a cave, a tomb, that could not keep him as its permanent resident." She spoke with the animation of an unanticipated epiphany and as in an aside to the personal history she was giving.

"I was reared in nearby Sepphoris, a great and sophisticated Roman center of commerce which afforded good employment for my family. My parents were Anna and Joachim. The city was called Autocratis, 'the Ornament of Galilee.' When I was very young, just thirteen, I first saw Joseph one Sabbath during the Feast of the Tabernacles when I had walked away from my family for a stroll along the pathway connecting the many tents in our town for the occasion. He was the most striking young man I had ever seen—tall, thin, bronzed, and gentle. I could tell that the moment I passed him. We didn't speak. Respectable Jewish girls never did that. But I felt a kind of magnetism that I couldn't resist or explain.

"I did go back to my tent and ask my father about the young man as was the fitting decorum for a young Jewish girl. Father knew all the people who came to our village. He told me the young man's name was Joseph and that he was the son of Heli. He said Joseph worked in Sepphoris. My father, esteeming the family of high enough merit for formal introductions, arranged for a meeting with Heli and his son. Joseph was older than I; he an established young adult and I merely a child. He was a carpenter by reputation, but in reality he was a construction craftsman, a tekton. In our area of Galilee, there were so few trees that he worked largely with stone and wood, not merely wood as a carpenter would."

Mary looked a little dreamy though she was far past those tender and impressionable years. "Though I was young when our families made an arrangement for our marriage, I had some time to mature since most often a marriage didn't occur within a year. Joseph and I already belonged to each other, though we had hardly said more than hello. The contract was so binding that if the male died in this period, the 'unmarried' girl was referred to as a widow!"

As Mary spoke she occasionally stroked the inordinately affectionate tabby cat that had emerged from the open house. The music of the sea lapping against the shore and the melodious chatter of birds were soothing, conducive to her reminiscent mood.

Mary continued to tell us about Joseph and the amazing event of divine conception of which all the followers and enemies of Jesus had heard. "I was going about my life, seeing Joseph only on occasions of family gatherings when I saw an angel one day as I was walking in the meadow near our home on a morning free of the usual chores assigned by my mother. The angel didn't suddenly or startlingly appear, but seemed at home walking among the wild flowers and absorbing all the beauty of the morning. I knew intuitively he was an angel by his immense beauty, by his perfection. Too, an aura of soft yellow light seemed to surround him. I had heard of angels from the old days, but no one other than Zacharias, husband of my cousin Elizabeth, had reported seeing one in four hundred years. An angel came to tell him that he and Elizabeth would have a son. Elizabeth was old, but God gave her a son. He was John the Baptist—a miracle child. I'm sure you know of him as he was quite well known in Jerusalem.

"Rather than startling me, the angel just emanated an amazing majesty. Anyone watching would have said I was frozen in fright. Actually I was transfixed with awe. Though the angel had not frightened me, as he spoke he calmed any apprehension I felt. I listened and found consolation in his words, but still I trembled inside at what I heard. I was to have a baby, a boy whom I would name Jesus, a ruler whose kingdom would never end. I didn't even know about husbands and babies. The angel saw my consternation and told me not to be afraid.

"My first impulse, I well remember, was to run to my mother who would surely explain what the angel meant. But some gentle force compelled me to stay. I immediately felt like crying in fright, but the warmth of the angelic presence somehow calmed me, so I just sat on the nearby rock and let the illogical news I had just heard take root in my heart. And when I was soon strengthened by the reassuring gaze of the angel, the heavenly being said goodbye after turning me toward home and assuring me God had orchestrated this plan and this moment."

It was clear that the impact of her encounter with the angel still lingered in Mary's demeanor and conversation to this day—now nearly thirty-four years later. "That walk home was a long one. I did rush directly to my mother. She simply held me to her and told me she would always be there beside me, particularly until Joseph and I were married. She was a woman who understood that the ways of God are not our ways, so her calm helped me through those first days. How she handled the news with my father, I never knew. I just knew that he watched me closely but seemed content not to question me. I regretted any shame my impending motherhood would cast over our family. But I was determined to trust what I had experienced and not what a misunderstanding and uninformed people were sure to say."

Looking out at the sun just beginning to touch the ocean's edge and as though she were peering into the past, Mary sighed and continued. "When Joseph and I took Jesus to the temple to be dedicated, an old man, Simeon, who seemed to be waiting there for us, said to me, 'A sword shall pierce your soul.' That was a strange word to share with a young mother. Little did I know that he was saying that the greatest of all privileges which would be mine would result in the greatest of all sorrows. Simeon knew that with the piercing of the body of my son with that hideous Roman lance, my heart would be pierced by indescribable agony.

"I knew being an unwed pregnant girl made me worthy of stoning according to our laws. But I never feared for my life greatly—maybe since the words of the angel on that sloping hillside that spring day always echoed reassurance to my mind: 'With God nothing is impossible.' If ever that truth of impossibilities being possible with God were verified, it was established by my conception and now by His resurrection. And very important to me, Jesus' resurrection confirms my virgin conception of Him. Apart from the wonder of God, there is no explanation for either. As Jesus grew, I didn't reflect much on Simeon's words. I just meditated upon the miracle I had experienced and enjoyed sharing the childhood of my son and watching him grow and learn."

"Mary, surely Joseph must have been a remarkable man too since God chose him as your partner in this great cosmic assignment." I needed to know more about Joseph for myself and for his role in Jesus' life.

183

"I feared telling Joseph, but he told me first that the angel had told him that I would deliver a special child before our marriage had ever been consummated—a child who would become the Savior of the troubled world. Joseph was so kind and understanding. And he was wise. I say was because Joseph died of a high fever when Jesus was young. It was Joseph who helped me understand my womb was chosen and blessed—would become the 'workshop of God' is what he said. He explained how God was combining two natures: a human, my son, and a God-man, His son. The child that develops in the womb, Joseph explained, does not get its blood from the mother or father. It is miraculously generated in the child itself. Now I can see what Joseph must have known: Jesus' blood that would stain the streets of Jerusalem and flow on the gray stones of Calvary was not human blood, but the blood of God.

"Joseph, gentle Joseph, never thought of making a public example of me. He, instead, endured the mockery and I the shame. Every ill-willed person in the village slandered us. Yet Joseph believed my story about the angel messenger with calm confidence. He believed because he too had been chosen by God and had been visited by a heavenly being.

"Yes, as surely as I was chosen by heaven to be the mother of Jesus, Joseph was elected to be the foster-father. He shielded me and shared my shame. The stigma of adultery overshadowed both of us, but Joseph bore the heartache right along with me. Believers extol my virtue; but they should at the same time extol Joseph's character. I endured no pain that was not also common to Joseph. Surely, Joseph, perhaps understanding more than I at the time, took his place in the divine drama and remained faithful to God and to me."

It was clear that Mary had loved Joseph and understood the magnanimity of his character. "Though Joseph was not Jesus' paternal father, he prided himself in serving as His earthly father," she continued. "He always enjoyed people saying, 'That's Joseph's boy.' He often told me and others of Philip who told Nathaniel he had found the one of whom Moses spoke; He was Jesus, son of Joseph. Once while Jesus was teaching, people commented, 'Isn't this Jesus, the son of Joseph?' The people of Nazareth commonly called Him the son of Joseph. Of course, Joseph just smiled and nodded, realizing that the truth of Jesus' conception was much too complex for any ordinary person to comprehend at that time."

Mary tossed a few crumbs of bread that she found in her apron pocket to a seagull which had joined our conversation, and then she smiled broadly, her even white teeth contributing to her aura of youth. "Joseph gave me such an explicit illustration, one I still meditate upon. He said in civil affairs for a person to be a mediator, he must be equal to both parties in order to bring them together. Now I see. For Jesus to mediate between humanity and God, He had to be equal to both. God knew I needed Joseph, a principled man and a man of wisdom, to teach me, to explain something to me that would last through a lifetime of amazement about what God did. I do miss Joseph, but he is with me. And our son is with me."

Just then Mary's eyes took on a particularly warm sentimentality. "I live by the complex axiom that my mother taught me. It will describe for you my joy after such despicable horror—after the sword of agony as Simeon told me. In fact, I've memorized Mother's proverb and sing it out over the waves sometimes as they clash against the shore near my cottage: 'The length of wait multiplied by the depth of anticipation equals the height of joy.' My heart now more than ever floods with joy. Now I understand what I could not fully comprehend when Gabriel, God's most beloved angel, told me long ago who my son would be. What often began as fear is continuing to turn into incomprehensible joy."

Mary's thoughts turned once again to her family and husband. "Joseph and I once brought Him to Jerusalem to the temple for the first time. As a youth Jesus witnessed the sacrifices of the lambs on the altar. He watched as the priests let the blood of the animal and caught it in a basin with a rounded bottom to prevent it from being set down before the blood was offered. He observed the blood poured on the altar. He was witnessing a long-standing temple tradition—a prototype of his own death."

Mary's look of exhilaration had given way some time back to a look of resignation and inevitability. "It was I who would later watch that prototype become reality. I would watch helplessly as God's Lamb, His Son—and my son—was sacrificed on the altar of Calvary. The sword . . . the sword . . . the sword of anguish had pierced my heart just as Simeon had said when Jesus was a baby and I a young, optimistic mother. Now I understood."

Mary choked back the tears. She stood to shake off the mood of oppression which had seized her. We followed her, rising somewhat stiffly from our seats of sand and stone. She walked slowly toward the seashore as if to warm in the rays of the late-afternoon sun. We followed silent in respect for her resurfaced pain. "Jesus' first visit to the temple stands out in my memory. I can still see it so clearly. We had concluded our visit to Jerusalem and the temple. Returning to Nazareth, we noticed He was not with us. That was not unusual because we most often traveled with friends and family for safety. Assuming Him to be with other children whose parents we knew, we asked about Him. He wasn't with any of them. Immediately we concluded He was still in Jerusalem. Returning, we found Him three days later in the temple. He was sitting on the temple floor in the midst of the teachers listening to them and asking questions, astonishing them with His profound understanding. Some of those were among those who years later condemned Him to be crucified.

"Candidly, like an anxious mother, I chided Him saying how

anxious we were and asking why He had stayed behind in the temple. His answer puzzled me: 'Did you not know I must be about My Father's business?' At first I thought it impudent. But at this point, Jesus went back to Nazareth with us and obeyed us as a child and as a young man. We watched Him as he became more and more focused on his 'Father's business.'

"Back home in Nazareth, Jesus and I still enjoyed a lot of together time. I often played with Him in the bright sunlight. Like a boy, He enjoyed frogs, but He also enjoyed touching lilies of the fields and watching birds. Once in a most revealing moment when He was maybe ten, we had paused to observe in detail the elliptical leaves and cleft edges of the poppies. Jesus looked at me and said, 'I understand the flight of the birds and the cycle of life for the lilies and poppies. I touch them and I feel their life. I watch them and know their source. They are alive. My Heavenly Father gives life.' I could only look at Him and marvel at what I heard. I didn't feel threatened by what He said or outside His realm of knowledge and experience. He was able to make our world connect to heaven. We both understood the moment and took comfort in it. Jesus never spoke to me again of such things. I knew He was letting me know that even in His learning and playtime that He had comprehension of life far beyond that of His mother."

Mary was enjoying sharing her memories of her child. The sun was getting low in the sky, and she, knowing we must depart soon, led the way back toward her cottage. "As we walked the streets, we shared observations of the pathos and drama of the village and the silly pomposities of arrogant passers-by. We talked of the heroism with which humble people endure adversity. We would often share the beauty and riches of our favorite Psalm. Jesus would try to tell me intricacies of the law and deeper wisdom of the prophets, but He would soon see I was responding shallowly, not understanding as He, so we would take the conversation back to a mutual level of understanding and enjoyment.

"Jesus grew in decorum, in knowledge, and in respect from God and men. That was clear. His development was almost tangible, almost measurable. His life was balanced. Though Jesus had a fun-loving side, He lived in the utmost sobriety a pure and righteous life. He was so intense at times that often His siblings quipped about not being as perfect as He. Jesus never chided back though. He would just smile—quietly, peacefully, knowingly. If Jesus' at-home character had not inspired approval from those of His own family and community, He would never have found acceptance among the masses of people He attracted."

Mary seemed to leave the role of mother reminiscing now and moved toward a disciple portraying Jesus—a woman herself knowing who her son was and recognizing His role as her Lord too. The childhood ties, she conveyed, were past. "Those years of playing in nature and of deep sharing of life—and of the nagging among siblings—were much too brief. After thirty years, Jesus left home. Once His public ministry was begun, I did not see Him until a wedding at Cana of Galilee. It was a festive, joyous celebration when there was a moment of embarrassment for the host. He ran out of wine. I, forgetting that the boy had become a man, sought a solution and implied to Jesus in front of his disciples that he should do something about the problem.

"'Woman, what have I to do with you? My hour is not yet come.'" Those were the words I heard coming from my gentle son's mouth. At first His response appeared curt. The 'sword' struck again. Jesus was letting me know that it was His 'Father's business' which was priority to Him now. I too understood and walked away after mumbling to the disciples, as if I needed to, that they should do as Jesus instructed them. Ultimately, I interpreted what He said not by His words but by the spirit I knew Him to have. He had not been rude but had addressed me by the respectable Hebrew title woman. Jesus did as I requested—or as

He willed—and turned the water into wine, rescuing a distraught host. This was His first public miracle. Since then, Jesus was no longer my son. He was my Lord, and I His subordinate."

Mary had to stop briefly under the willow, the bulbul having retreated to the forest for the evening. Physically she was out of breath, and the lingering pain of motherhood conceded welled fresh into her face once more. "I was a slow learner at first. Once when He was visiting Nazareth, Jesus became absorbed in His ministry of teaching. I was concerned He would exhaust Himself. He had not eaten, and I was afraid He would deplete his energies. There were also rumors some wanted to seize Him and throw Him from a nearby cliff. I took my other sons and went to caution Him not to overextend Himself. I appealed to Him to eat and leave before His life was further endangered. I was trying once more to be mother and use my other sons as support.

"Basically, He said to me very clearly that in working toward the world's redemption, the only relationships He could acknowledge were spiritual. I tried to accept that truth which I had known since that day in the meadow with the angel. But it has been an ongoing struggle as you might perceive. Little did I see of Jesus after that incident. The sword that was to pierce so harshly at Calvary had begun its severing effect."

Just then we heard a plop in the water just beyond the shore and looked back to see the wake left by the surfacing of a big fish. Mary smiled and made one last fond, reminiscent comment about Jesus: "Jesus always knew where the fish were even as a child. I sometimes let myself believe I was the mother teaching the child, but both of us knew the truth. Jesus grew up with four brothers: James, Joses, Judas, Simon, and several sisters, whose names, because of Jewish tradition of protecting women, have never become public. They were dear girls. Jesus loved his siblings and knew well how to live in community and survive. Never has there been a child who loved like He. Though Jesus was deeply committed to His family, the other children never really understood Him and frankly at times thought Him insane. During His life none of them believed in Him. It was for that reason He entrusted me to John, his dearest friend, from the cross.

"Even from the cross, Jesus' loving nature showed. Jesus saw me as a mother once again—if only for a moment. For Him to be concerned for me while He suffered is a love that any mother would be blessed to have. It is as if God allowed the roar of derision from the crowd to subside for a moment enabling me clearly to hear Jesus' words. He lifted His eyes and fixed them on me, and I heard when Jesus instructed John to look after me. A flood of recollection swept through my mind. If I could have, I would have taken Him in my arms and comforted Him as a child. With a criminal on each side of Him and soldiers below Him, He mastered His pain, controlled His spontaneous groaning, and embraced me with His words as surely as if it had been by His strong arms."

Mary's happiness in recalling the public acknowledgment and affection of Jesus was visible. But soon the sobriety of her son's death returned. "It was Roman custom to offer some mercy to dying criminals by giving them a sedative to dull the pain, but Jesus refused the narcotic drink offered Him. He wanted to remain alert and involved to the conclusion of His earthly assignment, consciously dying in love, not only for those of us standing around that cross but for the global and cosmic implications of what was happening. His body was suffering in excruciating pain, but His soul was pouring out love. He rejected His own release from pain and gave us an elixir that day that consisted not of frankincense, myrrh, and herbs, but of love.

"I was not alone at the cross, not totally abandoned in my grief. Jesus' brothers and sisters stood on the fringes of the crowd at Golgotha that day and saw their brother die. But it wasn't Jesus' death that made them believers in Him—as powerful as that was with all of the earth convulsing and rejecting the evil of the day. It was the resurrection that changed Jesus' family. When it was known He arose from the grave, all of Jesus' siblings gathered with us in the Upper Room. The room was above the clamor of the noisy street and beyond prying eyes. This room, presently watched by the authorities, was well known at the time only by His devotees. All of us were seeking a sanctuary. The apostles gave us comfort. It was a sanctuary of love."

Interrupting, Joseph redirected our attention on our mission by posing a deliberately naive question, "Mary, did you speak to Him while He was on the cross?"

"Others sat, but I stood. I saw up close the child of my womb die that despicable death. Only Jesus Himself could have given me the stamina for such an ordeal. I did not speak to Him, too overcome with horror, pain. Throughout His life I had expressed myself to Him freely. Now I could not speak," she said, dropping her head again in silence.

"Mary," cautiously I said in a low voice, "you did not need to speak. Your presence showed your abiding love and uncompromising devotion. He knew! No mother ever showed more fortitude. We are impressed with your valor. To stand by in times of trouble is a divine art—a sympathetic presence itself speaks negating any need for words. Have no regrets, Mary. Jesus understood your language."

Again I queried, "Mary, not to belabor the point or to imply doubt, let me ask a simple but significant question. Was that Jesus who died on the cross?"

We saw her look of astonishment which said, "Why do you ask such an ill-informed question?" Mary answered emphatically, "In a word: Yes! Do you think I would not know my own child who lived in our home for thirty years? The hand I held when He was an infant was the same hand nailed to that cross.

"As I watched, I did reaffirm that was not my son on the cross.

My child, yes, but God's Son. I knew He hung there for a purpose. The sword that would pierce my heart was not in the hand of a Roman soldier, but in the hand of God. God had a plan. All the sin that had ever been or would ever be committed converged on Jesus. God had placed the guilt—past, present, and future—of all humanity on my child. My child, God's son, paid for the pain inflicted on us all by sin."

Mary paused. There was a troubled empty stare on her face as one glimpsing a re-enactment of a tragedy. Then she continued, "That day, the sun stood at its meridian in a clear bright sky. Then suddenly, it began to darken as though a dark funeral veil were being drawn over it. All nature responded. Sheep were bleating in fright, birds fluttered frantically about, and the calloused crowd wrung their hands and trembled. It was an abysmal midnight at midday. The paradise of heaven never seemed further away. I heard Jesus cry out, 'Eli, Eli, lama sabachthani.' I had taught Him that Scripture as a child: 'My God, My God, why have you forsaken me?'

"Like the claw of a vulture, this cry tore at my heart. Three long hours of black silence were broken by those words of abandonment. He was made the sacrifice for sin that He might be the sufficient Savior from sin. His sacrifice was the price for our redemption. The punishment of sin was not removed from Him in order that He might remove the agony of sin from others. The Jews and Romans who crucified Him did not take His life. He willingly gave it. He had been isolated by those who denied Him, those who rejected Him, and those who forsook Him. Now He was isolated from heaven. Hell, I've realized, is where God isn't, and He was not with Jesus on the cross. How inconceivable that God should be separated from God."

Mary continued, her voice having grown more shrill and tense in remembered pain. "I know that cry wasn't a defiant cry, but rather a cry of His human heart expressing the horror of separation from the Father. Even in the darkest hour of His soul, He still acknowledged God. Life would leave His body shortly. He would bodily die. But this cry of separation was, in essence, a cry of spiritual death. He was agonizingly separated from his Father so that we may never have to suffer separation from God. Yes, God did really turn His back on Him that He may never have to turn His back on us."

Joseph and I looked at each other in silent acknowledgment that as profound as Mary had spoken as a mother, she now elaborated on Jesus as disciple. "Ironically, some said Jesus was calling for Elijah. Others said it was as a cry of anguish offered to the very God He served on earth. It was neither. I taught Him the words of our prophets and the Psalms of David. In teaching Jewish children, parents use a drill to get them to quote certain portions of Scripture. Those words of drill are the opening line of a Psalm by David, a psalm that speaks of the suffering of the Holy One of God. David's vision was fulfilled in the cross. I know what Jesus meant in that cry. He was teaching even from the cross, 'If you want to know what is happening here, look it up in that prophetic Psalm that begins with those words.'

They pierced My hands and My feet; I can count all My bones. They look and stare at Me. They divide My garments among them, and for My clothing they cast lots.

Also, David verified the events of the cross when he wrote:

All those who see Me, laugh Me to scorn; they shoot out the lip, they shake the head, saying, He trusted in the Lord, let Him rescue Him, since He delights in Him.

Those are almost verbatim the words of the thieves on the cross and those gathered around the cross."

Mary was intent now as teacher and explicator. But she didn't want us to miss the verification of David that Jesus was indeed the Son of God. "At a time when the crucifixion had not been perceived as a criminal punishment, those prophetic words were written by David. Without divine revelation, he could not have described the event well in advance. That prophecy of centuries earlier was fulfilled at the foot of the cross."

Mary continued to answer our inquiry directly. "I, too, would know intuitively that it was Jesus on the cross. His body was mutilated by the flagellation almost to the point of being unrecognizable. But His voice was unmistakable. It was He who shouted on the cross. It was He who gave John responsibility for my welfare. Yes, there is no doubt. It was Jesus who died on that cross.

"I recall also how the one whom David spoke of as being in conflict came forth triumphantly. And indeed, Jesus triumphed over the grave. His empty tomb validates that. I knew my son on the cross when I saw and heard him there, and David knew of Jesus on the cross centuries before the event. So from two sides of history, two points in time, there is verification that Jesus, God's Son, my child, died on the cross."

I queried again. "As before, I pose a question to which I think I know the answer. Do you know for a fact that He bodily resurrected?"

"I have strong, convincing personal evidence that Jesus rose," said Mary, her resonate voice ringing in the clear seaside air. "In light of all I have said, the answer is obviously yes. There is extensive evidence, beyond what my heart tells me, as to why I know He arose. That night in the Upper Room after the reports of the resurrection had circulated, I was there. The apostles were there. Why? Because we were drawn together by the reports of those who had seen Jesus. Who was there with me? His brothers, they who had at times while growing up thought Him irrational, they who did not have faith or confidence in Him, they were there now assembled with believers. The answer is clear. They, some of His longest and harshest critics, believed He was alive.

"Jesus' siblings, as I, had seen Him die. Their rejection would have sealed them in unbelief were it not for the resurrection. It is hard for any of us to admit we are wrong about anything, especially Hebrew men. Yet, Jesus' brothers were by their presence admitting they were wrong about Him. Their and His sisters' presence was a confirmation of the resurrection. Doubters, critics, detractors, unbelievers—now all were believers."

Mary spoke with energy and vitality, now having resolved the pain that had gripped her earlier. "A second reason we gathered was the apprehension about what would happen to those of us who knew of the resurrection and insisted on telling others about it. Already the Sanhedrin had convened to discuss how to deal with the rising tide of belief. Our lives were in peril because religion and government refused to accept what we knew to be true. Jesus' siblings knew the eminent danger. It was common street talk. The antagonists who falsely accused Him obtained the right to crucify Him on the basis that He was a danger to Rome, a rival to Caesar. Still, Rome has little sympathy for followers of Jesus, especially those from Galilee."

Mary obviously felt she needed to explain some of the reasons for the Roman antagonism. "The Romans remember Jesus riding through the camp on the southern end of the Mount of Olives at the time of the Passover. They know the populace shouted 'Hosanna.' To them that was a challenge, like a gauntlet cast. It was unlikely they would have more pity on us than on Him. They would delight now to identify members of His household, His brothers. Doubtless they would like to do to His brothers what they did to Him. His brothers saw His fate and know it could be theirs, but they cannot deny the resurrection. If believing Jesus' divinity to be true subjects followers to death, they accept that destiny with boldness and confidence. Again I say their conversion proves the deity of their brother, and that proves the resurrection.

"Let me tell you the final thing that convinced Jesus' family of His deity. It was the primary thing that caused them to be willing to share our faith. About five hundred of us gathered on the Mount of Olives about forty days after His resurrection. The interest of Jesus' brothers had been heightened by the reports of those who had seen Him since the crucifixion. Nine times He had appeared to individuals or groups of people. There were many infallible proofs of His appearing. His brothers, along with five hundred people, were on the mountain when He appeared. There, Jesus warmly spoke words of comfort to us. He promised to enable and empower us. He charged us to tell the good news to all people. Then with open-mouthed astonishment, five hundred people gasped simultaneously as we watched Him rise up into the clouds on His way back to His Father.

"It's amazing how God just keeps teaching and reassuring us through repetition. Interestingly, at the tomb two men in white apparel standing by spoke the glorious news of the resurrection. That day women in white apparel made an announcement on Olivet. They said that just as He was taken up, in like manner He one day will come back. It was a confirmation of what we had heard Him speak of in better days. Once it was a puzzling statement, but now a statement exciting expectation and invoking faithfulness. That event of Jesus ascending into heaven ultimately sealed the belief of His brothers. They now stand with those of us who acknowledge Jesus as God."

Mary's voice grew somewhat hushed as she conveyed the reality of the threat to public followers of Jesus. "Already the Sanhedrin has convened to select from their number a chief investigator. It is rumored it will be the brilliant, ruthless Saul of Tarsus. He is the most intellectually astute of the court. Saul was a witness to the crucifixion and the chief executioner at the stoning death of Steven, a man who died because He believed in the resurrection and told others of it. The Sanhedrin knows his knowledge of the Law. He has a reputation as a stern disciplinarian, a Pharisee of the Pharisees, lacking compassion. This is the occasion for him to prove himself to them. If he can stamp out those who profess to believe in the resurrection, he will have given the court great pleasure. Besides, it would virtually insure for him the eventual role of high priest, the office to which he aspires. If Saul is ever appointed, many will suffer grievously."

Mary stopped near her doorway, erect and undaunted, and turned to look us fully in the face, first me and then Joseph. "Nicodemus, Joseph, yes, I believe in the resurrection and now all my household with me. Had any among those of us who trusted in Jesus stolen His body, as alleged, we would have gladly returned it to His executioners to spare ourselves and our friends the persecution we face. None would have been so selfish as to have perpetrated the theft of Jesus' body, endangering all His followers, and not have exposed it in the current political furor.

"The members of the court feel compelled to prove He was not resurrected in order to exonerate themselves. They who did not act honorably have no honor. They are so blind as to further debase themselves and the court by persisting in expunging all followers of Jesus if they can. It is rumored that even in the Roman garrison, there are those who covertly believe in Jesus' resurrection. Some who were baptized by John in the Jordan when Jesus came to Him have professed their faith at great risk to themselves." Mary's countenance showed an encroaching deep sadness. "I do have one persistent regret perhaps, or maybe not. God's plan was for Jesus to die so sinful people who chose death might have the option to choose life. But I do occasionally think of the what-ifs. I might have saved Jesus from death because upon receiving convincing evidence affecting a court decision, even in route to crucifixion, the Sanhedrin custom is that the accused may be taken back and the trial resumed."

'One charge against Him was that He said He was the Son of God. This they considered an untruth. Perhaps, just perhaps, I could have spoken out and declared the report of my virgin conception of Him to be a lie. Then he might have had a retrial and would have been less threatening to the Jewish and Roman authorities. Jesus could be alive and sharing this visit with us today. Of course, that is merely a passing, selfish thought with me. I could never have refuted my own son's divinity—would never have participated in a lie even in an effort to save Jesus' life. It would not have been a part of God's plan. Anyway, Jesus is alive—just in another dimension of time and space than we are experiencing. One day, as He promised, we will live with Him in the home He's preparing for us just as he promised. He truly is alive."

A glow came back into Mary's face at the thought, the knowledge that Jesus arose and was presently living. "Surely, Jesus' appearances after His resurrection should be the most convincing evidence of His living, tangible body. I've already told you of some of them, but let me affirm for you once more the incidents of Jesus' post-resurrection appearances—appearances He made to various people during the forty days before He ascended after the resurrection. These incidences are conclusive, irrefutable evidence that He indeed is alive:

1. At the tomb, he spoke to Mary Magdalene.
2. Then several women near the tomb saw him.
3. Peter saw him.
4. Two men walking to Emmaus saw him.
5. Ten disciples validate His appearance in the upper room.
6. Thomas and the other disciples experienced Jesus walking through the door, defying physical laws. Jesus spoke to Thomas, asked Thomas to touch Him.
7. James, my son also, saw Jesus who seemed to come to reassure His brother.
8. Seven disciples saw him at once on the shores of Galilee.
9. In Bethany, on the Mount of Olives, a crowd of five

hundred rejoiced as He ascended to His Father.

"There is no doubt. He arose." Mary was very calm now, very affirmative. "We were all slow of heart, and He had to open our minds to the truth ever so gradually. I know the truth now. I reflect on it every day and often at night in the quiet of my home as I listen to the pulsating creation outside. Jesus is with me even now. And I know that Joseph will be resurrected. My other children will never die. We will never literally die. Jesus did that. He gave us life—life to all who will believe and follow Him."

Mary seemed finished when she said in some comprehensive way a conclusion she must have reached as she had agonized with her son in His death and now exhilarated in His restored life:

All people know virgins cannot conceive, stars cannot appear and disappear, a host of angels does not just emerge and vanish, and deity does not condescend to enter into human form. That is, until God intervenes and the supernatural amends the natural.

Yes, Nicodemus and Joseph, you have to write the truth. You can't let the power of Jesus be lost in a distorted, twisted world. There is good news to be told."

By our demeanor, it was clear we all recognized our time together was at an end. Mary had not only been the consummate hostess; she had been a refreshing reservoir of facts and faith. Her composure after such trauma revealed the confidence she had in the resurrection. Her resurrected sprit itself was evidence of the life that Jesus instituted through His resurrection.

Just as the sun was beginning to rest briefly on the horizon of the Sea of Galilee before it also bid farewell to the day, we said good-byes to Mary. John, who had spent the day in his own private reflection in the gently rocking boat, took us back to the busy end-of-day commerce on the Galilean shore. We would leave this captivating seaside once again early the next morning in search of our next subject, Andrew. Andrew held valuable information for us because he had been a follower of John the Baptist before being called by Jesus. Perhaps from him we could gain insight regarding one of the era's most colorful personalities. And through learning of Andrew's faith in Jesus, we could gain insight into Jesus' earlier years. A surprise awaited us. The sun finally dipped below the horizon, reclaiming its light from a rewarding day. It would arise on a day of intrigue.

SCROLL XII

A VISIT WITH ANDREW AND JAMES

Peter had told us where we were most likely to find Andrew. Having been a follower of John the Baptist, Andrew had learned to love the area near Jericho along the Jordan. So, our journey took us south along the banks of the river. We began our scenic journey to Jericho before dawn. The fabled land offered us a variety of beauty. Following the road was a guessing game. Leaving the tended terraces of carob, quince, almond, hazelnut, and olive trees, we began our trek. The verdure banks of the Jordon formed an elongated oasis through a desert. Even with all this water, there were areas where walls of sand spilled into the riverbed. Outcroppings of white blooming plants blanketed the sands with their fleecy white flowers near the water.

At points the slippery ascents were made a bit easier by animals having gone before us. The tracks of a fox shifted back and forth. A sand rat scurried about collecting food for its lair. Camels meandered around in total freedom. The horizon glistened with waves of heat. At one point we were captivated by the sight of a white Oryx, the most elegant of all antelopes. Striding along with its stiff-legged canter, it appeared as though it were strutting. Its horns were arced close together and straight, giving it the appearance of a unicorn.

Stopping along the way, we refreshed ourselves at a cluster of prickle pears. We took special care to be sure the yellow blossoms had faded, the thick peel was about to burst, and the flesh had turned a yellowish-red. Before picking them, we tested the direction of the wind. We knew it unwise to pick the fruit facing the wind lest the tiny thorns blow onto the skin inflicting major pain.

As we munched on our succulent treats, we were startled by the whistling sound of a fast-rising chukar partridge. This swift bird vanished almost as quickly as it appeared. After a tiring day in travel, further along our route, I called out, "Joseph, the day has been long beneath the Judean sun. Our animals are tiring. Let's end our day a bit early." Realizing I spoke what he was feeling, he yelled back, "See the smoke curling up from campfires in that oasis ahead? The waters of a spring there flow into the Jordan. Let's camp there." Riding into the lush oasis, we were the objects of stares and snide remarks from the other campers. Some evidences of our rank, if not our role, must have at once been evident.

Our mules, ever silent, and our camels, ever belching and bellowing, drank deeply from the springs. We filled our canteens as our servants busied themselves setting up camp. Fallow deer drank nervously at the unoccupied far end of the spring. Acacia raddiana growing near the water's edge gave fidgety animals a bit of a shield. We saw a giffon vulture circle overhead and knew some had not made it to the water.

Ira, one of our servants, called out to two young men nearby, "Dara! Joel!"

More nervous than the deer at having been recognized, Dara turned toward us quickly. Slowly he and his companion walked toward us.

"Nicodemus and Joseph," said Ira referencing us. "Sirs, you should recognize these two. They are apprentice scribes of your prestigious court."

Dara spoke for the two of them, "Your Excellencies, we recognize you and know of your role in the Sanhedrin."

The second of the two, Joel, with a tone of uncertainty in his voice, asked, "May we sit and visit with you?"

"Of course, be our guests and join us. Ira, prepare our guests wine made from the fruit I condensed from the grapes in my vineyard. Add to it some of the fresh cool spring water." This method, used by our ancestors for years, is a wonderful way to have fresh tasting unfermented wine all year.

"Joel," said Dara, "you speak better than I about this matter. Let's ask about our dastardly deed."

His eyes downcast, Joel began. "As young aspiring scribes, we were commissioned by a small group of members of the court to write about Jesus."

Joseph and I were hopeful for a moment as Joel continued.

"They charged us to write spurious accounts regarding Jesus, accounts defaming Him. Pretentiously, we walked with His followers for some weeks and gathered insight. Our submission to our elders drove us to write what even we didn't believe."

"Such as?" I inquired.

"I wrote of His birth."

"What of it?"

"I fantasized His conception resulted from His mother, whom I said was a streetwalker, secretly consorting with a Roman soldier. Her friends in the village, out of shame, sought to give legitimacy to her pregnancy by speaking of a mystical conception. 'All knew she was not a virgin,' I wrote."

Dara spoke, "I recorded that Jesus consorted with Mary from Magdela and even said they were eventually secretly married and had plans to leave this land and go to the distant land of the Franks."

"I am hearing this in disbelief," said Joseph. "You surely know these are damnable lies. They are complete distortions of the truth. Absolute fallacies."

"No one knows that better than we," affirmed Dara.

I rushed to ask, "Where are those bogus writings? They must not be allowed to have a life."

"That is our shame," offered Dara. "Days before His crucifixion, we turned them over to our superiors. They are now in their charge. We knew even at the time of our writing they were baseless, but our loyalty to our charge prompted us to compose them. Now, as a result of what happened the third day after His execution, we are all the more remorseful. I would that my hand had never learned to write."

Joseph, grief stricken, remarked, "Those who have these writings are sure to use them to support their deeds and to defame Jesus. I hope these lies will have a short life."

"No," I said, "they are sure to have periods of popularity and fade only to resurface among future generations. Only the truth can refute them."

"Our sorrow has driven us here to the desert in a vain attempt to escape our grief. But our pain has not abated. How can we ever be forgiven for what we have done?" It was Dara who made the inquiry.

My anger was controlled by hearing Dara invoke that word forgiven. Could I forgive them? I realized that not only must I forgive them but that the One about Whom the lies were written died to forgive them.

"Men, you know of His death!"

Joel interrupted, "Not only do we know of His death, we were there. We know of His resurrection."

"You spoke of His resurrection. Do you believe in it?"

"Having walked with Him and heard Him teach, we know in retrospect that it was only logical that such a miracle should have happened. Yes, we know of the reports of resurrection. We know and believe. The thought of having written as we did tears at our hearts. Were He here, we would beg His forgiveness."

Compassionately Joseph sought reconciliation for these distortionists of history, distortionists of eternal truth. "Did you hear Him speak from the cross? One such utterance was a prayer, 'Father, forgive them for they know not what they are doing.' The scope of that prayer includes even you."

Confusion slowly drained from their faces. Continuing, I

explained, "To forgive does not mean to forget. It means never to hold a thing against the offender again."

"You mean He would forgive us? If I, we, believed that," he said nodding toward Ira and receiving a nod of confirmation, "we would gladly beg His forgiveness."

I replied, "Forgiveness belongs to those who have faith to believe that His death for sin provides it."

"You mean that if we ask Him to forgive us, He will do even that?"

"Even that."

What followed was the two, along with us, bowed. And they, having changed their minds about Jesus, asked His forgiveness. As they did, I prayed silently thanking Jesus for the forgiveness He had granted me. I was no less in need of forgiveness than they. Their salty tears added to the desert sand was evidence of their contrite spirits. The radiance now showing on their faces was a tribute to Jesus' forgiveness.

A relieved Joel, rejoicing, said, "We thought we were destined to drift in these desert sands wallowing in our guilt all of our lives. His forgiveness gives us release to live."

"To live for Him!" said Ira.

Our conversation lasted long into the evening as we sought to affirm them further. The wail of a distant desert dog signaled it was time to end our day. A melodious desert lark sang us to sleep.

The next day's journey took us to Andrew sitting pensively in the breeze on the banks of the Jordan near Jericho. From Peter we had learned a bit about Andrew. Born in Bethsaida twenty-five miles east of Nazareth on the Sea of Galilee, like his brother Peter he was a fisherman. Fishing was a seasonal occupation, so he had taken a leave of absence to go south through the Jordan valley to a place near Jericho. As suggested, we did find Andrew there where Jesus was baptized by John. It had been here Andrew left John to follow Jesus. John had commended such a transfer of loyalty by saying of Jesus, "He must increase and I must decrease."

I greeted him, "Andrew, shalom. We were told we'd find you here, a man more likely to be working with his head than his hands. We are fellow seekers and followers of Jesus. I am Nicodemus and this is Joseph, priests of the detestable Sanhedrin and now followers of Jesus as you. You've likely heard it was Joseph who gave his tomb for Jesus to have an honorable burial. He and I, no doubt, further severed our ties with the Sanhedrin when we asked for Jesus' body. Since then, we've felt a strong compulsion to get the truth of Jesus' resurrection to dispel the false information that is beginning to circulate about Him. We've talked to many of your friends who traveled with Jesus. And because of Peter's generosity, we now have found you to get your perspective on Jesus."

"I never thought I'd meet you two," Andrew replied. A smaller man than Peter and Thaddeus, he was actually more like John, maybe Matthew, a more studious man. His initial glances showed us that he indeed believed us, trusting Peter perhaps more than just two strangers who came his way. "Thank you both for caring for our Lord when we couldn't. In fact, most of us disciples who loved Jesus ran away when He was taken, fearing for our own lives. I'm ashamed of that now, but I know Jesus didn't blame us. He understood us better than we understood ourselves. He knew it would take time and contemplation for us to finally realize our mission. Now, too, I know God will use even our fear to drive us to other cities and lands to spread the words of Jesus."

We sat down beside Andrew in the soft grass. "Tell us, Andrew, of your meeting with Jesus." It was I who led us straight to the point of our visit.

"To tell you of Jesus, I have to tell you of John the Baptist who pointed me to Jesus. Jesus respected John's appeal to the masses. Many wondered what it was that drew the crowds into the Judean desert to hear this man. Jesus explained by asking if they expected to see a man like a reed blowing in the wind. Indeed not. John was like a sturdy oak. He was not only a prophet. He was the subject of prophecy. His role had been fore-told as the one who should prepare the way for the Messiah. The prophet Malachi said he was born especially to prepare the hearts of the people.

"It is little wonder Jesus said of John, 'Assuredly, I say to you, among those born of women, there has not risen one greater than John the Baptist.' Doubtless such a compliment resulted not just from John being the forerunner but from the way he fulfilled this role. When Jesus came to the Jordan to be baptized, John announced His arrival upon the scene as Messiah. Gesturing toward Jesus, John declared, 'Look! The Lamb of God who is tak-ing away the sins of the world.'

"John himself had emphasized that repentance was the only way a person could enter the Messiah's kingdom. He recognized it was Jesus who would provide the pathway of repentance. Finally, he willfully receded into the background when the One he had come to introduce arrived."

Sitting beneath an acacia tree, Joseph and I assured Andrew we were not alien to those with faith in Jesus, but earnestly sought to confirm reality. "Tell us Andrew," said Joseph, "of your meeting Jesus."

Fondly Andrew persisted in speaking of John the Baptist. As he did, he looked to our left. It was a distant, faraway look as if he were expecting someone or something. "John was a rare man of God, an ascetic. His strengths were many. He was a purist in spirit, body, and even diet. His father was Zacharias, a priest after the order of Abijah. His mother was Elizabeth of the orders of Aaron. John automatically held the priesthood of Aaron with the right to baptize. Jesus' mother Mary and Elizabeth were cousins. John was born six months before Jesus.

"This son of a priest who left his promising role to become a desert dweller often subsisted only on the carob-like beans of the locus tree and wild honey, a more than sufficient diet for a period. His attire was well suited for the desert. The hide of the camel remains flexible for years, the pores closing when wet to help keep one dry and opening when hot to provide cooling. John attracted great crowds with his simple and singular message: 'Repent.' Though stated many different ways that was ultimately his message. 'Repent and be baptized!' he shouted with clarity of tone and intent. Many did. Among them were contemptuous tax collectors and deplorable soldiers.

"John's candor was most uncommon. He preached, 'You brood of vipers, who warned you to flee from the wrath to come? Therefore bear fruits worthy of repentance. Even now the axe is laid at the root of the trees. Therefore, every tree which does not bear good fruit is cut down and thrown into the fire.' When soldiers once asked John what they should do, he almost shouted in response.

'Stop intimidating people or accusing anyone falsely. And you tax collectors, don't collect from the people any more than you are entitled to collect. Be content with your wages.' They were accustomed to taunting the public and grumbling about their conditions. Such a proposed change was radical. Like me, many were moved to repentance by John's message and have become followers of Jesus.

"Some of the soldiers even became covert students of Jesus. They availed themselves of every opportunity to hear Him. It is rumored that some of those recently transferred back to Rome are secret believers. They had friends who were among the execution squad that put Jesus to death. Some under the command of a sympathetic officer, Gaius, who has been touched by the reports of the resurrection, have openly avowed their allegiance to Jesus. What fate awaits them in Rome is questionable.

However, based on the power of the resurrection, the question might be what fate awaits Rome when believers return and share the good news. They might well establish the faith even in the household of Caesar."

Again, Andrew looked to the left. Nicodemus could contain his curiosity no longer. He looked. There on the crest of a vast Judean sand mountain that stretched for miles was a tiny, solitary figure slowly making his way to the west. Andrew didn't seem alarmed, so I dismissed the individual as a mere wanderer. Then came a matchless moment," Andrew continued. "John was busy baptizing those who repented of their sins. We who followed were excitedly helping him. John looking up and seeing Jesus, instantly identified Him saying, 'Behold, the Lamb of God who will take away the sins of the world.' In astonishment the crowd turned to see Jesus whose loving eyes and warm smile indicated His pleasure at the comment by John. A murmur went through the crowd." There was no way we could comprehend the great cost of this day to him. All the lambs offered in the temple were but a foreshadowing of this Lamb."

"Did you immediately realize who Jesus was?" I asked.

"Immediately? By no means. Only lately have I come to understand who He was. We were all slow to comprehend who He was. I mean Jesus' true self. The resurrection has confirmed for us He was Immanuel, literally God with us. God in flesh and blood—God with a certain skin tone, eye and hair color, a certain height and weight."

Picking up a bit of clay and beginning to knead it, Andrew continued. "This is clay. Look, I have shaped it like a sphere. Its form is that of a sphere. In its essence, that is its true nature, its essence, clay." Then working the malleable clay, he shaped it like a cube and explained, "It's shape is now that of a square box. However, it is in essence still clay. The form changed but not the essence or nature of the clay. So in eternity Jesus was God in essence, equal to the Father. At His birth He took on the form of a servant like us. He had changed His form, but not His nature. He was still God in essence. His very nature was that of God.

"Radical? Yes. There is no other explanation for what He did on His earth walk than that He was divine. Candidly, after all we saw and heard, we should have expected the resurrection to be the natural result of His self-sacrificing death. Yet, we caught not a clue it was coming. It caught us by complete surprise."

Again Andrew looked left toward the horizon. I turned quickly again and saw coming over the ridge a large flock of sheep following their shepherd. Without much thought, I concluded this was a natural occurrence for the location.

Joseph asked, "Andrew, you did not suspect the resurrection?"

"Suspect the resurrection?" Andrew echoed with incredulity. "We did not expect His death, much less His resurrection. We humans expect what we have experienced. Never having seen a person self-resurrected, we had no cause to expect it. True, when we traveled with Him, we shared in three experiences that should have awakened our minds to the possibility. There was the time in Nain that He gently spoke to the corpse of a little girl commanding her to live. All within the house were amazed as she came back to life. Then there was the time we came to the home where a lad had died. All present knew of his death. He too was brought back to life by Jesus.

"The capstone experience that should have alerted us to His power over death took place when we came to the tomb of Lazarus who had been dead four days. With the power of heaven in His voice, He commanded, 'Lazarus, come forth!' Somewhere in the darkness of the tomb, Lazarus' lungs inhaled, his heart once more beat, and his pulse throbbed. Lazarus did come back from the dead. His suddenly standing in front of the tomb on the stone that had locked him away was the most miraculous thing I have ever witnessed. We should have realized Jesus had the power to unmask death and reveal it as the imposter it is."

"Andrew, who died on Calvary?" pressed Joseph.

"Why do you persist with this question? The answer is simple, Jesus. I was an eyewitness. I heard His cry suspended in the hot air, 'I thirst.' He was truly a man, or He would not have thirsted. He was truly God, or He could not have forgiven. He was the God/man-man/God. I watched as death's dark veil was pulled over the Light of the World. He, Jesus, assuredly Jesus, died."

"What then?" Joseph insisted.

"He was removed from the cross by you two as you were attended by the soldiers. I saw the nails pulled from His hands that healed others and from His feet that had traversed the land in love and forgiveness. His stiffening body you carried away under the watchful eyes of the guards and the large contingency that followed you to your tomb, Joseph. I marveled at the haste with which you men worked to insure the interment before the Sabbath began.

"Then the grinding sound of the grave stone, I remember, rolling and then thundering into its groove. Guards at the tomb later said they slept as His followers stole His body. How ludicrous to think they could have slept through the removal of that stone. The volume and length of the sound would have awakened the most weary. Only if the stone were supernaturally relocated might they not have awakened. Either way, there is divine action inherent in the movement of the stone. I am left with but one conclusion: He arose."

Then with a virtual incandescent smile and with a knowing twinkle in his eye, he said, "Besides, I have seen Him. He is definitely alive. This is no aberration. I have seen Him with the clarity and definition with which I now see you. I have heard Him as clearly as I hear that sheep bleating."

Hearing the sound of the approaching sheep, Andrew digressed. "He often taught us lessons based upon sheep and shepherding. Once He reflected on the Shepherd's Psalm of David. He assured us of the Father's provisions for us, and I am sure it is true now. He called our attention to a large 'V' formation of rocks on the hillside and spoke of how it got there. We were from the Galilee where fresh water is plentiful, but not so here in the arid region. Here the shepherds would find caves going directly into the ground rather than in a hillside. Using these as cisterns, the shepherd made a large 'V' on the hillside with the point of the 'V' being at the mouth of the cavern. It rains here only three months of the year. When it rains, the water is funneled into the cave which serves as a reservoir. It is stored here for use during the long dry months. In the absence of light and air, such water remains fresh indefinitely. It is called 'still water.' He told us how the Father in Heaven has already in store for us everything we need long before we need it. He was always assuring us and building our confidence in our Great God.

"Jesus noted also David's reference to 'the cup' and it running over. He explained how the shepherd would hew out of a large bolder a trough called a cup. The shepherd would draw from the cistern and pour water into the cup. Sheep would take turns drinking, never crowding another out. The cup was of such size that with the sheep crowding around it, the shepherd could not see his own feet. But when he felt them getting wet, he knew the cup was full and overflowing, providing an abundance for the sheep. Again Jesus used this to teach of the abundance of God's provisions.

"When we tended to be a bit unruly on one occasion, He gave us another lesson drawn from sheep. He said there are four essentials for a flock of sheep to lie down together as David wrote. First, they must be free from predators. Sheep are jumpy when a wolf or jackal is in the area. Next, they must be free of nuisances like these pesky gnats. Third, they must be well fed before lying down. Finally, there can't be any infighting in the flock for them to be at ease.

"Then Jesus pulled the convincing illustration together by saying the Father's goodness and mercy protect from predators and deliver us from nuisances. He spoke of the bounty of spiritual food afforded us. Then the clincher. He knew how to hit us hardest and for our good. He said it was our responsibility to avoid infighting. We failed to learn that lesson well. It wasn't long before James and John played one-upmanship asking for favored positions in His kingdom. Jesus answered, 'Whoever desires to become great among you, let him be your servant. And whoever desires to be first among you, let him be your servant, just as the Son of Man did not come be served, but to serve, and to give His life a ransom for many.'"

Joseph and I were patient listening to Andrew. Besides, we were learning from the teachings of Jesus. However, we returned the conversation to our earlier questions. "Tell us of the beginning of your journey with Jesus," Joseph said.

"After John baptized Him and He began to walk away, two of us who had followed John started walking after Him. He turned and saw us and said, 'What do you seek?'

"'Rabbi, that is, Teacher, where are you staying?'

"He said, 'Come and see.'

"We stayed with Him this time only one day, and He bid us farewell and ventured into the desert. I returned to Galilee to tell Peter what I had seen and heard. Jesus later spoke of this time of fasting forty days in the desert. Having come from the exhilarating experience of His baptism and the audible endorsement by the Father, He now was subject to temptation. I surmise that the purpose was to prove His character through testing.

"Like our forefathers before us, He was tempted in the desert. Jesus told of how he was famished after the forty days of fasting. Seizing the moment to capitalize on His need, Satan visited Him. The wily one addressed Him: 'If You are the Son of God, com-

mand these stones to turn to bread.' This archenemy who leads
the evil spiritual host sought to entice Him in a moment of weakness. It was not only a temptation to seek His will and prove He
was God's Son. It was an enticement to use His Sonship in a
manner contrary to His heaven-ordained mission on earth. It was
an appeal to abandon the Father's will.

"Jesus told us of those lonely, difficult days. He said the Word
we would be charged to share with all nations was the weapon
Jesus used in answering Satan. From our prophets He quoted,
'Man shall not live by bread alone, but by every word that proceeds from the mouth of God.' Tempting Him yet again, Satan
took Him to the pinnacle of the temple, the highest point of the
temple complex which soared over the ravine below.

"Satan's temptation involved the misuse of the Word of God.
'If you are the Son of God, throw yourself down.' Jesus would
hear similar words of derision and taunting spoken by a thief on
the cross: 'If you are the Son of God, save yourself and us.' With
this distortion of truth, Satan declared that God had promised
that His angels would have charge over Him and bear Him up.
Jesus quoted the Word of God correctly. 'It is written again, You
shall not tempt the Lord your God.'

"For a third time Jesus was tempted. Once more Satan solicited Him to evil by taking Him to a high mountain. From there he
showed Him the mountains of Nebo, along which ran one of the
primary caravan routes of the world. Along that ridge all nations
were represented by their tradesmen. It was a scenic summary of
all nations.

"Satan offered Jesus the kingdoms of this world if He would
fall down and worship him. This of all the temptations was the
most ridiculous. It was impossible that the Creator could be
tempted by that which He had created. The kingdom and power
were already His. This ostentatious offer was repulsed: 'Away
with you, Satan! For it is written, 'You shall worship the Lord

your God, and Him only you shall serve.'

"With this, the temptations ended. Jesus came out of the wilderness and shared with us disciples what had happened there so we could teach others to resist Satan. As soon as He did, He heard John the Baptist had been put in prison. Herod Antipas had jailed him for his scathing denunciation of Herod's marriage to Herodias, the former wife of Herod Philip I, his own brother.

"Herod and Herodias had become lovers on a trip to Rome. His legal wife, the daughter of an Arabian, King Aretas of Petra, learned of it. She took up residence in the fortress Machaerus on the Eastern shore of the Dead Sea near her father's throne in Petra. From there she made her way to her father. Outraged by the rejection of his daughter, King Aretas declared war on Herod nearly annihilating the army of Herod.

"John's message of repentance had compounded Herod's problems, and Herod looked for an opportunity to get rid of him. He resorted to use a political ploy as an excuse and had him beheaded. His disciples buried his headless body and told Jesus of his death. To some of the Jews the destruction of Herod's army was seen as just retribution by God for what Herod had done to John. "After hearing of John's arrest, Jesus left for Galilee in the regions of Zebulun and Naphtali. There He began preaching: 'Repent, for the kingdom of heaven is at hand.'

"It was while in this region the war erupted between Aretas and Herod. Before leaving the area of Jericho, however, Jesus responded to our inquiry about where He was staying. He took us up into a high mountain where eagles and ravens nest. From there we could see the vast Jordan Valley. The area Jesus had chosen as a refuge had a strong history. From the opposite side of the valley atop Mount Nebo, Moses had first seen the land of promise which flowed with milk and honey. The sin of Moses in striking the rock at Meribah had resulted in his being prevented from entering the land."

Reflecting a moment Andrew continued, "But I suppose it was only a delayed entrance. Though years had lapsed, Peter, James, and John told us of going up into a high mountain with Jesus where He was transfigured. It was there they saw Jesus with an incandescent glow about Him. With Him were Moses and Elijah. Moses had apparently made it to the greater Promised Land. The highlight moment on the mountain was a voice coming out of a cloud saying, 'This is My beloved Son, in whom I am well pleased. Hear Him!' Such a voice had been heard when John baptized Him.

"The three special disciples condemned themselves for their lack of comprehension. Jesus instructed them not to tell anyone of this 'until the Son of Man is risen from the dead.' Preoccupation with the glorious moment blinded them to that ultimate revelation regarding the resurrection. On another occasion in Galilee, Jesus pointedly said, 'The Son of Man is about to be betrayed into the hands of men, and they will kill Him, and the third day He will be raised up.' How could He have been more clear? How could we have been more lacking in understanding?

"Jesus not only told us these things we did not grasp, but He went so far as to tell us He will come again. Though it has been some days since we have seen Him, He is coming again at a time not known. As a sentinel calling for attention, He has heralded His coming. '. . . the sign of the Son of Man will appear in heaven. Watch therefore, for you do not know what hour your Lord is coming. Blessed is that servant whom his master, when He comes, finds faithful.' He warned regarding deception related to His return.

"Jesus often referred to Himself as the Son of Man. Once in Caesarea Philippi He asked His disciples who people said He was. That was after John the Baptist had been beheaded, so it was reasonable when they answered, 'Some say John the Baptist, some Elijah, and others Jeremiah.'

He asked, 'Who do you say I am?' By you He meant all of us. Peter, my dear brother, wisely answered for all of us, 'You are the Christ, the Son of the living God.' Peter never ceased to amaze us. This time he was more correct than even he realized. Of all his statements, this was his most soul-stirring one. By referring to Jesus as 'the Christ,' he meant the Anointed One, the one who is the Mediator set apart by the Father.

"Jesus made a sterling statement to Peter. Again addressing Peter with a blessing applied to all of us, He said He was giving him the keys to the Kingdom. He said whatever was loosed on earth would be loosed in heaven, and whatever is bound on earth will be bound in heaven. Startling at the time!

"The imagery has become increasingly clear. When young rabbis were in training, they would go with the chief rabbi to the cabinet in which were kept the sacred scrolls, the Word of God. Carefully he would use the key to unlock the cabinet and remove the scrolls for their teaching session. After the lesson, the Word of God was once more locked in the cabinet with the key. When the young rabbi had learned his lessons well and knew the Word of God, he then was given a key to unlock and lock the scroll cabinet. What Jesus was saying to us was that if we kept His word unto ourselves, not even heaven could release it. However, if we dared share, that is, loose His word, the power of heaven was loosed to enable its efficacious working. This promise now is more encouraging than ever. The Living Word is to be loosed into the world from which it can never be removed.

"After coming down from the mount of the transfiguration, Jesus was asked why it was said Elijah must come before this manifestation. Then came the shocker. 'Elijah is already here,' said Jesus. You see, one like Elijah was spoken of as needing to come before Messiah. When he said, 'Elijah is already here,' He was speaking of John the Baptist. There on the bank of the Jordan that day 'Elijah,' that is John the Baptist, met the Messiah, Jesus. We were oblivious to the meaning inherent in the moment.

"I, along with John, was the first to follow Him. At first I was a follower, then a disciple. I sought out Peter and told him I had found the long-awaited Messiah. We three and Philip soon followed Jesus, His mother Mary, and others to a wedding in Cana, six miles north of Nazareth. There we saw Him perform His first miracle, turning water into wine. The last of the wine was the best served. It signified the reality that of His miracles, He saved the best till last, His resurrection."

Again refocusing on the mission, Joseph invited Andrew to share his convictions regarding the crucifixion and resurrection.

"He was dead. It was without a doubt Jesus who died. Calloused Roman soldiers who gambled at the foot of the cross attested to His death, declaring in a written document: 'He is dead Envious elders, whose deception led to His condemnation, attentively attested: 'He is dead.' Sadducees, shunning the supernatural, sneered: 'He is dead.' Pompous Pharisees prided themselves with their achievement and gloated with gladness: 'He is dead.' The prophetic sword of the old man Simeon spoken at His dedication pierced the heart of His mother Mary: 'He is dead.' All His acquaintances and the women who followed Him from Galilee watched the flame of life that had shown so brightly in His eyes flicker out. They, too, knew He was dead. Regressive remorse, blind bitterness, and personal piety caused them to lose their spiritual and emotional balance. Soon He who was born under the Star of David lay under a shroud. He was indeed dead.

"Oh, but that day, the day death died changed life. He forced open from the other side the door of death that had been locked since Adam died and came back the Lord of Life. In every closed bud of winter that blossoms in spring, He has left us the promise of resurrection. He deserves not only our compliments for His work but our obedience to His will. I will spend my life sharing

His Word that the power of God may be manifest in lives."

The friendly apostle had indeed shown himself friendly by being so transparent with his new friends. "Pardon my distraction while talking. I noticed you also saw the shepherd and sheep, Nicodemus," said Andrew. "Now look further to the west. The shepherd had a set course with the sheep following closely. Look even further to the west toward that boulder, and you will see a spring of water cascading down the mountain leaving in its wake the green vegetation. From the depth of the hot, dry desert, that shepherd has brought his sheep to the much-needed water, guided only by his instincts."

I was transfixed by the scene. It brought to mind the saying of Jesus: "I am the Good Shepherd. I know my sheep, and they know my voice." In this desert it takes a very good shepherd to know where there is water and how he is to lead his flock to it. That scene resulted in an instant analysis. Like that good shepherd, Jesus knows where our needs can be met and how we are to be guided there.

"John pointed me to Jesus, telling me to 'Follow one greater than I.' I did follow Jesus. There was no resisting His compelling personality and spirit, though He himself said there was none greater than John the Baptist, no one 'born of woman,' that is. Of course, none of us understood the implications for Jesus' own deity in that statement."

Just as Andrew had finished his memories of his days with Jesus and had added so much to our investigation of the validity of the resurrection, very much to his delight, he was interrupted by the arrival of James. As I had noticed Andrew looking toward the horizon of the hill to his left several times during our discourse, I had feared he was alert to possible search parties from Jerusalem. We were pleased to see it was only a gentle shepherd who had emerged. Too, we now learned another reason Andrew had been scanning the horizon. He said he and James had planned to meet in this secluded spot to compare their experiences of recent days.

James came rather suddenly over the hillside, almost as if he knew when Andrew would finish his visit with us. He told us he had continued to proclaim the resurrection, had received death threats from Annas still intent on destroying every influence of Jesus.

"James," I said, "like you, we are believers subject to the wrath of members of the court because of our newly established allegiance to Jesus whom they condemned. We are men of age, you more youthful. We subdue our fears of the fury of our former colleagues. Does the likelihood of punishment restrict you in sharing what you know?"

"What I know I must share. I know doing so might well cost me my life. However, truth must be given freedom. Within the court there is conflict. The blame game has begun. Each sect is blaming the other for creating the confusion that has erupted. There is little wonder that they should target me."

Having already spoken with Mary, Joseph and I knew of James as one of the four sibling half-brothers of Jesus. This gave him a life-long perspective like no other person. To gain a unique insight into Jesus, we asked that he tell of their life together.

"Jesus was born of Mary. I was the oldest son born to Mary and Joseph. As His younger brother for nearly thirty years, we ate practically every meal together," he began. "Six days a week we worked together, and on the seventh we went to the synagogue together. Never has anyone had a better older brother. Sure we were sibling rivals, but friends. I didn't always understand Him, but I had every reason to respect Him as different. His entrancing and enigmatic nature was often bewildering.

"Being older than I, Jesus went to Jerusalem for Passover when I was still too young to go. I was captivated by His accounts of the temple and sacrifices. He told of the Tyropoeon flowing

through the city, the valleys of Hinnom and Kidron, and the lovely gardens of Gethsemane with their luxuriant foliage. His vivid
recall made it seem to me as if I had visited also. Within
Jerusalem, terrace upon terrace rose until the temple overshadowed all. Not in ancient or modern times has there been a sacred
building to compare.

"Jesus and our mother told of how the family camped on the
southern end of the Mount of Olives amid the grove of myrtles,
stately cypresses, and two giant cedars. Along terraces, olive trees
with their dark green and silver leaves grew. Here the children
were free to play. Families had fellowship and renewed acquaintances. They talked hopefully of the day Messiah would come.
Jesus told of the grandeur of the palace of the high priest on
Mount Zion. The Ophel, the crowded suburb of the priests, and
the Maktesh, occupied by bazaars, were beyond belief to us
growing up in little Nazareth.

"It was the temple platform and exquisite temple itself that
drew Jesus' most sustained attention. The temple was covered
with plates of gold that made onlookers turn away as if peering
at the sun itself. The rabbis say of the glory of the temple: 'The
world is like an eye. The ocean surrounding the world is the
white of the eye; its color is the world itself; the pupil is
Jerusalem; but the image within the pupil is the sanctuary.'

"The city was Levitically clean. No dead body could be left
overnight, and no burial within the city walls was permitted. Not
even domestic fowls were allowed, and no vegetable gardens
were allowed lest decaying vegetation should defile the air. In my
childish mind, I relived His every step as He recounted His first
visit. Now, I'm astounded how a city so bent on purity could tol-
erate such an impure and unholy act as occurred there.

"Of all He saw there, the sacrifices of the bullock for the sins
of the people most impressed Him. Now I know why. He told of
the solemnity with which the priest took off his golden vest-

ments, bathed his hands and feet and put on his linen garments. The bullock for the sin-offering stood between the Temple-porch and the altar. It faced the south with the high priest standing facing the east and the worshipers; the head of the bullock was turned to the west facing the sanctuary. He then laid both hands on the sacrifice's head and recited the confessional.

"The people bowed with their faces to the ground and responded: 'Blessed be the Name; the glory of His kingdom is forever and ever.' I listened as an admiring little brother, never knowing Jesus would be the offering made for sin once and for all. Though impressed by Him growing up, neither I nor my brothers believed in His messianic role. It never occurred to us. We were cynical and not sympathetic. The family was perplexed by Him. There were disputes and divisions in the family over Him. As He grew and His fame spread, there were moments of elation when our hopes for Him as a leader rose. Fear and uncertainty prevailed at other times.

"We grew up amid Nazarites who practiced what they believed to be holy conduct. They drank no wine or strong drink, neither ate animal flesh. No razor ever touched their heads. They wore no wool, only linen. Their scruples incited their pious wrath at times. By their standards His laxity regarding the traditions of the elders was offensive. He was too joyous and free-spirited to be considered pious as they preferred.

"Once when we went to the synagogue, He read from Isaiah: 'The Spirit of the Lord is upon Me, because He has anointed Me to preach the gospel to the poor; He has sent Me to heal the broken-hearted, to preach deliverance to the captive, and recovering of sight to the blind, to set at liberty those that are bound, to preach the acceptable year of the Lord.' The priests knew who He was, son of Mary, and allowed Him to read from the sacred text. No bastard child was allowed to enter the synagogue. How they understood His birth, I don't know, but they did not consider Him unworthy to read in the synagogue. Only when He related what He read to Himself did the priests turn on Him.

"At times young Jesus was saddened by our lack of confidence in Him, even by concerns for His mental stability. In no way could I believe that the boy with whom I was reared, my sibling playmate, could in reality be the Holy God and perfect man. That concept transcends the thought of scholars, much less the mind of a youth. It is the conundrum of the ages. I was astounded the day Andrew came with excitement saying, 'We have found the Christ.' I stood speechless when he said the Messiah was Jesus. No, there was no way I could accept that. That was then; this is now.

"I was absorbed by the complexity presented by growing up with Jesus. The emergence of the baby boy Jesus into the Christ was puzzling. Now I know what was incomparable then. I gladly acclaim Him my 'glorious Lord Jesus Christ' and profess myself to be His servant, one to whom I give my undivided loyalty. I call Him Jesus. It speaks of his human nature. I call Him Christ as acknowledgment of Him as the Messiah, the Anointed One. I call Him Lord because I now attribute to Him equal honor as the Father. As the Father is Lord, so also is Jesus. So Jesus Christ is God as is the Father. I attribute to Him equal honor as the Father. The puzzle finally has come together for me."

"James," said Joseph, "you have made the journey from dark unbelief to light. Your faith has been made clear, even to acknowledging a willingness to die for what you believe. I want to hear in your own words what made the change."

James, already animated, became more eager to share. "After the reports of the resurrection one day, I heard my name called by a familiar voice. I turned and there stood Jesus. Of all people, He had singled me out to visit. As children we were close but grew apart because of my inability to understand what was happening. He was always patient with my unbelief. Deep down I wanted to understand and believe but could not. Obviously He knew this and was patient with me. Now He honored me by granting me a private interview. His words in that conference were convincing, but His very living presence even more so. I knew Him to be dead.

"Seeing Him alive communicated His Lordship even more clearly than words ever could. In that moment all doubts were dispelled. By His resurrection I was compelled to believe. Not only did I believe. I went immediately and shared with our family. Their many life-long questions about Him were answered, and understanding came to us because of the resurrection. That is why we all were in the Upper Room that night after the resurrection when a hundred and twenty believers gathered. If we who had the furthest to travel on the road leading from unbelief to belief can make the journey, so will millions. To acknowledge His resurrection is the starting point of belief."

Jesus' brother had voluntarily believed in Jesus as the Christ, His sibling, His servant. Not knowing where our parting paths would lead us, we had to bid each other farewell, they to go to Galilee and we to Jerusalem. We knew full well this could be our last time to see each other. The pressures on each of us were growing.

As we said good-bye and expressed our deep gratitude for sharing with both Andrew and James, Joseph and I had found the commitment of these two to be true for all who believed in the resurrection. Still further confirmation could only strengthen our cause. Now we would return to Jerusalem and meet with an inquirer with a thirst for truth as great as our own quest. His life had been spared by the death of Jesus.

From here in Jericho, our route to Jerusalem would challenge us physically and enthrall us emotionally. The ascent would take us through the baron Wilderness of Judah, up the valley David spoke of as 'The Valley of the Shadow of Death.' Ultimately, our final climb would be up and over the Mount of Olives and across the Kidron Valley back to Jerusalem. Our mules provided the best of transportation. Few self-respecting Jews would dare ride a horse. The animal was too closely identified with the Romans. Donkeys were for farm labor and short trips around towns. Camels were principally for commerce and use by desert nomads. So mules were our select mode of transportation.

Though sure-footed, Joseph's mule stumbled, throwing him on sharp rocks. His lacerations were significant and his bruises numerous. I made a poultice from a loaf of wild figs. The compress began its healing effect at once. His clothes tattered, dusty, and blood stained, we resumed our journey.

Slowly the sand mountains gave way to the desert floor. Walking the seemingly endless desert made us feel small. Or maybe it was simply our tiredness which diminished us. The unrelenting wave of time had enabled the water spilling down from Jerusalem to erode the desert, forming the Valley of the Shadow of Death. It is so named because of the narrow ledges along the steep rock walls and the human and wild animal predators that populate the caves along the ledges. The valley is so narrow that the sun rarely visits its bottom, making it even more ominous.

During our overnight stop near the upper end of the valley, a lonely jackal sang its eerie song as though the moon were its only audience. None too soon the rising sun began to chase the last of the night's shadows from the landscape, heralding a new day and opportunity. We were soon up and on to Jerusalem.

Joseph and I were unaware of what had transpired in the court in our absence. In Jerusalem the caldron of hate was boiling. The Shammai had persuaded the venomous Caiaphas to convene the court to consider further attempts to silence those who advocated the resurrection as reality. False philosophical and erroneous physical efforts to refute it had failed. Now Caiaphas and a small number of members of the Sanhedrin were convinced radical steps must be taken to eradicate believers. Yet, knowing of the court's concern for us and having been away for weeks, we dared not enter yet another meeting of the Sanhedrin.

We had confidants on the court who respected our beliefs and served as insiders to inform us of what transpired in the session. We knew the setting well and absorbed every insight shared with us by our colleagues in the session.

We knew the beauty of the meeting room was a contrast to the bitterness it housed. The whitewashed stucco walls were embossed and adorned with large, marginally carved stones; the ceiling was decorated with triangular and hexagonal tiles, the floor mosaic. The building ranked with the best in the Roman Empire. The aesthetics of the lovely room did nothing to temper the vindictive leaders.

The number willing to attend was less than imposing, but there were more than the twenty-three required to take official action. Some members stayed away because they were neutral, some had enough involvement, and others had come to believe privately in the resurrection. Caiaphas, assuming his position of power before the seated semicircle of jurists, argued, "Already this blasphemous heresy of a resurrection is spreading through every village and camp of the region. Men of many languages are speaking of it. There are reports of a band of believers in Damascus and others beyond the Great Sea. We must appoint a chief investigator with authority to stop those spreading the false doctrine wherever he finds them."

The unctuous Theudas ben Levi, a well known sycophant, as always aggressive, was the first to respond, "We need a forceful person not afraid to impose the death penalty on such heretics, a man of action." This was his ploy to call attention to himself and indirectly solicit support for himself. It was well known by members of the court that he had independently been intimidating believers. His imposing stature and stern face were in themselves threatening.

Joshua ben Hananiah, a more bookish member of the court, rose, adjusted the folds in his blue- and gold-trimmed robe, cleared his voice, and spoke. "A man known for his intellect is more suited for this role—one whose integrity will be further verification of the absurdity of a resurrection, a man who when he speaks will solicit confidence in his actions. He need not be physically forceful himself but nevertheless willing to use force. It is his intellect for which he should be known. There is no one more respected for his scholarly disposition, his intellect, than the venerable Gamaliel." Gamaliel, indeed, fit this description. As a fellow reluctant member attending this session, Gamaliel rose and addressed the court. "My research and writing on other matters make it impossible to assume this assignment. Besides, I could not in good conscience fulfill this role because I know there are good, honorable people of letters who believe in the resurrection. I could not act against them. We now know that we were among those to whom he made reference as being 'honorable people.' His colleagues shuffled and murmured disapprovingly. Yet, Gamaliel was a man of such repute none dared confront him.

Saul, a younger member of the court, was enraged. He reflexively snorted his disapproval of his venerable teacher. Having long been a student of Gamaliel, Saul was considered an outstanding scholar. His physical stature, his deformed back, and limited eyesight had caused no one to consider him until the matter of intellect was mentioned as being admirable in this effort. Instantly, his shortcomings were overshadowed by the assets of his sharp mind and tenacity. Ultimately it was his brilliance that won him the role of prosecutor.

Saul spoke, "If contempt for the theory of a resurrection qualifies one for this role, I am fit for it." He seemed almost eager to undertake the task.

"Yes," injected portly Baruch, "and Saul has the background that will support his findings as creditable in several significant circles. From the day he joined this court, I have known him well, knew his father also. Saul was circumcised of the stock of Israel the eighth day after his birth according to our laws. He is of the lineage of Benjamin, a Hebrew of Hebrews. Concerning the Law, he is a Pharisee. Regarding righteousness which is in the Law, he is blameless. In the matter of zeal, he is without a peer."

Around the room persons were nodding affirmation. The lips of Caiaphas curled with glee at the thought of Saul leading efforts to discredit those who believed in the resurrection. Saul's passion was such that even the most long-standing friendships would not shield a person from his wrath. He was well suited.

"The intellect of Saul," noted Elaias, a man steeped in the traditions of the court, "will be a great benefit in this challenging effort. Gamaliel, Saul has been one of your most outstanding students and, as such, a favorite of this court. He has gained favor with the body in every assignment given him. His arguments before the Sanhedrin have always been powerful and persuasive."

"There is reason for little further debate," said Caiaphas. If chosen, Saul would be Caiaphas' surrogate, his well qualified proxy. "The findings and actions of Saul will once and for all validate the actions of this court in sending that radical imposter Jesus to His justified death," concluded Caiaphas. One by one, members of the court affirmed Saul as the man to investigate thoroughly the rumors of the resurrection.

To the chief scribe Caiaphas said, "Write the document authorizing Saul to seek out and extract by force confessions denying belief in the resurrection. Also let it show he has this authority by the magistrates of this court who now confer it upon him. Make certain the document gives him all the power, once and for all, to eradicate this growing lie."

Gamaliel demurred and excused himself from the room. He

had great regard for his former student but little sympathy for the actions of his colleagues this day. Saul boasted, "I can assure this prestigious assembly I will vindicate the honor of the court. I will prove beyond a doubt there was no resurrection. Proof will be amassed that will show that as in life so in death Jesus, the imposter, was a fraud. You can be confidant I will utilize the authority invested in me by this august court to ferret out the deluded and misguided who insist Jesus arose from the dead. The honor of this venerable body, not His honor, will be vindicated. No one among the advocates of a resurrection will be shown any favor. No pain will be considered too severe to be used in exacting renunciation. I shall seek to reason with believers, but if that fails, I will resort to whatever is necessary to squelch this myth."

Pleased with what they had set in motion, members of the court nodded their pleasure at such resolve. Now Saul was unleashed to savage the believing community. One by one his colleagues congratulated him. Some suggested Saul give immediate attention to the growing colony of believers in Damascus. He concurred. His hunt began.

Caiaphas now had his ideal inquisitor, an imposing iconoclast, his very own alter-ego through whom to carry out the purge. This self-righteous, pompous bigot would keep his own hands ceremonially clean—if not his heart.

With this action the Sanhedrin, known as "the great court of justice," reached its nadir. Saul would serve as their "public whip," their tormentor. From this time, Saul would be known as the intimidator.

SCROLL XIII

THE LAST GATHERING

Our return to Jerusalem afforded us a needed respite. Much had been done, but more remained in our quest to chronicle events that validate the resurrection. Joseph and I stopped first at my residence, finding most of my servants had fled for fear of reprisal from the Romans or members of the court. Some had been interrogated and threatened. The most faithful had remained loyal to me and confirmed their faith in the resurrection. We were told that during the intimidation, threats were made against us. Fear had now become our accepted companion.

We delighted to share some details of our odyssey with those loyal servants. In turn, they related how daily more people in the streets were confirming their faith and speaking openly about it. The number of believers was growing so fast the city officials themselves were beginning to be intimidated by the increasing assertion of faith.

The warmth of the servants' reception reached a zenith with a delightful meal. We enjoyed my favorite salad consisting of mint, rue, coriander, parsley, chives, green onions, lettuce, coleroot, thyme, carmint, green fleabane, and celery. A pie of fish hash was the main course. Dessert was a succulent honeycomb made by the bees in Bethany. It was good to get back to such sumptuous dining after the amenities of the highway. Such comfort and accommodating grace speeded our renewal. We decided to stay the night with my family and go to the home of Joseph for a visit to the tomb early the next morning.

In the early morning, the sun's rays, like arrows piercing the sky, lit a new day. We walked in the garden again and mused about what we had been hearing. Incredibly, our attention was diverted by a young man kneeling near the open tomb. Cautiously we approached not knowing his purpose. Joseph spoke softly, "Shalom." Startled, he turned and backed away.

Our words of welcome caused him to stop for a moment. He stared knowingly at us. "You, you are the two members of the Sanhedren that buried Him!"

Realizing our guest was fearful of us, we did not approach him but encouraged him to be at ease and asked if we could be of help. "No," he said at first and then asked, "do you, I mean, can you. . . ?" his voice trailing off. "Are you men who believe the stories circulating about what happened here?"

That aroused our suspicion. Was he a secret spy seeking information to incriminate us? Emboldened by what we knew, we answered, "Yes, but who are you?"

"You don't know?"

"Why, no."

Looking around as if to see if there were others present, he said, "My name," hesitating, "my name is Barabbas." Frisson in his voice chilled in the air.

"Barabbas!" we exclaimed in chorus.

"Yes, I, the son of a rabbi, am the one they released. I am the one in whose place Jesus died."

No one spoke for the longest time, spellbound by our unlikely meeting in this setting.

"Tell me," he continued, "what do you know of a certainty?"

"First," said Joseph, "tell us what you know."

"I was there at Calvary in the jeering crowd. I had every reason to be there. And I believe the one who hung on that cross had no reason for being there.

"The crowd chose between us. They knew very well the Roman blood I had shed. As a Zealot, I had killed many Romans. I raided their camps and pillaged their supplies. I have taunted and cursed them from afar. I have even deceived and stolen from my own people. Had this been known, I would have disgraced my father's name. He a rabbi, a man sworn to justice, was an instigator advocating my release. Knowing I had shed Roman blood, the Jews wanted my release that I might kill again. But seeing my replacement die, I can kill no more. I heard Him cry for the Father to forgive. His gaze seemed to focus on me. Can it be that He can forgive even me?"

"He has forgiven us. Yes, He can forgive you. All of us have sinned, and there on the cross, He accepted the evil of us all. You said there was no reason for Him to be on that cross, but there was. He assumed our guilt in offering Himself. We know now He had the power to save Himself. No one could have taken His life had He not allowed it."

"But what can I do to gain this forgiveness?"

"He forgives us not because of what we can do, but because of what He has done. He accepts us not because of who we are, but because of Who He is. Yes, He not only can, but will forgive you."

Slowly moving forward for the first time, looking at the open tomb and then turning to us, he asked, "Will you walk to the tomb with me?"

We nodded affirmatively, and the three of us walked to the tomb. At the entrance, he paused and asked if he could go in. It was a transfixing moment as he responded to our consent. He entered alone, and after a long silence, we heard him pray: "Father, He called you Father like a humble, obedient child. I, a man of blood, I come to you obediently yielding my stubborn will to yours. I was not on that cross because He was. I am here because He isn't. As He prayed for me and gave His life for me, I pray as He, 'Father forgive—forgive me!'"

There was no glow that came from the tomb at that moment, but great joy prevailed in it. There was a radiance on his face as he came out. The old person was left in that tomb never to come out. The man who came out of the tomb was a new one. With his face much less stressed, he said, "I, too, believe. He is risen."

We spent time reassuring him. Joseph took him to his house and gave him new clothes and several days' provisions. We shared with him where a secret gathering of believers would welcome him. For safety reasons there was a password which would gain him entrance, "He is risen." When given and the response "He is risen indeed" returned, someone from inside would open the door. With much relief and hope, Barabbas departed.

Now Joseph and I sat alone in Joseph's home reflecting before we ourselves joined the meeting arranged for later in the day with other believers. Feeling it expedient to make our chronicles complete, we reviewed the religious and political climate that created the atmosphere leading to the crucifixion. Experientially, we knew bitter rivalry existed among members of the Sanhedrin. We Pharisees prided ourselves in our scholarship and piety. The very name Pharisee meant "to separate." To insure our purity, we avoided Gentiles, any non-Jew, at all times and were strict in our obedience of the Law, even to eating the proper herbs. Pharisees, we knew, were about six thousand strong at the time. As Pharisaic priests, we served in two primary roles, the Temple and synagogue. The dominant authority of Pharisees was not expressed through the Temple. The power-brokers there were the despised Sadducees. Their formality was much greater than ours, making their actions mechanical and ritualistic. More than to us, Christ's lifestyle was repugnant to them. He was a perpetual offense.

The Sadducees postured themselves as descendants of Sadoc, high priest in the time of David. They considered themselves the true guardians of the faith. Yet, they were dualistic, believing in strict enforcement of the law while living urbane and worldly lives. They were among the aristocratic segment of society who dealt with the Romans and desired full political acceptance so they might carry on their lucrative businesses. In reality the Sadducees were Hellenistic in their beliefs while professing loyalty to the laws of Moses. They did not believe in an afterlife and hence the possibility of a resurrection. They perceived of angels and demons as figments of the imagination. Individuals were responsible for creating their own 'heaven' on earth.

Herod appointed and dismissed the high priests at will for political reasons. This made aspirants all the more eager to appease him. Annas, a man steeped in intrigue, had been deposed as high priest by Valeris Gratus, predecessor of Pilate. His discharge resulted from his imposing illegal death sentences. He continued to run the court through his son Eleazar, who was high priest for a time. He then ruled through his son-in-law, Caiaphas, who presided for eighteen years.

Among the populace the pendulum of popularity swung more toward the Pharisees with the passing of time. They were more nationalistic. The Sadducees were committed to bringing God down to man. The Pharisees were committed to lifting man up to God. Both failed miserably. This complexity of contending parties fueled the flame consigning Christ to the cross. Having been participants in this party strife, both Joseph and I had become disenchanted long before encountering Jesus, now finding ourselves increasingly estranged from our former colleagues.

The hour was late. The time was approaching for the meeting on this Sabbath. Peter had arranged for us to come secretly to the Upper Room. From other believers who used this meeting place regularly, we would gain further insight into our inquiry of the resurrection. As I understood, the Christ-followers waited until after dark to gather and only let those enter who gave the password we had shared with Barabbas. Once Joseph and I arrived and had identified who was owner of the tomb and who was the accomplice in the burial of Jesus, we listened as some of the people in the room identified themselves. Others just observed silently. Peter explained well who would be joining the group and why. Though the assembled group knew our mission, I confirmed our purpose to prepare each of them to tell of his unique experience with Jesus.

Introductions ensued. "I am Cleopas of Emmaus."

"My name is Bartholomew, but most often I am called Nathaniel, Bartholomew, meaning son of Talmai, King of Geshure. As descendant of a king, I am the only member of royalty honored to be numbered among the apostles."

"My name is Greek, but I am Jewish, Philip from Bethsaida in Galilee."

"Thomas is my name. Being a twin I am sometimes called Didymus. Like Nathaniel and Phillip we were apostles of Jesus."

"Greetings, I am Luke, a physician. My home was Antioch."

"I am from Bethany, known as Lazarus."

Pleasantries having been exchanged, all those fifteen or so present took seats, some leaning against the wall, some sitting by a column, some reclining on mats belonging to the room. I spoke. "Joseph and I have come seeking information confirming what is rumored about the resurrection of Jesus. Your candor will be honored and any skepticism respected. We do not desire to bias you in any way. Be assured, if there is any suspicion that our presence is a part of a plot to betray you, we have as much to lose before the Sanhedrin as you. We have heard of each of you and would like now to hear from each of you."

Almost interrupting because of an eagerness to share his experience, Thomas spoke. "Before that dreadful day in Jerusalem, I last professed my ardor for Him in Jericho. We had heard from travelers coming from Jerusalem what the mood was there. It was a frightful moment. Jesus had set His face. Declaring His hour had come, He was determined to go to Jerusalem. I knew this moment was different. Though He had often said, 'My hour is not yet come,' this was the first time He said it had. He knew what that meant. We could only imagine."

Joseph injected, "Did you envision the crucifixion?"

"By no means. Nevertheless I insisted we not go, reminding Jesus, as if He needed reminding, they had tried to stone Him the last time He was there. It was to no avail. After a bit of rankling about it and seeing His resolve, I remembered what He had taught us: the person who desires to save His life will lose it, but whoever loses his life for Jesus' sake will find it. Bolstered by this thought, I said, 'Let's go up to Jerusalem and die with Him.' My bravado would be tested, and I am ashamed to say that in Gethsemane I failed the test. The night of Gethsemane we met in the Upper Room for the Passover meal. Jesus sought to prepare us for what was ahead. He spoke in language which now can only be understood because of the resurrection. He told us that He was going to prepare a place for us and that we could come to be with Him. He appealed to us not to let our hearts be troubled. He made His promise all the more personal by saying He would meet us in that place of many mansions. Then He said, 'Where I am going you know, and the way you know.' I didn't know, so I said I didn't. Inherent in His response was the promise to meet us at our death and take us to the Father's house. He is the way home."

"Thomas," Joseph injected, "who was that hanging on that cross at Calvary? Do you have any doubt?"

"Doubt? No, absolutely no doubt. Emphatically it was Jesus. After what He did, you have the audacity to question that it was He?"

"Thomas, I have my answer and am sure, but I did not want to bias yours. Do you have any doubt about His resurrection? Don't tell me what you think I want to hear. Tell me what you know."

"On that first day of the week after the resurrection, I was detained when the apostles assembled behind locked doors for fear. When I finally got there, they told me Jesus had been right there with them. I am a pragmatist, I like empirical evidence. I was skeptical. Being skeptical isn't necessarily bad. It means a person doesn't have an answer but wants one. I was in no way cynical. I believed there was an answer, but I didn't have it. I said I would not believe He was alive until I saw His scarred hands and wounded side.

"In demanding proof from Him, I was not trying to lord over my Lord. Overpowering and conclusive proof became mine eight days later. This time I was in the Upper Room with the other ten. Jesus appeared and greeted us, 'Peace to you!' That is what I sought, peace. Standing before me, He said, 'Stretch out your hand and touch me.' I didn't. I couldn't. I didn't need to. I did what my spirit compelled me to do. I fell to my knees and cried out, 'My Lord, and my God!' My witness redounded to the acknowledgment of His glory. I called Him not Jesus but by two names ascribed to deity, my Lord and my God. Only such a One could resolve all our fear of death by proving that death has no power over a believer. Jesus justifiably somewhat chided me. He said, 'Thomas, because you have seen me you believed. Blessed are those who have not seen and yet believe.'

"Some say He was a mere man. If He were only a man, He could not have returned from death. Some say He was God only. If He were only God, He would not have died. He was the God who became a man for a season. God incarnate. Yes, I believe in the resurrection. Yes, a thousand times yes. My life has been transformed by that single moment."

Cleopas, who had stood near a window in the night breeze, could contain himself no longer. "Early on I recognized Jesus as a prophet mighty in word and deed. I had heard His authoritative teaching and seen His deeds. I was convinced that no man could do such deeds and know such truth unless God was with Him.

Late on the afternoon of the reports of the resurrection, a friend and I were on our way out of Jerusalem on the short road to Emmaus. The two towns were only about seven miles apart. As we walked, we reasoned in our hearts that He would have been the one to redeem Israel. In honesty, we like many had hoped this redemption, in part, would also be deliverance from our Roman oppressors.

"I had been there and seen the chief priests and leaders of the people deliver Him to the Romans to be crucified. At the cross I heard the derisive shouts hurled at Him. One was a challenge about which I wondered. One near me cried out, 'If you are the Son of God, come down from that cross and save yourself.' He showed that love is purest that withstands provocation and does only good to the one who offends." With pathos Cleopas' voice rose, "I wanted Him to vindicate Himself by coming down from that cross, silence His detractors, and proclaim Himself as the Christ. In my heart I made the same plea, 'Save yourself.' I left there knowing not only was He dead, but recognizing my hopes and ambitions died also. He was crucified, dead, and soon to be entombed forever. History would lightly regard a disgraced rabbi who died a criminal's death in a remote part of the world. My conclusions were wrong.

"The Roman cobblestone road led through valleys and hills shimmering with gold and bronze grain in season. This day, the purple-green tones of the vineyards and the silver of the olive trees were stirred by a light wind. Strange," Cleopas mused, "I should remember such details and have been so insensitive to a man who joined us. We reasoned with our new companion as to whether there had really been a resurrection. Such a concept was beyond belief. Perhaps that fact kept us from considering that our new companion was actually the resurrected Christ. I concluded that any similarity of voice was just that, a similarity. His hood shielded His profile, but had it not we would likely have only thought Him to resemble the Jesus we knew. We were completely oblivious to the possibility that was unfolding.

"This Stranger talked with us as we walked. He gave us an opportunity to be open by asking, 'What is this resurrection about which you are talking?' I thought how uninformed and said, 'Are you the only person in Jerusalem who doesn't know about this?' Assuming He didn't know, I told Him in detail of the Prophet who was crucified I called Him a prophet. His death left little reason to call Him anything else. He then referenced the prophets, asking if we didn't know the prophets of old foretold such things regarding the Christ. He then began to explain the teachings of Moses and the prophets. As He did, I thought it reasonable Jesus should be resurrected, but logic quickly suppressed such consideration. We enjoyed the company of this Stranger so much that when we got to Emmaus, we invited Him to dine with us and spend the night. He accepted. While we were dining, it ever so subtly became evident who this Stranger was. He, Jesus, was right there with us. The hands that had broken bread the night He was betrayed had now broken bread with us that we might believe.

"We realized that only a few have or will see Him. Therefore it is all the more vital that we who have such an honor make it known to others. We rushed back to Jerusalem that very night. The eleven and a few others were gathered. They were so excited they could not sleep. They were saying the Lord is risen. Our exuberance drove us to interrupt the stories of their experiences to tell them of ours. Wonder filled the room. Joy reigned. Wanting to give us additional assurance to anchor who He was, He had explained certain of the laws of Moses, the Prophets, and the Psalms, showing the necessity for the Christ to suffer and rise from the dead the third day. Lacking understanding of the word of Moses and the Prophets, we did not think it reasonable for the Promised One to suffer and die. Now I know it was foretold and essential.

"Our mourning the loss of a Friend has passed. Joy has overcome it. We have lost nothing. We have gained much. We are gathered here this night in privacy. However, since that night, there are those who have frequented the temple, thanking and praising God. We may yet reclaim the temple as the House of God. We do this with awareness there is a growing resentment against us by those who crucified Him. Some have even been tortured as a result. Yet our joy isn't diminished. His vicarious suffering was for us. It is reasonable we should suffer for Him. If you, Nicodemus and Joseph, desire to know if I believe in His resurrection, let my witness be recorded. My undeniable experience leaves me no other conclusion. Yes, with all my heart, I believe He is risen!"

Having copiously studied Moses, the Prophets, and Psalms, I marveled over the explanation given by the Christ to Cleopas. I commented, "My colleagues and I have had our eyes blinded to these great truths by our prejudices and biases. Our arrogance and prejudice closed our hearts to who He was for too long. The priests intended it for evil, but God intended it for good. In Christ He was working all things together for our good. May we see this truth in all of life. We sat in judgment on the One who will judge all men justly. Except for the forgiveness and the pardon He offers, we would all stand condemned. His grace is sufficient."

Cleopas digressed to illustrate his point. "There is a story told of a person who noticed a rare flower growing on a ledge on the face of a precipitous rock. To gain it would be at the peril of his life. There was no way to reach it except by lowering someone from the top by rope. The man wanting the flower brought a young boy and offered him a reward if he would get it for him. Immediately realizing the danger, the lad demurred. Finally the lad agreed on one condition. He said, 'I will do it if my brother holds the rope.' This is an example of complete trust under perilous conditions.

"Thomas, like you, I was skeptical. Not having answers but believing there were answers, I went to Him at night and found transforming truth. He, obviously was referring to Himself when He said, 'God so loved the world He gave His only begotten Son that whosoever believes in Him should be saved.' In this significant statement are three great testimonies like three primary colors that make one white beam of light of God's love. He loves the world with a love that is so self-sacrificing that He gave His own Son. Having given us the greatest gift, we should know He wouldn't withhold any good thing from us. We must learn to interpret the events of life in trust of His love, not with questioning, doubting, or denying.

"God died for us. Indeed, God, the Mighty Maker. Before there was anything, time, space or matter—Jesus was with God as an equal. He spoke and worlds came into existence. We think our world is enough. Jesus commanded and around us myriads of other worlds came into being. He stretched out the heavens and bound the icy-blue stars of Pleiades. He established Orion, the blazing hunter who climbs upon the eastern horizon, followed by his faithful dog Sirius as they hunt Torus, the bull, in the night sky. He is the Morning Star who is now risen in our hearts.

"Those who grope for knowledge of ultimate reality behind and above the universe only have to look at Jesus Christ. As the colors of the rainbow may be found in every ray of silver sunlight, so Jesus is seen in all creation. This Creator made of Himself a man that He might remake us. A tear vial can't contain the ocean. Neither can the mind of man contain the truth of God, the Eternal. Only Jesus who created the physical world had the authority and power to recreate the crowning glory of His creation–mankind, the highest of His order. It is for that reason we seek to establish for all generations the mystery of the resurrection."

Thomas spoke, "He had love, as He said to you, Nicodemus,

for 'whosoever.' I heard His lament on the Mount of Olives, 'O Jerusalem, Jerusalem: you that kill the prophets and stone those sent to you, how often I would have gathered your children together, as a hen gathers her brood under her wings.' Then He sobbed. 'But you would not.' Though he meant Jerusalem, I know this cry reveals His compassion for all. He knew the hatred and hostility of those in Jerusalem whose anger boiled against Him, yet He loved even them. In that prayer, as in all of His life, He was doing what He told us to do: 'Love your enemies, bless those who curse you, do good to those who hate you, pray for those who spitefully use you and persecute you.' On Calvary He was our matchless template of all He taught."

The clatter of camels' hoofs and gruff voices distracted all of us in the Upper Room for a moment. Accustomed to fear, we stopped our discussion and waited until the noise passed.

Resuming our focus, Luke spoke with caution. His Greek mind inclined him to be a seeker of knowledge. He was a professional disciple, quite different in experience from the fishermen. "As a physician I have great interest in Jesus. I talked with His mother Mary about His conception. I've concluded that "in" a lonely manger in benign Bethlehem, two events occurred simultaneously. Of the celestial bodies as numerous as the sands of the sea, one of them, this orb, became . . . the visited one. In a simple cave used for a stable, Mary's child was born. It is my persuasion the prophecy longed for was fulfilled. I am convinced Jesus, born of Mary, was Immanuel, God with us.

"Ends are always present in beginnings. His birth began with a miracle, so it is reasonable His death should result in a miracle. Having defied the laws of nature by His birth, it is logical He should defy the laws of death by His resurrection. Jesus Christ had His portrait verbally painted in colorful broad strokes seven hundred and thirty-two years before His birth. Messiah's coming had long been desired and expected. God the Father determined to define His Son well in advance so that He might be indisputably known. The voice that called worlds to be born from the darkness was, for a time, to be limited to an infant's cooing."

Luke continued to explain himself methodically. "The second event that occurred in Bethlehem was the greatest mission Jesus began. The long-awaited moment had come. What was to unfold was not what was most anticipated. It was far better." Luke proved to be poetic, bringing additional insight to the significance of Bethlehem. "As a physician, I have over the years attended many of those involved in the drama of the cross. My acquaintances are extensive and varied. I had access to the chambers of Pilate. I was there when Gaius gave the priests the death report. I saw him, heard him, personally. Regardless of what others may say, the reports stated He was dead.

"Also as a physician, I know life and I know death. The One taken from the cross was dead. No vital signs of life were noticeable. The body entombed could not have been resuscitated. Nothing less than resurrection, the reinstatement of life in a lifeless body, enabled Jesus to return to life. At the crucifixion, another struggle for life surely was lost. The finality of death never was so awful. It seemed evil had won. The Miracle Worker did not save Himself. Many witnesses watched as He died. No one left thinking anything but that He was dead."

The room was hushed as Luke, known in the community as the "beloved physician," continued to speak. "One of my patients is a member of the Sanhedrin, a man of learning. We have often met to discuss weighty issues, having a mutual respect for each other. He is critical of my openness to miracles. He bristles at the idea of the resurrection. The man of whom I speak is Saul of Tarsus. Because of his brilliance and tenacity, he is the Sanhedrin appointee to investigate the resurrection. I must warn you all. He is empowered by documents entitling him to interrogate, intimidate, and even kill anyone he considers worthy, persons like you

Joseph and Nicodemus. He has sole discretion regarding life or death.

"It is ironic that Saul was chosen investigator because he is a poet and philosopher. Yet, he is the lance in the hand of the Sanhedrin assigned to rid any public discussion of the resurrection. As unlikely as it may seem, I have an encouraging hope regarding Saul. The facts of the resurrection are irrefutable. He will find the truth. There is no doubt about it.

"When all this is over, he will know more about this entire affair than anyone. He, too, has seen the death certificates and heard the verbal report of the guards. He knows Jesus died. The impossibilities the resurrection poses to his logical mind are one reason he is intent upon proving Jesus is still dead. Mary understood the reason for the birth, even in the absence of logic. All she has to do is remember 'With God nothing is impossible.' The conception was not impossible. The resurrection was not impossible. I want us all to remember this--neither is the conversion of Saul impossible."

There was a shuffling in the room, persons glanced at one another, and some gasped. All wondered at such a remote possibility. The most they could hope from Saul's investigation would be that he would be more tolerant than the Sanhedrin led by Caiaphas. But converted? Not likely.

"Nathaniel, What are your thoughts?"

"From our first encounter, I knew Jesus was different. I could see He had a spirit of discernment. At times it seemed as though He knew things before they happened. I thought of Him as having a gift from God. But being God? Never. Such a concept defied my understanding. More than how God could be a man is why He would be. I was in Galilee when Phillip came rushing to me saying, 'We have found the one Moses and the Prophets spoke of. He is Jesus of Nazareth. Come and see.' When Philip told me from where He came, I exclaimed, 'Can anything good come out of Nazareth?'"

Nathaniel continued to define his amazement about Jesus. "As we were approaching Jesus, before anything else was said, He said of me, 'Behold an Israelite in whom there is no guile.' Indeed, I had endeavored to live such a life. But how did He know? With my first comment, He knew of my candor. I asked Him how He knew me. He said when I was under the fig tree, He saw me. Few people knew of my affinity for that tree. A characteristic of fig trees is they spread out their limbs forming a canopy around the base. The foliage is so thick no one can see beneath the tree. In the heat of the day, it is the coolest place around. I often crawl under its sheltering limbs and enjoy the cool and quiet. He said He saw me under the tree. No way. At least, there is no natural way He could have seen me.

"At first this was somewhat frightening. Being around a man who knew such things was intimidating. Then I thought it was good that He could perceive how things were and that He would be my shelter. Such perception apart from divine revelation was impossible, so I settled for it being just that and nothing more— divine perception. When I marveled at His insight, He told me what I had seen was nothing compared to what I would see. He said I would envision heaven opening and the angels of God ascending and descending on the Son of Man. Such confirmation I have seen. He knew I would.

"When we all went fishing, my curiosity occurred again. We had fished long and hard without catching anything. He told us to throw our nets on the right side of the boat and we would enjoy a catch. With nothing to lose, we did. He was right. He knew where the fish were. Then there was the time He insisted we go through Samaria. The idea of going through the land of those people was an abhorrent thought. I had been taught as a child to have nothing to do with the despicable Samaritans. At Jacob's well, near Sychar, we met a woman. It was a revered place because Jacob gave it to his son, Joseph. Some of us had gone into town to purchase provisions when the woman came to the well. Jesus broke every taboo conceivable. He dared ask that Samaritan woman for a drink of water. A Jew making a request of a Samaritan was unheard of. Then to think of drinking water drawn by such a person was worse.

"The woman asked Jesus how He, a male Jew, asked her, a Samarian woman, for water. He said to her that if she knew Who He was, she would ask Him for a drink and He would give her 'living water.' She thought He was talking about some special effervescent water. Puzzled, she asked if He were greater than Jacob. Using water as a symbol, Jesus told her if she drank the water He offered, she would never thirst. She asked for it, not really understanding as yet. We didn't either. 'Go get your husband,' He instructed her. Embarrassed to say it, she acknowledged she had no husband. He knew it, and His answer was a shock to her and even more to us. 'That is right. You have had five husbands, and the man with whom you are now living isn't your husband.' Again, I pondered, how did He know that?

"Jesus attracted all ranks of people. Once in Capernaum a centurion came asking Him to heal his sick servant. He said he knew Jesus could. Humbly the centurion spoke of having servants under his authority, and he was confident Jesus had authority to command the healing of his servant. Jesus complimented his faith and told him to go home—his servant had been healed. We later learned that at that moment the servant was healed. Same issue. How did Jesus know that?"

Nathaniel's amazement was clearly visible—and the applications he made astounding. "Another moment when His foreknowledge was shown came our last night together. We had been with Jesus a long time and had come to realize He knew who was doing what. We had no idea what surreptitious deeds Judas was plotting. If anyone should have known it, logically it would have been one of us apostles. We didn't. Jesus did.

"Jesus spoke of being betrayed by one of us. We all asked if we were the one. It is the custom at such a feast for the host to break bread and pass it among those present. Jesus said the one to whom He would give the sop would be the betrayer. We were all given bread, but no one noticed that Judas was the first to whom He gave the sop. We still did not understand when Judas left the room. When Jesus said, 'What you do, do quickly,' we thought Jesus was sending Him on an urgent assignment. We didn't know what Judas was going to do. Jesus did. Judas had set out on his furtive mission. How did Jesus know that?"

Nathaniel sighed, comfortable in his touching a bit of heaven. "Now I know the answer to my many questions. Jesus being Divine knew all things. That is how He knew that I was under the fig tree, where the fish were, that the woman in Samaria had been married five times, and that the centurion's servant had been healed." A deep sense of appreciation for Jesus settled over us.

Philip had been contemplative during most of this conversation. He slowly began reminiscing. "Did you know that I was the first to hear His inviting words, 'Follow me'? I had no idea how blessed I was to be called by Him. I was so excited I ran to tell you, Nathaniel. I was aflame with excitement and wanted Nathaniel to share in it. Jesus had a plan. By it I am blessed as are all people.

"Whereas Peter was an extrovert, I am an introvert. Still, He used me by making me in charge of supplies. We were once in the Galilee and He was teaching nearly five thousand people. The noon hour approached, and He turned to me and asked how we could feed them. Imagine Him asking me! I knew math, but I was about to get to know Jesus. It only took a moment to calculate the impossibility of the situation, and I replied there was no way to feed that mass. All the money we had was equivalent to two hundred days of meager wages. That would only provide a scrap for each person, if anything at all for some.

"Andrew overheard our conversation and reported to Jesus the presence of a lad with five barley loaves and two fishes. Five loaves and two fishes! How inadequate, I thought. I missed an opportunity, but Jesus never did. There was no banquet table with white linen, but there was much green grass. Jesus had the disciples seat the people as orderly as possible. Miraculously, He fed that crowd. The fish and bread multiplied as we shared the meager food. To this day, it still amazes me. As He later broke bread and gave thanks in the Upper Room, He did so there. The crowd responded with popular approval, saying He was a prophet. Not realizing He had a kingdom not of this world, they shouted to make Him their king. Most men would respond affirmatively to such an appeal. He merely walked away to be alone. He was so often alone."

Andrew interjected, "Philip, tell about the time the Greeks came looking for Jesus."

"That is one of my most refreshing memories. Because of the trade routes along the Galilee, news of Jesus was broadly known. A group of Greeks who had come on pilgrimage to the feast asked to see Jesus. I suppose they asked me because of my Greek name. Rumor was they wanted Him to go with them to Greece. Were He seeking popularity, He most assuredly would have gone. Instead He further taught us of Himself in terms even we who traveled with Him failed to grasp. Now I see them clearly:

> The hour has come that the Son of Man should be glorified. . . . Most assuredly, I say to you, unless a grain of wheat falls into the ground and dies, it remains alone; but if it dies; it produces much grain. . . . What shall I say? Father, save Me from this hour? But for this purpose I came to this hour. . . And I, if I am lifted from the earth, will draw all people to myself.

"Now I see Jesus' statement revealed. He understood the

timeline of His life. Later in Gethsemane, He prayed asking the Father to let the cup pass from Him. He was no martyr seeing a moment of glory. Surely He had a well defined mission. His divine nature kept Him focused. He knew what He was to do and when. Having heard of the horror of crucifixion, He shuddered, terrorized by the horror of the moment approaching. His human nature was repelled by the thought of it being subjected to crucifixion. His final submission came in His last prayer of ultimate surrender: 'Nevertheless Thy will be done.' The die was cast."

Philip began to look remorseful. "There was one moment in which I showed the least understanding of all. In the Upper Room, the night of ignominy, Jesus said if we knew Him, we knew the Father. I posed an appeal, 'Show us the Father, and it is sufficient.' The very One who is as the Father was right there with us, and I failed to realize it. As He looked transfixed at me, He must have thought I was a slow learner. He must have felt I didn't really remember what He had taught and what I had seen. My appeal to see the Father was like an orphan child asking for its father. My heart's craving was for the Father. I know now that the entire Father was to the Son, the Son is to us and that the entire Son was to the Father, we are to be to the Son.

Resolve now replaced regret as Philip insisted, "Jesus told us to tell His story the entire world over. One region of which He made note was Samaria. I would never have gone to that outcast area had He not taken us there. Since then, I have gone back and preached telling them Who the man Jesus was Who spent two days with them. I have shared regarding His crucifixion and resurrection. Many responded and submitted themselves to immersion, signifying their obedience to Him, but it was my first time to act independently. It was just as though He were there with me.

"Leaving Samaria, I felt compelled to go south of Jerusalem into Gaza. It was a hot, long walk, and a charioteer offered me a ride. He, a eunuch, was reading from Isaiah, and I asked if he understood what he was reading. He exclaimed he could not unless someone explained it to him. My moment. I took up reading from the writings of the great prophet.

> *He was despised and rejected of men, a man of sorrows and acquainted with grief. . . . Surely He has borne our griefs and carried our sorrows...He was wounded for our transgressions, He was bruised for our iniquities, the chastisement for our peace was upon Him and by His stripes we are healed...He was oppressed and He was afflicted, yet He opened not His mouth; He was led as a lamb to the slaughter. . . .*

"As I explained how this described what had happened to Jesus, he was enthralled. I continued reading,

> *And they made not His grave with the wicked, but with the rich at His death, because He had done no violence, nor was any deceit in His mouth...When you make His soul an offering for sin, He shall see His seed, He shall prolong His days, and the pleasure of the Lord shall prosper in His hand...He bore the sin of many, and made intercession for the transgressions."*

"Remarkable!" my charioteer exclaimed.

"It was my joy to explain that long in advance, the Father revealed to Isaiah what had now historically happened. This was done by the Father as a way to identify Messiah definitively. I related that there were over three hundred identifying prophecies related to Messiah that were fulfilled in Jesus. The odds of that just happening were impossible. It was a defining point. I explained how Jesus had established baptism as an act to show obedience to Him. Just then as we were passing a pool of water, the eunuch stopped the chariot and asked why he couldn't be baptized. Confirming his faith, we both went into the water. He went on his way carrying the truth in his heart to be related in Ethiopia.

"From there, I went to Azotus, and starting there I preached all the way up the coast of the Via Mara to my home in Caesarea. Many believed and were baptized. By the resurrection, Jesus had been set free from the chains of death, free to be shared with the entire world."

Joseph, ever thirsty for more testimony, asked further, "Philip, your insights clearly indicate you believe in the crucifixion and resurrection. Are there even more personal reasons?"

The response was fast, sharp. "I watched as Jesus, suspended on the cross, had His life's blood drained. I saw Gaius as he thrust the sword deep into His side. He confirmed Jesus was decidedly dead when taken from the cross. As the exactor mortis, Gaius had to stay at the cross to confirm the end. People who postulate the myth that He did not die lie. I saw Gaius sign His death certificate as did the witness assigned by the Sanhedrin. Yes, I believe in the resurrection. Apart from the resurrection, there is no way to explain the boldness with which we now tell His story."

I arose and looked around. "You have spoken of your faith, your confidence in God's character. Of all the utterances He made from the cross, the one that inspires my faith most is: 'It is finished.' He said it as His earthly work was completed, His life's task fulfilled. The victim had become the victor. The dreadful darkness was passed. Never again would the countenance of the Father be denied Him. Never again would His blood be shed. All that remained was the easy part, death. The Law had been satisfied. He had redeemed those under the Law. The wage of sin was paid. It was finished. No one ever has to add anything to what He has done on the cross.

"We had heard his words of desolation: 'My God, My God, why have you forsaken Me?' His words of lamentation linger: 'I thirst.' Then came His word of jubilation: 'It is finished.' His anguish was ended. He could now ascend to the Father and report: 'The work you sent Me to do, 'It is finished.' That single word of grandeur that rent the air, 'TETELESTAI,' is used by us variously to mean 'paid in full,' 'made an end of,' 'it is performed,' and 'it is accomplished.' I ask of you and pose my own answers. What was made an end of? Our sin and guilt. What was performed? The ultimate requirements of the Law. What was accomplished? The work to do given Him by the Father. What was paid in full? The price of atonement. Through death He had destroyed Satan who had the power over death, His adversary in the wilderness temptations, the devil, Satan, was now the defeated foe."

Now the somewhat reserved Joseph recounted his musings on the sayings from the cross. "His last utterance redounded to His glory. 'Father into your hands I commend my spirit.' This the Hebrew evening prayer lifted from the Psalms of David that was taught Him as a child by His mother, Mary. In reverting to this prayer of His childhood, He added one word, 'Father.' With that He expelled His last breath. This quote from the Psalms reveals on the cross He had His mind on the Word of God. His first word from the cross was a petition of intercession addressed to the Father. His last word was His final commitment. With confidence and calm, He placed His life in the hands of the Father.

"This word was not a farewell to friends on earth but a greeting to the Father in heaven. He who had been delivered into the hands of His enemies now delivered His spirit to the Father. With that, He made His exodus and walked through the Valley of the Shadow of Death into the presence of the Father."

Yet another voice was to be raised in the room where these testimonials were being shared. He spoke, "I am blessed and refreshed by what has been shared. Let me tell you of an encounter I had recently with an inquisitor. A Roman soldier approached me on the street. After a brief interchange, he asked if I were a believer in the resurrection. Having heard stories of intimidation, I knew I could not conceal the truth. I conceded I was a believer. In threatening tones, he instantly demanded that I recant and renounce such a belief. Humbly, but emphatically, I told him I could not deny what I knew to be true. He became more threatening and commanded me to denounce belief in what he called heresy.

"Again with resoluteness, knowing the potential consequence, I avowed my belief in the resurrection. 'Very well then,' he said, 'I will have to kill you. In order that I might report, what is your name?' I began to laugh. Assertively he demanded, 'What is your name?' I could hardly quit laughing. Finally constraining myself I said, 'My name . . . my name is . . . Lazarus.' Thinking me to be a harmless dreamer, he let me go. I too believe in the resurrection."

There was just one more thing . . . one more person who would not let the night pass without speaking. He had sat a silent observer all the evening, had sat as one stunned by all he had heard and seen. He spoke slowly, falteringly. But what he said was unforgettable. "'He is risen.' Those are the words that gained for me entrance into this room tonight. 'He is risen.' That is the truth that has gained for me entrance into the Kingdom of God forever. Jesus, in every sense of the word, died for me. My name is Barabbas."

Joseph's voice now rose to one of exaltation. He moved to the center of the room and embraced all those there in his confident gaze. "Like Lazarus, we can now walk proudly and triumphantly in the presence of death. Jesus has conquered it. His resurrection has set us free from the prison of fear." Those in that room needed to hear Joseph's message of how to live in the face of threats. With all our fears alleviated, we felt confident we could refute any resurrection heresy.

As we parted, I passionately related one last word of exhortation: "Don't fail to tell the story of your journey to faith. It is not intended for you alone." Making our exit, I realized many of these vanguards of the faith would pay for their beliefs with their lives in order that the truth might live. Also, they knew that when the court was angered, the vengeful leaders would stop at nothing to exact retribution. The crucifixion of Jesus was evidence of this. These confident crusaders were to live in this context of conflict as lights in the darkness. The blood of these martyrs would nourish the roots of the faith now sprouting. An air of resoluteness made me confident theirs would be lives well spent.

Joseph and I proposed to rendezvous one last time. It was to complete the cycle and go back to where we began—the tomb. We had indeed found that what happened there was not a tactical theft but truly a transcending miracle.

SCROLL XIV

FRIENDS CONFIRM LIFE

Our journey ended and our principal questions answered, Joseph and I returned to Joseph's home to visit the tomb once more. As we had walked the circuitous roads through valleys and hillsides, retracing the path and visiting the personalities Jesus intimately knew, we had reasoned and exulted in the layers upon layers of truth we had encountered. From having walked where He walked and having talked to people to whom He had talked, we ourselves were changed and empowered from some existential reservoir of truth from both outside and deep within ourselves. Jesus could never be to us merely an abstract thought, a bloodless theory, a historical figure. He was a risen King, a risen Savior, and now the God who coursed through our bodies and lived in our souls.

Joseph was glad to be home, his wife relieved to embrace him after our two-week absence from Jerusalem. "The many insights, the facts we gained first-hand, and the information shared in every case confirm the initial report of the women at the tomb three days after Jesus was executed. "Indeed," Joseph noted, "the best news the world ever heard did come from a graveyard just outside Jerusalem, came from this very place, a place God, in some supernatural way, allowed me to design and nurture for the greatest event of all history. Jesus arose right here. Here He defeated death for every believer. Here He made all true philosophical assertion begin and end.. And here He invalidated every other mere religion of all the ages. Here Jesus took charge of the world for all times. He is risen. When life gets hard and circumstances have drained all the pastels from our sunrises, we must remember what happened here is for all people and all times. Life changed. Goodness prevailed. Evil was defeated."

No comment could have enhanced this moment of confirmation of Joseph's faith in the most fundamental and greatest truth of the entire universe. We drew cool water from the garden cistern to refresh our physical thirst, our thirst for knowledge having been quenched.

As I plucked a shoshan lily and savored its bracing sweet odor, I managed a quiet comment, "Joseph, our quest began here. When the angel told His followers He had risen, He also said. 'Come and see,' meaning come and get an understanding of what has happened. God did send us on a mission to document the truth of the resurrection. We did that. But the full reality of what happened here we'll only comprehend in eternity."

Joseph understood the import of what I said, but his response revealed that he too could not fully wrap his mind around the cosmic truth of what had happened in his humble garden, in his tomb. "Part of the truth is that this tomb wasn't a tomb after all. It was only an anti-room occupied for a few days by Heaven's Prince, by the Creator Himself, on His way back home at the end of His earth walk. He came to stage a daring, selfless rescue of a people subverted and held hostage by the subtle, perverse power of Satan and the sin with which he devours personalities and souls. That is the greatest of all acts of kindness and compassion—to give back life that was taken away by the Great Deceiver. And that, perhaps, is as clearly as we can define the reality of what Jesus did here. He gave back life to those who had fallen to the death imposed by Satan. I can only shake my head and marvel in astonishment."

Because of Joseph's insight and because of his suddenly discovered ability to articulate the profundity of what had occurred in this spot, I was moved to offer a prayer of gratitude:

"Lord, I do not ask for the patience you showed Peter.

I don't demand the love you showed John.
I won't plead for the mercy you gave the Zealot.
And I dare not ask the kindness shown Matthew.
But, Lord, I do ask for the grace you showed the
dying thief,
And I ask for your empowerment that I may go
tell others that Your grace is available for all who will
trust You. Amen."

I turned to look fully at my friend, to study his face, as we stood there in his garden with his words still settling in my soul. Misty-eyed in love and appreciation for my friend Joseph and my Savior Jesus, I managed to speak some of what I was experiencing. "Joseph, you will always be remembered as a man who longed for the kingdom of God. You had been a secret disciple of Jesus, but it was your boldness in requesting of Pilate the right to bury him that encouraged me. It was your courage that inspired me to align myself with you in preparing His body for burial. It was your daring that prompted me to leave the ranks of spectators and become a devotee."

Joseph, no doubt, was dealing with his own emotion and appreciation of friendship. Surely Jesus and John might have shared such a moment. As he spoke, a thrill of exaltation suffused me. "Jesus taught openness. He said, 'Whosoever shall confess Me before men, him also will I confess before My Father in heaven.' That call to public participation in His life is the reason I could contain myself no longer as I felt the impact of His life and death at the trial that day. Moved by love for the man I saw submit to the evil around Him, I knew it was my time to reveal my loyalty by asking Pilate to let me take His body for a decent burial. Even when we touched the crusted blood of his taunt, tortured body, I had no way of knowing the significance of what I was doing."

Joseph continued his mental sorting. "It was important that the crucifixion take place in a public arena to nullify any thought that Jesus survived. His post-resurrection appearances are known so broadly no one can deny He was thereafter alive. Yet, His adversaries must try every possible ploy to discount and disprove it, or they will suffer embarrassment and the very forces of hell experience defeat. Those who assiduously dispute the resurrection argue against a mountain of evidence supporting the miracle as rare as if the sun should rise in the west. Belief in the resurrection has not resulted from the passing of time, memory fading, and a myth emerging. Many witnesses to it still live. It is not merely the figment of the imagination of unlearned men. In fact, Gamaliel, publicly heralded as one of the greatest thinker of our times, now defends the truth of Jesus and the resurrection."

We still lingered at the well near the tomb area—the water, the trees, the lush vegetation seeming to sustain our own entranced spirits there. Joseph, with the practical, methodical logic of a designer, continued his synthesis of events. "Those who came that dawning had no comprehension of what rising from the dead meant. After His transfiguration when the Father confirmed Him, He told His followers not to tell anyone about this until the Son of man has risen from the dead. They said they kept it not knowing what He meant by 'rising from the dead.' When teaching them, He spoke in such terms as laying down His life and taking it up again or being as a grain of wheat that falls to the ground and springs up again. They doubtless thought He was speaking purely metaphorically about some nominal event. He often taught in parables, and such a conclusion might follow. The thought of a resurrection was beyond them. That in part is why they were so frightened by seeing Him alive. We hear only what we want to hear. They were totally unprepared for the resurrection."

"You are right," I injected. "If the resurrection was beyond the perception of the believers, certainly the reality was even further outside the consideration of public leaders and common people. Though only recently past, it is already a history that Jesus was crucified, the government authorities having acknowledged the event. His crucifixion has been recorded as a bloody, revolting, heartless travesty and has defined Jesus as a man caught in a vice between religion and politics, Rome and the Sanhedrin. History, authentically recorded, will continue to affirm the injustice of Pilate's ordering His execution. And history is reliable enough it will record the fact and date He died.

"Though Jesus' life and death are accepted fact, right now, there is no historical proof of His resurrection—that is, in the sense it was observed by eyewitnesses. No one saw Him being resurrected. But, the resurrection is a conclusion reached from reliable witnesses having seen Him alive. There is no way, apart from the resurrection, that this dead man could have been known to be alive. In the interval between when He was certified by legal authorities to be dead and the time He was known to be bodily alive, something happened here at this tomb. Many witnesses attest to His being dead because they saw Him, touched Him, and buried Him. And many witnesses attest to His being alive because they saw Him, touched Him, and talked with Him. Logic, inductive reasoning alone, leads to only one conclusion: He was resurrected. The bodily resurrection of Jesus Christ at a certain moment in time and from a specific place, this tomb, is foundational to the establishment of faith.

"Faith is not needed to establish a historical fact. However, historical facts are a marvelous encouragement to faith. Those who initially came to this tomb came without faith. His historical appearances stimulated their faith. The visitors here that early dawn were convinced He was dead. They brought spices to complete His entombment. They had no faith, no hope. They brought no doubts with them, only certainty, the certainty of His death. It was not faith that created the experiences of appearances; it was the appearances that created belief in the resurrection."

Joseph seemed finished with his venture into logic. His work-worn hands had pounded from fist to palm throughout his discourse to clarify the logic in his own mind. But Joseph couldn't let his rationalization go without one more summation. "The Sanhedrin—and yes the Roman government, too—is working so frantically to refute the truth because Jesus' resurrection is an indictment against all human effort which ignores the Divine and against all forms of religions which don't acknowledge Jesus. The resurrection means that life matters and that it matters what we do in life."

"So, Joseph, now that you've so clearly verified the resurrection in terms of logic, let me summarize my most concrete— more Law-based—conclusions after having taken the journey following Jesus' trek and having talked with those most intimate in His life here." I sat on the stone of the cistern, head in hands, as I struggled to arrange my own logic. "As personal accounts have now correlated and as we have attested in our own spirits, Jesus was Messiah. Our prophet Isaiah gave us signs to identify the Messiah: 1) He was despised and rejected, truly a man of sorrow. 2) He was taken from prison and judgment. 3) And this, Joseph, His grave was assigned to be with the wicked, yet He was buried with the rich, in your tomb. 4) Another consideration is that Pilate hates us Jews and especially those of the court who started this execution. And it is most unusual he allowed you to be the custodian of His body. In doing so, he enabled a divine prophecy to be fulfilled, for never is a criminal, as Jesus was accused of being, allowed to be buried with the rich."

It wasn't easy to summarize my own conclusions. My heart and the head were overstepping each other in their excitement and effort to arrive at the clearest explanation. "It was in this tomb He was buried. That we know. But groping for ways to denounce the reports, non-believers might well say it was not to this tomb the women came that morning."

"But it was this my tomb." Joseph's ability to compress more practical logic asserted itself now. "There are no other tombs in the garden. Besides, why would the Temple Guard have been here rather than at the other alleged tomb? I came soon after the report and saw for myself it was this, the very same tomb in which we buried Him. This thing was not done in secret. Others knew where He was entombed, and it was to this site they came after the news spread."

I made careful note of this comment by the erudite Joseph as he continued nodding his head, his jaw set in solid affirmation. "It was Jesus who died on the cross. There was no switch when Simon of Cyrene carried His cross along the route to Calvary. Many things would have made such a switch obvious, not the least of which is the swarthy complexion of the Cyrenians. He was declared dead, and thereafter His body was missing from a guarded tomb. I've concluded there is only one explanation for Jesus' missing body: Jesus arose by a miracle of God, rose because He was God.

"The logic, again, is so obvious. Jesus' enemies could not have removed the body. If members of the Temple Guard who kept the tomb had, they would have produced it and exonerated the conclusion of the priests that Jesus was an imposter. They have been scurrying all around Jerusalem trying to find who might have taken the body. Without success, they offered a sizeable monetary reward for anyone producing a successful lead regarding the missing body. Also, had the Romans stolen the body, they would have delighted to make a mockery of the reports of a resurrection by publicly displaying His lifeless form. There is one conclusion that keeps recurring no matter the path of reasoning we follow: What happened between the time He was certified dead and when He began making appearances has only one explanation— He arose from the dead, the living Lord Jesus Christ."

Joseph and I both stood from our resting place on the carefully stacked-stone mouth of the cistern. We stretched, looked about the garden, and inhaled the fresh, life-giving air abounding in the place. I moved the arranging of perception from Jesus now to His followers. "Believers in Jesus will not be ground like wheat nor stored like barley in a sack; we will be like the grain planted in the earth and multiply a hundred fold as Jesus' parable had taught. The story of the ages will change those of all ages to come. Some who profess belief in the resurrection have been threatened with death, some tortured, and some have died standing by the fact of the resurrection. Friends and family members begged His devotees that if they had the lifeless body to return it and spare themselves. They gave their lives knowing He lives."

I shared some information I had learned of the disciples' whereabouts, actually information I had gathered from reliable sources on the streets. His apostles had already met and decided how they would carry out His mandate to share this good news to the ends of the earth. Matthew was going to Ethiopia, Andrew and John to Greece, Peter to Rome, Simon the Zealot to Persia, Nathaniel to Armenia, Philip to Asia Minor, Thomas to India. And James, the son of Zebedee, along with James the Lesser would remain in Jerusalem as vanguards of the faith each. Together we had the opportunity to share an influence that would last longer than we.

"You and I have now come back to the place where we started and truly know this place for the first time. The chronicles we assembled are not by accident, but by design, Divine design. Resounding in my heart, and I pray on the pages of our chronicles, is what a difference we feel in life now that we see the resurrection clearly—now that we see Jesus more clearly:

> ~What a difference that we see a life changed from raging insanity to bliss in Mary Magdalene.
> ~What a difference that we see an undisciplined rogue fisherman changed to controlled discipleship in Peter.

~What a difference that we discern the sad mother of Jesus transformed into a blissful believer.

~What a difference that we see once-intimidated men now emboldened and committed to carry the truth as are the disciples.

~What a difference that we see firsthand the change of heart in Gamaliel, the most scholarly and empirical thinker of the times, from a dissident to a defender.

~What a difference that we see a man's-man soldier like Gaius conquered by the gentle compassion of Jesus.

~What a difference that we see a man three days entombed awaken to the fresh, bright air of a new morning as did Lazarus.

~What a difference that we see men once living routine, uneventful lives, become obsessed believers with purpose and zeal as we.

~What a difference Jesus made everywhere He went. . .

- *teaching* the unlearned, expounding to the learned,
- *healing* a leper or the lame,
- *feeding* thousands of hungry adults and children a substantive meal,
- *restoring* life to a dead man or a child,
- *refocusing* the lives of confused, needful women,
- *forgiving* abhorrent sin,
- *refuting* hostile, vengeful jurors, priests, and temple officials,
- *teaching* radical laws of loving our enemies,
- *altering* the laws of nature to walk on water or make water into wine,
- *multiplying* what exists to create what is needed as with five loaves and three fish,
- *transforming* from the physical to the metaphysical to walk through doors,

- *ascending* into heaven before the eyes of those He loved.

This was Jesus . . . but there's one more thing. . .

- *coming,* surely coming, as He said to take His believers to where He is."

"Oh, Joseph, the reality is almost too heavy, too marvelous to bear, too profound to comprehend." The wonder of what God had just spoken to me about Who His Son is forced me to a bowed, submitted posture. The well was my altar. Then after that meditative moment, I spoke, "Joseph, please come to the tomb with me." In awe we approached the most revered site in the entire universe, and in reverent tones I spoke affirmatively for us both:

"Oh, God we praise you that we have been blessed to see your fulfillment of your word like that spoken to the prophet Hosea:

I will ransom you from the power of the grave;
I will redeem you from death.
O Death, O will be your plagues!
O Grave, I will be your destruction!"

Then my affirmation turned to joy, joy that wouldn't be controlled. Standing, with Joseph beside me, just at the tomb's entrance, I cried out, "Where is He?" Maybe it was in exuberance for His resurrection, maybe in defiance of His death. But mostly, it was a cry of sheer confirmation of ageless truth.

I was pleased to answer my own question:

"Let loose in the world where no human or supernatural force can restrain Him!'"

. . . .

A lone dove rose from the cranny above the open tomb and soared heavenward, leaving the empty tomb as a silent empirical witness to the resurrection. We stood in utter silence and reverence for the place, for the truth of the resurrection, and for the difference this resurrection and this Jesus would make in the lives of believers for all generations.

Only a gentle flurry of the leaves and the melody of a distant lark touched our euphoria. Just then something foreign to this glimpse into heaven intruded into our reverie. We turned from the tomb, and there with a contingency of armored guards stood the dreaded intimidator. . . Saul.

EPILOGUE:
GOD'S SCROLL

Markus, sitting in the courtyard of the villa provided for retired Roman soldiers, put down the frayed parchment scroll he had been reading. With astonishment he turned to Lucius, a fellow chronicler for his regiment having just returned to Rome from Caeserea. "Where did you get these scrolls? They are revolutionary. I know reliable documents when I see them. These meet all demands of historical reality.

"In Jerusalem I heard Jesus speak on several occasions on the Temple Mount. My friend Gaius, mentioned in these scrolls, has led me to believe in Jesus as my Lord. However, I have never read anything regarding Him with such details. These scrolls preserve early and verifiable testimony. How did you come into possession of these?"

"Before his martyrdom, Ethal, a displaced scribe for Nicodemus, summoned me and gave me The Chronicles, telling me Nicodemus had written them and given them to him to keep for posterity. They have been in my care for these thirty years, but for fear of losing them or being charged for subversion, I have kept them secretly. You, Markus, my life-long friend, are one of the few with whom I've shared a word of *The Chronicles*.

"Ethal was a devotee of Christ, slain in the purge in the Circus Maximus, an ardent believer in the bodily resurrection. When Ethal gave me these scrolls, I asked him about the fate of Nicodemus and Joseph. He related that Saul and his contingency imprisoned the two of them. After cultivating the confidence of the prison guards, Nicodemus and Joseph shared with them the truth regarding the resurrection as established by their research.

Drucillus was the first of the guards to respond to their testimonies, questioning why they would risk their lives for the most hopeless of causes.

"The damp rock walls and cold steel bars of their cell certainly gave no cause to hope. Nearby cells were crowded with others who had professed faith in Jesus, groaning from the torture designed to elicit confessions and renunciations. Nicodemus and Joseph had themselves been tortured, and Saul had announced to them that he would see to it that more torture followed unless they too renounced their heresy.

"Then, the miracle. Late one night Drucillus and another guard came to their cell. As quietly as possible they unlocked the barred door and told the two prisoners to follow them. Uncertain as to what trickery might be involved, Joseph and Nicodemus complied.

"Once outside in an alley, Drucillus spoke of his acceptance of Christ and His resurrection. Ethal did not know the details of their escape, but he did report on Nicodemus and Joseph's departure from each other. Joseph would remain in Jerusalem, continuing to work through the cell of believers there. Nicodemus would travel south to Bet Gamal on the Coastal Plain southeast of Jerusalem.

"Joseph was later apprehended. Though subjected to extensive interrogation, he refused to recant his story. By virtue of his long tenure on the court and service to the community of Jerusalem, he was released and kept under house arrest. Even with these limitations he continued to share his story with the many who covertly came to his residence. Among those were some sympathetic colleagues with whom he had served in the court. He lived out his life in relative peace and was buried in another chamber of his tomb where Jesus had been placed.

"Nicodemus made his way to the estate of his venerable old friend Gamaliel at his estate, Bet Gamal. He and Gamaliel had tutored Stephen, the first devotee martyred for Jesus. Gamaliel's regard for Stephen had prompted him to ask for his body which he had buried at Bet Gamal. Nicodemus had come not only to visit his old friend but to visit the grave of Stephen.

"After a cordial time of visiting with his dear friend beneath the green canopy of a grape arbor, Nicodemus asked to visit the grave of Stephen. Then Gamaliel guided the stooped old man well worn from the depleting last months to the gravesite. Wearied by his journey but not his mission, Nicodemus knelt at the site of the grave and began to weep. It seemed the impact of all that had started the day the court condemned Jesus and had culminated in the death of Stephen bore heavily upon him. His weeping, at first silent, became convulsive. Then one last gasp was followed by silence. At the grave of Stephen, another faithful servant of Jesus died.

"The purge in Jerusalem and Rome went on. Rather than admit their dramatic error, the Romans and Sanhedrin officials sought to destroy a part of history. They stopped at no cost. The deaths in the Circus Maximus attest to the oppressors' passion. Reports were that Nero sought the annihilation of all partisans of Jesus in Rome. Since the building of the Circus Maximus, the facility had not seen such savagery as expressed against believers. One fourth the population of Rome often gathered in the expanded arena for the slaying of Christians. Amid all this, the Emperor was oblivious to the universal significance of the events and to the savagery of it all, posturing himself as a charioteer, singer, musician, and poet.

"Still, despite the slaughter in the Circus Maximus, belief in the resurrected Jesus was so strong that people abided by their faith even in the face of death. Many gladiators were won to a belief in Jesus by the courage of those of the faith. The deaths of the martyrs attested to the reality of the resurrection. Scarcely would they have died such deaths for a lie.

"You see," said Lucius, "our faith has been confirmed by the blood of the martyrs who were there and had empirical evidence on which to base their faith. Many, like Nicodemus, a jurist, and Joseph, a councilor from Armimathea, were pragmatists. They died confident in their beliefs in Jesus and the resurrected life."

Later that night, in Rome, July 18, 64 A. D., fire broke out in the merchant area near the Circus where it adjoined the Palatine and Caelian Hills. Fanned by the swirling summer winds, it spread rapidly. Hearing of the raging fire, Nero returned to Rome from his retreat at Antium. At first he tried to direct efforts to save the city. Seeing the futility, he decided to use the blaze to rid the city of those he deemed undesirable, the Christians. While Rome burned, Nero watched from his palace. Standing on his rooftop, he played his lyre and sang of the burning city of Troy.

Screams were soon heard in the streets of the ancient city; already smoke emanated from the Jewish quarter. Marcus and Lucius, along with others, fled for their lives. They escaped the flames but not the Roman execution squads. Nero persisted in signing the order for the death of Jesus' messengers and message.

From a balcony window, awaiting his fate, an aged man, a former member of the Praetorian Guard and chief executioner of Jesus, Gaius Cassius, took one longing look at the Palatine. He sighed, thinking to himself, I, Gaius Cassius, brought from the foot of the cross into the household of Caesar the good news of forgiveness. Gathered there with him were former members of the Praetorian Guard who had joined him and lived out their faith influencing many. They had hoped one day to see a Caesar sit on the throne of Imperial Rome who was a believer. To that end, they had worked and prayed. Now this devastation was their reality.

Looking down into the street, Gaius saw by the light of the burning buildings those who believed in the resurrected Christ being consumed in the fire—many first falling to the sword—for the faith they shared. His eyes were dimmed by age, but not his memory. Knowing he soon would die with them, he lifted his face toward heaven and prayed:

> Dear God, they still do not know what they are doing.
> As your Son did for me, I pray for them, "Father forgive them."

For six days and seven nights Rome burned. When the flames finally abated and the conflagration ended, seventy percent of the Imperial City lay in ruins, leaving in its ashes . . .

The Chronicles of Nicodemus.

Gaius, like the multitude that would follow him, died virtually winking at death remembering the words of Jesus:

"I am the resurrection, and the life: he that believes in me though he die yet shall he live."